MEDJUGORJE: THE FIRST TWENTY-ONE YEARS

BOOKS BY THE AUTHOR

The Liturgical Revolution—Vol. I, Cranmer's Godly Order
The Liturgical Revolution—Vol. II, Pope John's Council
The Liturgical Revolution—Vol. III, Pope Paul's New Mass
Newman Against the Liberals
The Order of Melchisedech—A Defence of the Catholic Priesthood
Apologia Pro Marcel Lefebvre Vol. I
Apologia Pro Marcel Lefebvre Vol. II
Apologia Pro Marcel Lefebvre Vol. III
I Am With You Always
The Second Vatican Council and Religious Liberty
For Altar and Throne—The Rising in the Vendée
Partisans of Error—St. Pius X Against the Modernists
A Fireside Chat with Malcolm Muggeridge
The Tridentine Mass: The Mass That Will Not Die
Saint John Fisher
Dossier on Catechetics

BOOKLETS

The Liturgy Since Vatican II:
Cardinal Gracias Memorial Publication 1986.
Medjugorje: A Warning.
Agreement or compromise? An Anglican-Roman
Catholic joint statement on the ministry.
Open Letter to the Rt Rev. Hugh Lindsay,
Bishop of Hexham and Newcastle.
The Church 2000—Recipe for Ruin
Changes in the Mass
Archbishop Lefebvre—The Truth
The Tridentine Mass
The New Mass
On Communion in the Hand and Similar Frauds
An Open Lesson to a Bishop on the Development of the Roman Rite
Archbishop Lefebvre and Religious Liberty
Communion Under Both Kinds—An Ecumenical Surrender

The Legal Status of the Tridentine Mass
A Privilege of the Ordained. Angelus Press
The Roman Rite Destroyed
The Liturgical Revolution
Antony Roper memorial Lecture 1984 :
The Catechetical Revolution—Blessing or Disaster?
Saint Athanasius—Defender of the Faith
The Divine Constitution and Indefectibility of the Catholic Church
The Barbarians Have Taken Over
The Goldfish Bowl: The Church Since Vatican II
The Eternal Sacrifice. The Liturgy Since Vatican II
A Critique: Mass Facing the People
Liturgical Shipwreck: 25 Years of the New Mass
Medjugorje After 15 Years: The Message and Meaning
A Short History of the Roman Mass
The Catholic Sanctuary and the Second Vatican Council
The Great debate of '98: Questioning the
Status of the New Order of Mass
Liturgical Time Bombs in Vatican II
The Reign of Christ the King—In Both Public and Private Life

MEDJUGORJE

The First Twenty-One Years
(1981–2002)

A SOURCE-BASED CONTRIBUTION TO THE DEFINITIVE HISTORY

Michael Davies

Foreword by Peter Kwasniewski
A Reminiscence by Adrian Davies

This edition is the only authorized work available and is published with the permission of the Davies estate. In the interests of keeping Michael Davies's original writing intact, we have decided to retain all the footnotes included by the author at the time of its composition. As such, we cannot guarantee that the addresses and contact information included are still accurate.

Copyright © Davies Estate, 2023
Foreword © Peter Kwasniewski, 2023

All rights reserved:
No part of this book may be reproduced or transmitted, in any form or by any means, without permission

ISBN: 978-1-990685-39-2 (pbk)
ISBN: 978-1-990685-40-8 (hc)

Arouca Press
PO Box 55003
Bridgeport PO
Waterloo, ON N2J 3G0
Canada
www.aroucapress.com
Send inquiries to info@aroucapress.com

CONTENTS

Note on this Edition xi

Foreword, Peter Kwasniewski xiii

My Father and Medjugorje: A Reminiscence, Adrian Davies xvii

Preface, Bishop Ratko Perić xix

Introduction, Michael Davies xxvii

List of Principal Croatian Personae Mentioned in this Book xxxi

	1 The Six "Seers" 3
24 JUNE, 1981	**2** The First 'Apparitions' 10
	3 The Charismatic Connection 15
	4 A Preposterous Proliferation 17
	5 Credibility of the Messages 20
	6 Secrets 22
4 SEPTEMBER, 1981	**7** The Sign 23
	8 The Position of Bishop Pavao Žanić 24
	9 An Immoral Priest Defended 26
	10 Fraud on Film 28
	11 The Herzegovina Question 30
25 MARCH, 1985	**12** A Letter from Bishop Žanić to Father Tomislav Pervan 31
23 FEBRUARY, 1987	**13** Communiqué of the Yugoslav Bishops Concerning the Facts of Medjugorje 34
25 JULY, 1987	**14** Declaration of the Bishop of Mostar Concerning Medjugorje 36
20 JANUARY, 1988	**15** Letter to Mrs Marija Davies from the Bishop of Mostar 41
11 JULY, 1988	**16** Marija Pavlović Contradicts Herself 43
31 MARCH, 1989	**17** Visions in Alabama? 47

MAY 1990	18	*The Truth about Medjugorje*	49
13 JUNE, 1990	19	*The Irish Bishops' Conference Statement*	72
1991	20	*Alleged Miracles at Medjugorje*	73
	21	*The Medjugorje Industry*	75
MAY–JUNE 1993	22	*Sacrificial Giving*	77
1993	23	*Millions Are Deluded*	81
24 JULY, 1993	24	*A New Bishop of Mostar*	84
OCTOBER, 1993	25	*An Interview with the Bishop of Mostar (excerpts)*	88
10–11 SEPTEMBER, 1994	26	*The Pope Visits Croatia*	92
11 OCTOBER, 1994	27	*Synod Intervention by Monsignor Ratko Perić*	97
17 JUNE, 1995	28	*The Film* Gospa	99
31 AUGUST, 1995	29	*A Warning Concerning the Film* Gospa	101
23 MARCH, 1996	30	*CDF Letter to Bishop Taverdet*	102
16 JUNE, 1996	31	*The Ban on Pilgrimages Reaffirmed*	104
4 DECEMBER, 1996	32	*The Circulation of Texts of Alleged Private Revelations*	105
25 JANUARY, 1997	33	*Medjugorje: The State of the Question in 1997*	107
12–13 APRIL, 1997	34	*Medjugorje in the Light of the Pope's Visit to Sarajevo*	110
13 APRIL, 1997	35	*The Pope, Medjugorje, and the Provincial of the Herzegovina Franciscans*	113
22 JUNE, 1997	36	*What Kind of "Fruits" are These?*	115
NOVEMBER, 1997	37	*Medjugorje Incredibilities*	119
11 NOVEMBER, 1997	38	*The "Confirmation" in Čapljina and the "Charisma" of Medjugorje*	124
26 DECEMBER, 1997	39	*The Grievous Fate of the Truth*	130
19 MARCH, 1998	40	*Father Laurentin Visits Bishop Perić*	133
22 MARCH, 1998	41	*Father Laurentin Writes to Bishop Perić*	137

23 MARCH, 1998	**42**	*The Franciscan Rebellion in Herzegovina: Rome Acts* 138
24 MARCH, 1998	**43**	*A Letter from Monsignor Ratko Perić to the Abbé René Laurentin, Protocol Number 265/98* 140
26 MAY, 1998	**44**	*Beautiful Gift or Pathetic Delusion?* 142
21 JULY, 1998	**45**	*Private Visits to Unauthentic Apparitions* 151
15 SEPTEMBER, 1998	**46**	*An Unexpected Endorsement For Bishop Perić* 154
16 NOVEMBER, 1998	**47**	*Implementing* Romanis Pontificibus 156
21 NOVEMBER, 1998	**48**	*Dismissal of Three Franciscans From the Order of Friars Minor* 159
14 DECEMBER, 1998	**49**	*Further Implementation of the Decree* Romanis Pontificibus—*Communiqué* 161
	50	*January, 1999: With Truth Against Lies Concerning the Parish of Čapljina* 163
20 FEBRUARY, 1999	**51**	*The Franciscan Rebellion in Herzegovina: Rome Acts* 172
7 JANUARY, 2000	**52**	*The Position of the French Episcopal Conference Regarding Medjugorje* 176
11 JANUARY, 2000	**53**	*Death of Bishop Pavao Žanić* 187
24 JANUARY, 2000	**54**	Newsweek *Report:"Visions of the Virgin"* 188
7 FEBRUARY, 2000	**55**	*A Letter From Bishop Ratko Perić Concerning Father Zovko* 191
1 JULY, 2000	**56**	*Confirmation Homily by Bishop Ratko Perić* 193
3 DECEMBER, 2000	**57**	*A Medjugorje Canonisation* 198
28 MAY, 2001	**58**	*Communiqué from Monsignor Luka Pavlović, Vicar General of Mostar-Duvno* 199

29 MAY, 2001	**59**	*Communiqué of the Bishops' Conference of Bosnia-Herzegovina* 205
14 JUNE, 2001	**60**	*Homily by Bishop Perić* 207
10 OCTOBER, 2001	**61**	*Bosnia-Herzegovina Cardinal Critical of Medjugorje Franciscans* 212
	62	*Mostar, 2001: Final Chapter of the Book* Ogledalo Pravde ("Mirror of Justice"), *by Bishop Perić* 214
5 JULY, 2002	**63**	Catholic Herald *Report* 217
12 JULY, 2002	**64**	Catholic Herald: *A Defence of Medjugorje* 224
19 JULY, 2002	**65**	Catholic Herald: *My Reply to Monsignor Tutto* 228
26 JULY, 2002	**66**	Catholic Herald *Editorial: The Mixed Fruits of Medjugorje* 232
24 AUGUST, 2002	**67**	*A Bogus Papal Blessing* 236
	68	*October, 2002: Unexpected Support for the False Apparitions* 241
8 NOVEMBER, 2002	**69**	Crkva Na Kamenu: *A Pronouncement by the Congregation for the Doctrine of the Faith on the Current Spate of Apparitions* 251
29 DECEMBER, 2002	**70**	The Sunday Times 254
		Final Note 257

APPENDICES 259

17 FEBRUARY, 2004	**1**	*A Definitive Statement by Bishop Perić* 261
	2	Regarding the Events of Medjugorje: Part 1 278
	3	Extracts from the Diary of Vicka Ivanković 297

NOTE ON THIS EDITION

IN THE FINAL MONTHS OF HIS LIFE IN 2004, Michael Davies was revising and updating a number of his books, one of which was *Medjugorje after Twenty-One Years (1981–2002): The Definitive History*. In early 2004, I was asked by Michael to proofread his manuscript to ensure uniformity of presentation and content. Sadly, he died on 25 September, 2004, before the task was completed but his widow Maria, son Adrian, and I finished the work in 2005. The publishers I approached at that time declined to publish on the grounds that interest in Medjugorje was waning.

Somehow, a version of Michael's incomplete and unauthorised version, which includes my name as his proofreader, and which had not been approved by Michael or his family, started appearing on a number of websites at that time. Michael's family are delighted that Arouca Press has now published his book and wish to make it clear that this is the only authorised version approved by them as his executors. All other versions on the internet are unauthorised and should be removed.

Leo Darroch

FOREWORD

A Valuable Work Rescued from the Davies Archives

WHEN I WAS A GREENHORN (BLUEHORN?) MARIAN devotee in high school—this would have been right around the year 1988—a friend of mine who used to drive me to conferences, retreats, Rosary rallies, special Masses, and the like, and who had strained to breaking point his rearview mirror with the number of devotional items hanging from it, introduced me to the already-burgeoning phenomenon of Medjugorje. He avidly shared the messages and proudly displayed a Rosary the metal links of which had changed color. He was also an advocate of the Blue Army and Fr. Gobbi's Marian Movement of Priests.

Although I lost touch with this friend after college, I never lost my devotion to Our Lady; indeed, it has been a mainstay of my life ever since, particularly the praying of the Rosary and the wearing of the Brown Scapular of Our Lady of Mount Carmel (which, since July 16, 2021, has acquired a poignant new meaning as the symbol of our pleading for and our confidence in her heavenly help against the enemies of Tradition). I did, however, grow cold towards Medjugorje and the MMP. Instead, it was my love for the liturgy that grew warm, and as I immersed myself in it more, I found it to be the most substantial nourishment the Church offered. Moreover, as my intellectual life opened up through the reading of the Church's Fathers and Doctors, the contrast between their spiritual wisdom and the often puerile content of popular private revelations did not reflect well on the latter.

Yet I would sometimes wonder about Medjugorje. Why were so many "into it" in such a passionate, even obsessive way? Why did the repeated condemnations of the local bishop have so little effect? Why couldn't the Vatican reach any decision in the face of an embarrassing flood of messages (now in the tens or possibly hundreds of thousands) lasting for decades and characterized by sheer banality and imbecilic theological errors? What was really going on? But I did not have the time or take the opportunity to dig deeper. I suspect that this is the case with many Catholics: they are aware, peripherally, of popular movements or groups or causes or places, but they do not know what to think about them—and, more crucially, who they can trust to tell the story.

The book that we are now fortunate to see in print at last—the definitive version of Michael Davies's study of the Medjugorje phenomenon, a work he was revising right up to his death in 2004—is a valuable contribution to the growing literature on the subject. Although the work covers only the period from 1981 to 2002, it brings together and offers incisive observations on material that other treatments summarize rapidly or even omit altogether. It must be remembered that Michael's Croatian wife, Maria, was in a unique position to assist Michael with access to an abundance of information in her native language that would have been, and often still is, a closed book to researchers from other countries.

At the request of Michael's wife Maria and their son Adrian, the manuscript was tidied up by Leo Darroch in late 2005, but never found a publisher at the time, due to a perception—not surprising at the bright dawn of Pope Benedict XVI's pontificate—that interest in Medjugorje was waning. So far from losing its magnetism, however, the place of the alleged apparitions has continued to attract huge numbers of pilgrims from all over the world, especially since the Vatican under Pope Francis has given mixed signals (albeit generally construed as encouraging ones) about pilgrimages and pious exercises in connection with it. Alas, it is no reason for rejoicing that official attitudes seem to have "thawed," for, as Davies shows in these pages, the evidence that meets the inquisitive eye is disturbing. The local hierarchy unwaveringly condemned the claimed apparitions—not for "political reasons," as some maintain, but for theological, spiritual, and pastoral ones that remain as relevant in 2022 as they were in 2002.

While Davies's book is not the most comprehensive study of the subject,[1] it is one of the most helpful in its provision of original sources and one of the most thoughtful in its judicious observations. It is not every day that one finds a new book on an important subject tackled by a deservedly famous Catholic author. Davies sees the connection of Medjugorje with a variety of controversial issues in the Church today: the relationship of authority and obedience, the nature of the charismatic movement, the dangers of chasing after private revelations (which has, I'm afraid, invaded the traditionalist movement as well), the scandal of clerical immorality, and the lure of false ecumenism.

How easy it is for unwary and unstable human beings to let themselves be carried away and led down a dangerous road, at times into cult-like behavior! How readily Church authorities who attempted to critique or control the Medjugorje enthusiasm were ignored, and what a mess certain other authorities have made of the volatile situation! If the truth will set us free, as Christ proclaimed, then falsehood, with its origin in the enemy of mankind, will do the opposite. Sadly, many devotees of the so-called "Queen of Peace" of Bosnia-Herzogovina are so "locked in," so convinced of the heavenly origin of these visions, that they would consider a book like this one to be a temptation to be resisted or even a form of unfair persecution. My decades-long experience with the writings of Michael Davies persuades me otherwise: his books are the meticulous work of a man in love with the truth, with Our Lord, with His Blessed Mother, and with Holy Mother Church.

Peter A. Kwasniewski
November 21, 2022
Presentation of the Blessed Virgin Mary

---

[1] This description befits Donal Anthony Foley's *Medjugorje Complete: The Definitive Account of the Visions and Visionaries* (Brooklyn, NY: Angelico Press, 2021), which belongs in the library of any serious student of the subject.

A REMINISCENCE

My Father and Medjugorje

MY FATHER MICHAEL DAVIES WOULD, I THINK, BE surprised at the continuing interest in his writings more than eighteen years after his death and so much longer after most of his work was done. That was not only because he was a modest man, but also because he very well understood the difference between writing about events in the distant past and writing about events in the recent past.

The analysis and, dare I say, the conjectures of an author whose subject is the ancient world or the Middle Ages are much less likely to be rendered obsolete by the discovery of documents that cast a completely new light upon his subject than books dealing with current events or the recent past. However well an author deals with the materials at his disposal, if his subject is recent events, his work is apt to be superseded not merely by new perspectives, which are matters of opinion, but by the discovery or declassification of new materials, which might reveal new or at least hitherto hidden facts—a most unusual thing in classical or even mediaeval history, but only to be expected when the subject matter is the Catholic Church since Vatican II.

I know very well (since my father told me not long before he died) that he had not expected his great liturgical trilogy, written, it should be remembered, decades before his death in 2004, though revised by the author more than once in the intervening years, to continue in print into the third millennium. He would be astonished to find it still in print and much in demand in the third decade of the third millennium.

My father would be even more amazed that his turn-of-the-millennium writings about the "apparitions" at Medjugorje are being reprinted in 2022, since events have moved on in the intervening twenty years and more, but nevertheless his book has a particular value that few English texts about Medjugorje share.

My mother (now, alas, in very poor health) is Croatian and with her help (and even some help from me, since I learned Croatian as a child) he was able to access part of the vast Croatian literature about Medjugorje, and to put the phenomenon in its peculiar historical context, namely the sad quarrels between some dissident Franciscans (not ultimately supported by their order) in the Franciscan Province of Bosnia and Herzegovina and the bishops of Mostar, which predated the apparitions by some years, but became mixed up with the supposed visions when the dissidents took up the cause of the "seers."

My father was able to correspond with Bishop Perić, the scholarly and much respected Bishop of Mostar, who shared the scepticism of his eminent predecessor, Bishop Žanić, about the claims of the "seers," and so obtain a different perspective to that of the enthusiasts who continue to flock to Medjugorje in 2022—including, unfortunately, some high profile Croatian footballers of exemplary personal Catholic life, who in general terms offer vastly more positive role models for youth than their English counterparts.

This little book, then, has a continuing value and I am grateful to Mr Barbas and Arouca Press for publishing its final version.

Adrian Davies

PREFACE

The Truth Both Frees Us and Binds Us

THERE IS A GOOD NUMBER OF THE FAITHFUL throughout the world who strive for the purity of the Faith, respecting the Church's Magisterium and bearing witness to the spuriousness of the "visions" at Medjugorje. One of them is Michael Davies of London. When I assumed responsibility for the diocese of Mostar, I came to know Mr Davies, who is English[1], and his wife Maria, who is Croatian. They were friends of my predecessor, the late Bishop Pavao Žanić, who died on 11 November, 2000. I must thank Michael for the efforts that he has made to follow and criticise the unbelievable claims made about the events at Medjugorje, a theme that he develops in this book, *Medjugorje after Twenty-One Years*.

Why do I as the local bishop not accept the "visions" at Medjugorje as worthy of credence? I begin from the premise that I would truly like to believe that the "visions" are authentic, and that Our Lady truly appeared there. Indeed, not only there. Yet the truth both frees us and binds us! As I followed the events at Medjugorje in recent years, I was driven to the following conclusions.

Firstly, the story dating back to 1981 of the so-called "visions" of the six "seers" of Medjugorje, half of whom still see visions on a daily basis, while the other half see them only once a year, has long since spread beyond the borders of the parish and the diocese both by rumour and by reason of the travels through the world of the "seers" and their supporters.

There can be no doubt that the "visions" have made converts in the ranks of commercial travellers, who had a "vision"

---

1 You won't like that comment! [Note: This is a friendly joke on the part of Bishop Perić. Although I was born in England my father was Welsh and I have always considered myself a Welshman].

of very tangible benefits for themselves, whence they spread to the ranks of religious enthusiasts, who travel thousands of miles to make their confessions and say the Rosary at Medjugorje! The "visions" have not, however, been recognised by the Church, so no one is any way bound to believe in them.

Secondly, some Franciscans in Herzegovina as well as a number of priests throughout the world promote the concept of Medjugorje as the site of "supernatural visions and messages". A number of the faithful, moreover, persist in visiting Medjugorje, not only so as to bear witness to how "Our Lady appears" despite the Church's cautious stance, but also to bring pressure to bear on Church authorities, not excluding even the very highest, to recognise the events at Medjugorje as visions worthy of credence.

I have to ask how Christ's Church could on the basis of such pilgrimages to a single parish, motivated by a range of emotions from mere curiosity to fanatical zeal, proclaim such "visions" to be supernatural, when three ecclesiastical commissions of inquiry into the events at Medjugorje lawfully constituted on the direction of Bishop Žanić, the local bishop, and the Conference of Bishops [of the former Yugoslavia] in 1991 confirmed that they could find no proof that there had been "supernatural visions and messages". How could the Church, which is the pillar and support of the truth, recognise these more than questionable "visions" under pressure from such petitioners?

Thirdly, it is most puzzling why such priests and faithful who really thirst for visions and messages do not drink their fill from the sources of visions that have been recognised as authentic—for example, Lourdes and Fatima, though there are others besides—but instead turn to the unrecognised "visions" at Medjugorje, where "Our Lady" supposedly "appears" *sine fine*. The Church recognized some of the seers of Lourdes and Fatima as saints or as blessed after their deaths, but the champions of Medjugorje seem to be in competition with one another to see who can go the most times to a place where the Church has not merely declined to recognise the authenticity of the "visions" but has even forbidden private or public pilgrimages if they are based on the authenticity of the unrecognised "visions".

If indeed some bishops from other parts of the world come and stay at Medjugorje (some twenty kilometres from Mostar) for several days, yet do not even feel the need to make themselves known to their local counterpart, whether during or after the war [between Croatia and Serbia], then such servants of the Church show neither episcopal collegiality nor solicitude for the universal Church (1 Cor. 11:28) but rather a strange curiosity to see what "visions" might be seen on the stony hillsides of Herzegovina. Yet we bishops and priests constantly pray to God in the Canon of the Mass to confirm His Church in faith and charity on its way through this world.

Fourthly, the mere fact that many people, though they are believers, hold something to be true does not make it true; perhaps even the contrary is the case. Christ the Lord stood alone, but for His Mother and one disciple, at Gabbatha and on Golgotha. He was the only Truth opposed by the nameless masses, the superior and inferior clergy, and the national and international establishment in Jerusalem.

When Christ proclaimed that He was the truth, Pilate gave the jesting answer "What is truth?" (John 18:38), which is to say, that for them personal advantage, political position, and a temporary triumph were more important than any truth, human or divine!

Though the Truth died on that Good Friday, it rose again on the third day. Truth is not, therefore, necessarily in the greater number. So, all the valid confessions, communions and Rosary prayers at Medjugorje, though they confer grace as efficaciously as in other parishes, no more and no less, do not of themselves in any sense demonstrate the truth of the "supernatural apparitions" in that parish.

Fifthly, the "seers" who see visions on a daily basis and the endless apparitions themselves (33,333 to date, nor is there any risk of my being mistaken, for there is no end to the numbers of the "visions") are more in the nature of a religious show and a spectacle for the world than a true and faithful witness to the peace and unity of the Faith and love for the Church. Who can fail to see that these endlessly multiplying numbers should not be taken seriously? Shall we change our Catholic orthodoxy for fantastical superstition?

Sixthly, the many "messages" pronounced in the early years by the mouths of the so-called "seers", especially those that praised the disobedience of some Franciscan priests in Mostar, and berated the local bishop who conscientiously abided by canon law, that belittled the highest decisions of the Church regarding the administration of the diocese, which as such were obviously inspired by worldly considerations and not by heaven, brought far greater disorder and conflict than true peace and order to the Church.

Seventhly, our Croatian Franciscans, who accept Medjugorje as a place of "supernatural apparitions," have never, alas, distanced themselves publicly from this bad and untruthful message to the Church in Herzegovina.

Some Franciscan Fathers have performed many invalid confirmations. One of them, who falsely purported to confirm with a mitre on his head in the parish of Čapljina in 1997, claimed to come from Medjugorje and openly supported schism in that community by his sacrilegious and invalid confirmations. Now that he has been expelled from the Franciscan order, he has forcibly occupied the parish of Grude, where, two days ago, on the feast of Whitsun, 2004, according to a photograph which appeared in the daily papers, he once again carried out invalid confirmations, but this time without a mitre.

If the "seers" with their "visions" tolerate such schismatic scandals, without in any way admonishing those involved, and likewise those who support the "seers" and act as their public relations men, without ever distancing themselves from or condemning such local schisms, then in the name of the Mother of God, the Queen of Peace, yea, in the name of the Holy Trinity, one God, might that not be a sign that those involved in propagandizing in support of the supposed credibility of such "visions" do not have the Divine will at the forefront of their thoughts?

A group of Franciscans (eight living, one deceased) who have been expelled from their Order for their notorious disobedience to the decisions both of their own superiors and of the Holy See with regard to matters of ecclesiastical administration in the diocese, have forcibly taken over a number of parishes in which for some years now they have been administering invalid confessions, and officiating at invalid marriages, some even carrying out invalid confirmations, and generally carrying on in defiance of canon law, all in the immediate or general neighbourhood of Medjugorje, as the place where tens of thousands of "visions" have occurred.

It is indeed astonishing that the "apparition", which has passed on messages to thousands of the curious, including even American President Ronald Reagan and Soviet Premier Mikhail Gorbachev, and its supporters, has not yet expressed concern, whether about the blasphemy perpetrated against Christ's sacraments or the damage to the unity of the Church in the diocese of Mostar-Duvno. It is certainly remarkable that people come from all over the world to make their confessions in Medjugorje, but the expelled Franciscans and a few others who are in a state of disobedience to the Holy See, their Order and the local Church authorities, give thousands of invalid absolutions in the very neighbourhood of Medjugorje.

When this group of Franciscans, who even now wear Franciscan habits even though they were canonically expelled from the Order of Friars Minor in 2001, blasphemously and sacrilegiously sinned against the sacraments of the Eucharist and of confirmation by summoning an Old Catholic deacon (!), a schismatic not in communion with the Catholic Church, to celebrate an invalid Eucharist and to "confirm" hundreds of candidates in three parishes (Grude, Čapljina and Ploče-Tepčići), that deacon falsely held himself out to be a bishop, saying, "both the friars and I believe in the Marian apparitions at Medjugorje".

Alas, we heard not a word and saw not a sign of disapproval of such pronouncements. On the contrary, some still defend the visitation of the non-Catholic deacon who proclaimed himself to be a bishop. One of his colleagues, who lived in the same community for some time, tells how this deacon celebrated "Mass" in honour of the Blessed Virgin Mary in a church in Switzerland on the feast of the Assumption, all dressed in black! A requiem for the Mother of God on the day of her Assumption into heaven! What folly! A man who cannot celebrate Mass at all, since he is not a priest, so insults Our Lady, who reached a higher state of holiness than any other human being, yet he claims to "believe in the Marian apparitions at Medjugorje", and comes along to "confirm" Catholic children in Herzegovina. Yet that same colleague of his has given written testimony that this "bishop" does not recognize the sacrament of confirmation administered according to the Catholic rite, so he "confirmed" his friend a second time!

The scandal of disobedience, concerning which we have not heard a word of criticism from the "oasis of peace" at Medjugorje, has grown to such a level that some of the abovementioned former Franciscans asked an Old Catholic bishop in Switzerland to consecrate one of them as bishop! So that the schism in the diocese should deepen?

The Holy Father, John Paul II, who has never mentioned Medjugorje in any of his allocutions, has frequently summoned the superiors of the Order of Friars Minor to resolve the Herzegovinian question.

So, for example, on 16 June, 2003, the Pope once again asked the members of the General Chapter of the Franciscan Order to carry into effect the decision of his predecessor, Pope Paul VI, going back to 1975:

> Your missionary activity will prove fruitful in so far as it is fulfilled in harmony with the lawful pastors to whom Our Lord has entrusted responsibility for his flock. Bearing that well in mind, I once again warmly remind you of the efforts that have been made to overcome the difficulties that have long existed in certain areas. It is my heartfelt wish that, with co-operation on every side, that understanding with the diocesan authorities sought by my worthy predecessor, Pope Paul VI, should be fully attained. It has become

apparent that such an understanding is a prerequisite for effective evangelisation.

It would be desirable to have an unambiguous response from the Franciscan side to this exhortation by the Pope.

For my part, I have never publicized the immorality or the financial scandals associated with Medjugorje. There are other well-publicized disorders and evidence that sufficiently disprove the supposedly supernatural nature of the "visions" and suggest that it would be better to conclude *"constat de non supernaturalitate"* rather than *"non constat de supernaturalitate"*.

This book seeks to describe chronologically, analyse logically, and explain faithfully the many facts connected with the more than questionable "visions" at Medjugorje. May the true Queen of Peace help the author by her intercession with the most Holy Trinity.

Mostar, on the feast of the Blessed Virgin Mary,
Mother of the Church,
31 May, 2004,
✠ *Ratko Perić*, Bishop

INTRODUCTION

SINCE THE SECOND VATICAN COUNCIL THERE HAS been a grave crisis of authority within the Catholic Church. The ordinary faithful have not received the firm and unequivocal teaching and guidance from their ecclesiastical superiors to which they had become accustomed. Cardinal Josef Ratzinger, the Prefect of the Congregation for the Doctrine of the Faith, has noted the extent to which individual bishops have abdicated their authority to national episcopal conferences which, only too often, have been manipulated into propagating the opinions of so-called theological experts of dubious orthodoxy.

Parish priests have frequently abdicated their authority to parish councils, and Rome itself has sometimes appeared to speak with an uncertain voice. But certainty is what the faithful seek, and when they do not receive it from the Magisterium, they will seek it elsewhere. Some have sought certainty in the charismatic movement which, if examined objectively, renders the Magisterium unnecessary, for what need is there of a teaching authority when each individual Christian can communicate directly with the Holy Ghost?

Other Catholics have put their faith in one of the numerous apparitions which are allegedly taking place throughout the world. For the purposes of this book a distinction must be made between visions and apparitions. Donal Foley is probably the greatest authority on Marian apparitions writing in the English language today. He explains:

> The basic difference between a "vision" and an "apparition" in Catholic terms, is as follows: in a vision God produces a concept or image without there necessarily being anything external to the viewer, whereas in an apparition, God apparently causes something external to the viewer to be perceived through the senses, which act normally, even if the "seer" is in an ecstatic state.[1]

---

1 D. Foley, *Marian Apparitions, the Bible, and the Modern World* (Gracewing Press, Herefordshire, 2002), 100.

This distinction is not always made clear by those promoting Medjugorje. It is evident that what the so-called seers claim to receive are, according to Mr. Foley's definition, apparitions, but in Medjugorje literature they are described indiscriminately as seers or visionaries. This is not a matter of any importance, because, as this book will make clear, no individual associated with Medjugorje has ever been the recipient of either an apparition or a vision.

In the years following the Council a very clear pattern of behaviour has emerged among supporters of alleged apparitions. It is a tendency to make belief in the authenticity of a particular apparition the criterion of orthodoxy. *True* Catholics believe the apparitions, and the faith of those who do not is suspect in some way. Those drawn towards these apparitions tend to be conservative in outlook, the type of Catholic who might have been expected to defend the teaching of the Magisterium. Once such Catholics become "hooked" on an apparition, all their efforts tend to be devoted to defending and propagating it. They have thus been effectively removed from the battlefield for orthodoxy. There can be no doubt that spurious apparitions are one of Satan's most effective weapons in his war against the Mystical Body of Christ. The problem is, of course, to distinguish authentic from spurious apparitions. The principles for making this distinction are enunciated clearly in Appendix II.

I recollect very clearly that a decade or so ago I scandalised some devout friends by maintaining that the alleged apparitions at Palmar de Troya in Spain were inspired by the devil. I was asked how I could make such a claim in view of the piety manifested there: all-night vigils, heroic acts of penance, the Rosary, and financial sacrifices of staggering proportions. How could Satan have been responsible for such good fruits? I knew one devout and highly educated English Catholic who sold everything he had and abandoned his profession to go and live in Palmar. Later, when Clemente, the self-styled seer, proclaimed himself to be Pope and "excommunicated" everyone who did not recognise him as such, this friend and

Introduction

others withdrew from Palmar in horror, and admitted that they had been deceived. But the tragedy is that there are thousands who did not. Their faith had become identified with the authenticity of the Palmar sect. Satan had amputated them from the Mystical Body of Christ.

How can one reconcile the devotion that I have mentioned with diabolic inspiration? The answer should be self-evident. If a seer, claiming to be inspired by heaven, denied the doctrine of the Trinity or advocated free love, he would hardly be likely to deceive faithful Catholics. Satan will obviously seek to introduce error and separate the faithful from the Church under a veneer of piety.

There can be little doubt that when the time comes for adherents of Medjugorje to choose between the Church and the illusory apparitions, many will choose the apparitions, as was the case with Palmar de Troya. As Pope Leo XIII warned in his encyclical *Satis cognitum*: "The Church of Christ, therefore, is one and the same forever: those who leave it depart from the will and command of Christ the Lord. Leaving the path of salvation, they enter on the path of perdition."

In 1983 I was visited by some good friends who brought me a booklet written in Croatian about some apparitions allegedly taking place at Medjugorje in what was then Yugoslavia. They wished my wife, who is Croatian, to translate it. When they left, I asked my wife to give me a résumé of the alleged messages, and after she had done so with the first three, I told her not to waste a second of her time translating them as they did not possess a vestige of credibility. I am glad to say that these friends now share my opinion. Since that time Medjugorje has attracted more attention and more enthusiasm almost daily, and millions of Catholics now flock there from throughout the world.

Michael Davies
15 September, 2004
(The Seven Sorrows of the Blessed Virgin Mary)
Note: Michael Davies died on 25 September, 2004.

LIST OF PRINCIPAL CROATIAN PERSONAE MENTIONED IN THIS BOOK

IT MAY BE OF SOME HELP IF I PROVIDE A LIST OF the principal Croatian personae mentioned in the book, particularly as a good number of them have the same surnames. The reference OP refers to the book *Ogledalo Pravde* by Bishop Perić.

Father Petar Barbarić, OFM: expelled from the Franciscan Order for disobedience (see 23 March, 1998).

Father Slavko Barbarić, OFM: one of the principal mentors of the six seers and concealers of the truth concerning Medjurgorje. He died in 2000 and received an instant Medjugorje canonization (see 3 December, 2000).

Father Janko Bubalo: author of a book entitled *A Thousand Meetings with Our Lady*, consisting of conversations with Vicka Ivanković.

Jakov Colo: youngest "seer".

Bishop Petar Čule of Mostar: predecessor of Bishop Pavao Žanić.

Ivan Dragicević: "seer".

Mirjana Dragicević: "seer".

Archbishop Franić of Split: a Charismatic and the only prelate in the former Yugoslavia to believe the apparitions to be authentic.

Ivanka (Ivica) Ivanković: "seer".

Vicka (Vida) Ivanković: oldest "seer".

His Eminence Cardinal Franjo Kuharić: President of the Yugoslav Episcopal Conference.

Father Ivan Landeka: parish priest of Medjugorje in 1993.

Sister Leopolda: religious sister seduced by Father Ivica Vego.

Father Miljenko Mića Stojić,: parish priest at Medjugorje in 1997.

Marija Pavlović: "seer".

Father Tadija Pavlović, OFM: priest quickly disillusioned with Medjugorje (see 24 June, 1981)

Monsignor Ratko Perić: Bishop of Mostar-Duvno from 24 July, 1993.

Father Tomislav Pervan: parish priest of Medjugorje from 1984-1988, then Provincial of the Franciscan Province of Herzegovina.

Father Ivan Prusina, OFM: expelled from the Franciscan Order for disobedience, but reinstated on a legal technicality. Now lives in Germany and is not permitted to exercise any ministry in Herzegovina.

Monsignor Želimir Puljić: Bishop of Dubrovnik.

Father Bože Radoš, OFM: expelled from the Franciscan Order for disobedience.

Father Ljudevit Rupčić, OFM: forbidden to celebrate Mass or preach at Medjugorje.

Father Ivo Sivrić, OFM: author, *The Hidden Face of Medjugorje*.

Father Emilio Tardif, OFM: charismatic Franciscan who initiated "seers" into the movement (see "The Charismatic Connection").

Jelena Vasilj: "locutionist".

Marijana Vasilj (no relation): "locutionist".

Monsignor Pavao Žanić: Bishop of Mostar-Duvno, 1980-1993.

Father Jozo Vasilj, OFM: Franciscan Provincial in Herzegovina who was so disillusioned with the members of his province that he moved to Zaire and will not return.

Father Ivica Vego, OFM: laicised after making Sister Leopolda pregnant. Now married to her and still actively involved with Medjugorje.

Father Jozo Zovko: parish priest of Medjugorje when the "apparitions" began. Forbidden to celebrate Mass for the faithful or to preach in Herzegovina.

MEDJUGORJE
The First Twenty-One Years
(1981–2002)

1
The Six "Seers"

IN THE INTERESTS OF CLARITY, BEFORE ENTERING upon an account of the events at Medjugorje in chronological order, brief biographies of the self-styled seers are given below. In several cases they have the same surname, which tends to cause confusion. They are, in order of age:

Vicka (Vida) Ivanković, born on 3 September, 1964, is the oldest of the seers. She has been receiving daily apparitions since 24 June, 1981, although on some days there were no apparitions, while on others she received five or more. She has received nine of the ten secrets and still receives daily apparitions. Vicka is always willing to speak to any large number of pilgrims who wish to meet her, and to put their questions to Our Lady and to transmit her answers to them.

She claims that for two years, from 7 January, 1983, until 10 April, 1985, Our Lady recounted her life story in great detail, and that this autobiography will be published in due course. She also stated in an interview for an Australian television network, which I have on video-cassette, that Our Lady took her on a guided tour of heaven, hell, and purgatory. Jakov Colo, the youngest visionary, was also invited on the tour. Our Lady took Vicka by the right hand and Jakov by the left and they floated off. Vicka wondered how long the journey would take, and was amazed to find that it lasted only one second. The tour itself took twenty minutes. Vicka did not explain how she was able to be so precise about the time taken. Heaven is a very large room in which people wearing grey, yellow, and pink gowns are walking, praying, and singing while small angels float above them. Purgatory is a big space in which no one can be seen, but it was possible to feel that the souls there were beating and thumping each other. There is a large fire in hell into which the souls enter and emerge as beasts.

Another of her stories is of a taxi driver who had been given a bloody handkerchief which he was about to throw in a river. A mysterious woman in black—who, of course, turned out to be Our Lady—prevented him just in time, because had he thrown it the world would have been destroyed (see May 1990, Part 6). No open-minded person who reads Bishop Žanić's account of Vicka (see May 1990, Parts 6-11), or of her attempt to defraud Dutch benefactors of Medjugorje by telling them that Our Lady wished them to finance the construction of an hotel by the father of one of her friends, can escape the conclusion that she is an habitual liar (see November 1997, *Medjugorje Incredibilities*).

In January, 2002, Vicka married Mario Mijatovic, from the parish of Gradino. They live in the parish of Medjugorje.

Mirjana Dragicević was born in Sarajevo on 18 March, 1965. Her first vision was on 24 June, 1981, and after receiving the tenth secret on 25 December, 1982, she ceased to have daily apparitions. Mirjana said that parting from Our Lady caused her great sorrow, and they found it hard to part from each other even after being together for forty-five minutes. Our Lady assured Mirjana that she must return to a normal daily routine and live in the future without her motherly advice. She warned Mirjana that the first few months without their daily meetings would be very hard for her, and this proved to be the case. Mirjana fell into a state of deep depression, avoided everyone, and locked herself in her bedroom weeping, hoping that Our Lady would appear to her, and calling out her name. Our Lady bestowed a great gift to her, that of promising to appear on her birthday for the rest of her life. However, a year is a long time, visitors were coming from all sides, and so Our Lady had a change of mind. On 2 August, 1987, Mirjana received an internal locution, and from then on, on the second of every month, she has received an internal locution or an actual apparition of Our Lady, and sometimes they pray together for unbelievers. From 2 January, 1997, these visits ceased to be on a private basis. Mirjana is made aware of the exact time when Our Lady will appear, from 10:00 a.m. until 11:00 a.m., and this monthly meeting is now open to the public.

Mirjana has received all ten secrets. She claims to have received them from Our Lady on a parchment which has been examined by 'linguistic experts' who pronounced that it was written in an unknown language. That is fortunate as had this not been the case, they would no longer have been secret. The only precedent for a document in an unknown language is that of *The Book of Mormon*. One wonders why Our Lady would have given the ten secrets to Mirjana, who speaks only Croatian, in an unknown language, and whether by some miracle she is able to understand it. It is also claimed that, having been carbon tested for date and substance, the parchment has been documented as made from an unknown substance[1]. Mirjana was married to Marko Soldo on 16 September, 1989, and has two children: Marija, born on 8 December, 1990, and Veronica, born on 19 April, 1994. She is married and lives in Medjugorje.

Mirjana has the distinction of being the only seer to have had an apparition of the devil. He appeared to her on 14 April, 1982, while she was waiting for Our Lady to appear. He was wearing the same clothes worn by Our Lady, and had a terrible black face but with Mary's features. He stared at her with burning black eyes and offered her all the pleasures of the world, but she refused. A little later Our Lady appeared and said: 'I apologise, but you had to see him in order to know that he exists and that you will be tempted in this world.'[2] To the

---

1 See www.medjugorjeusa.org.
2 R. Franken, *A Journey to Medjugorje* (1999), 37. Father Rudo Franken is a Dutch priest who made a journey to Medjugorje to investigate the alleged apparitions. He was prompted to do so by witnessing its popularity among thousands of his fellow citizens. He has read almost all the books and pamphlets written concerning the alleged apparitions and quotes them profusely. I have made use of a good number of these quotations but in every case I have given the page in Father Franken's book where the quotation can be found. Every serious student of Medjugorje should obtain this book, which is recommended highly by Monsignor Ratko Perić, Bishop of Mostar-Duvno. The distribution of this book is made not only by the publisher Van Spijk B.V., but also by the author himself. 136 pages, paperback €10,. published September

best of my knowledge this is the only occasion when Our Lady has apologised to a seer, and no explanation is given as to why she did not command the devil to manifest himself to any of the other Medjugorje seers to prove to them that he existed.

Marija Pavlović was born on 1 April, 1965. She married Paolo Lunetti on 1 April, 1993, and went for a honeymoon on the Côte d'Azur in France. The couple now have three children. Mrs. Lunetti now lives in Monza, Italy, in a 'palatial' six-storey home.[3] She has received nine secrets, and still has daily apparitions. She is on such good terms with Our Lady that the Blessed Virgin allows herself to be caressed if Marija requests it. A nun who was present while Marija was witnessing an apparition relates:

> Marija asked me whether I desired to touch the Virgin. I said yes straight away. She then took my right hand and I lifted it to the Virgin's shoulder: she then guided my hand down telling me what I was touching. I myself neither saw nor felt anything. Thus, I caressed her right down to her feet.

Surely this ludicrous and almost blasphemous nonsense is enough to deprive Pavlović of any credibility.

Marija receives and reveals Our Lady's "Message to the Parish of Medjugorje and the entire World" on the 25th of each month.

Ivan Dragicević, who is not related to Mirjana, was born in Bijakovici, in the parish of Medjugorje, on 25 May, 1965. His secondary education took place in Citluk, where he failed to pass the first-year examinations. In August, 1981, he entered the Franciscan seminary for Herzegovina, where he claimed to receive daily apparitions and claimed that Our Lady always gave him the traditional Croatian greeting: "Praised be Jesus and Mary". It is somewhat surprising that Our Lady, who is

---

2002 (see p. 127). Available from: Rudo Franken, priest, De Hove 1, NL-6585 AN Mook, The Netherlands. rudo.franken@hetnet.nl. Homepage www.stichtingvaak.nl; Van Spijk B. V., P. O. Box 1230, NL-5900 BE Venlo, The Netherlands.
3   Ratko Perić, *Ogledalo Pravde* (Mostar, 2001), 31.

The Six "Seers" 7

our model of humility, would bestow praise upon herself! He failed to pass his first-year examinations after two attempts. It was thought that he might have more success at the seminary in Dubrovnik, where he was sent in the autumn of 1982. On one occasion, during the recitation of the Rosary, he informed his fellow seminarians that Our Lady had appeared upon a picture of Our Lord and said: 'This is your father.' (Our Lord did not once refer to Himself as our father in the Bible and is never referred to as such in the Tradition of the Church.)

Once again Dragicević's academic progress was poor and he left the seminary in January 1983 and returned home. He spent, and still spends, a great deal of his time touring the world, addressing large audiences, and never fails to delight them with purported apparitions of Our Lady. On 23 October, 1994, he married Laureen Murphy, an American beauty queen from Boston, and, of course, had a wedding-day apparition. They have four children. He divides his time between his homes in Medjugorje and Boston. He has received nine secrets and by 2001 more than seven thousand daily apparitions, and still has a daily apparition wherever he is in the world. He is now extremely wealthy and drives a custom-built BMW with "outside the series" wide sports tyres.

Ivanka (Ivica) Ivanković was born in Bijakovici on 21 June, 1966. She married Rajko Elez on 29 December, 1986, and has three children, Kristina, Josip, and Ivan. She has received ten secrets and ceased having daily apparitions on 7 May, 1985. Ivanka claimed that in this final apparition Our Lady had never looked more sweet and beautiful, and was wearing the most beautiful dress that she had ever seen. It sparkled with silver and gold. The Virgin was accompanied by two angels with matching outfits, and asked Ivanka if she had a wish. The wish was to see her deceased mother. Then, after embraces and kisses, there was a final message: "My dear child, today is our last meeting. Do not be sad. I shall return on your birthday every year except for this one. My child, do not think that I am not coming because you have done something wrong. You have done nothing wrong. The plans which my Son and I had, you accepted with your whole heart and you carried them out. Ivanka, the blessings that you and your brothers [the other seers?] have received have never previously been accorded to anyone on earth." After the conversation had lasted an hour, Ivanka gave a farewell kiss to Our Lady, who then rose aloft to heaven accompanied by the two angels.

She now has one apparition a year. She states that one apparition a year is sufficient for her since she has already received more graces than anyone else on earth. In 1997 the visit lasted for six minutes and the message was as follows: "Dear children, pray from your hearts so that you will know how to forgive and to be forgiven. I thank you for your prayers and for the love that you give me."

Ivanka claimed that when she was preparing to celebrate the New Year at midnight in 1982 Our Lady paid her a surprise visit and wished everyone present a happy new year. Marija, Vicka, and Ivan claim to have had only nine secrets confided to them, and hence still have daily apparitions.

Jakov Colo, born in Bijakovici on 6 March, 1971, is the youngest of the visionaries. He married Anna-Lisa Barozzi on 11 April, 1993, and has three children. He received daily apparitions from 25 June, 1981, until 12 September, 1998. Between 7 January, 1983, and 11 April, 1983, Our Lady told him the story of her life. During an apparition in 1993, at the height of the war, Our Lady asked him to pray for peace in the former Yugoslavia, and convinced him that his prayers could bring the war to an end. On 12 September, 1998, after visiting the United States, he came to the parish office in Medjugorje saying that Our Lady had appeared to him for the last time on that day. The apparition lasted for 30 minutes, from 11:15 to 11:45. He did, however, receive the promise of a regular visit on Christmas Day each year. The Virgin revealed the tenth secret to him with great sadness, but comforted him gently, saying: "Do not be sad, because like a mother I will be with you always, and like a true mother I will never abandon you."

Jakov has also had the privilege of shaking hands with Our Lady:

> On the feast of Our Lady's Nativity (8 September 1981), the Virgin appeared to Vicka and Jakov in Jakov's house. So Jakov held out his hand to the Virgin, saying: "Dear Holy Virgin, I wish you a happy birthday." Thus, it was that the little boy had the great good fortune to see the Mother of God shake his hand.

It is claimed that "Jakov's face, eager and upturned, is one of the most external outward proofs we have of the authenticity of the events." But if one reads the accepted criteria for discerning the authenticity of alleged apparitions, eager and upturned faces will not be found among them (see Appendix II).

According to the June 1996 issue of the *Medjugorje Herald*: "Marija, Vicka, and Ivan have each received nine secrets and so continue to have daily apparitions." This is very convenient, ensuring that the pilgrims and the money continue to roll in. The Medjugorje pilgrims expect, as part of their package trip, to see a seer going into ecstasy while experiencing an apparition. They are never disappointed.

Jelena Vasilj and Marijana Vasilj. In addition to the six seers already listed, there are two who do not claim to have apparitions but to receive inner locutions in which they hear the voice of Our Lady and see her inwardly with their hearts. They are Jelena Vasilj, born on 14 May, 1972, and Marijana Vasilj (no relation), born on 5 October, 1972. They have established a prayer group which the Virgin not only attends but actually leads through the two locutionists. Our Lady leads another prayer group which she directs through Ivan and Marija.[4]

---

[4] Richard J. Beyer, *Medjugorje Day by Day* (Ave Maria Press, Notre Dame, Indiana 46556, 1993). This information appears at the beginning of the book, which has no page numbers and consists almost entirely of alleged messages delivered to the alleged seers by Our Lady. If genuine, they would mean that Our Lady must be the most loquacious and boring woman in the history of the world.

2

24 JUNE, 1981

The First 'Apparitions'

THE ALLEGED APPARITIONS BEGAN ON 24 JUNE, 1981, when Ivanka Ivanković claimed to have seen Our Lady while out walking with Mirjana Dragicević. They later claimed that they were looking for their sheep when, in reality, they had gone out to smoke, a fact which they hid from their parents (see May 1990, Part 5). The apparition took place on Mount Crnica, now referred to by tour guides as Apparition Hill. A footpath leads up from the village of Bijakovici, where Ivan Dragicević was born, to the place of the apparition itself. This is sometimes referred to as Mount Podbrdo, which causes confusion because Mount Crnica, of which Podbrdo is part, is the usual name given. The path is now widened by the feet of millions of pilgrims. According to the official Medjugorje mythology, the girls ran up this hill over the rocks and thorns barefoot, not even following the path.

In an interview on 8 September, 1988, Vicka Ivanković described what happened on the second day:

> On the second day in the afternoon the three of us, myself, Mirjana and Ivanka, went walking. We said that we would go and see if Our Lady was coming. We expected to see her but still wondering if she would come. We went along the same road to the same spot as the previous day. Ivanka was again first to see Our Lady. I returned home to bring Marija and Jakov because after the first day they asked me, "Vicka, if you see Our Lady, come and get us. We do not have to see her but we would like to be with you." So, I went to bring the two of them but they were already on their way to the hill.
>
> We had nothing on our feet and it seemed that we were not walking on the ground but gliding above it. Suddenly we found ourselves at the apparition site. On

The First 'Apparitions'

that second day those who were not so shy could ask questions but mostly we were praying with the Lady.

On the third day I took a glass of holy water and sprinkled it at Our Lady, I said, "If you are Our Lady, stay with us but if you are not, leave us alone." The Lady smiled, and the water which I threw just flowed off her dress.

Eight days later the girls stated categorically that Our Lady had said four or five times that she would appear on three more days only, that is, on July 1, 2, and 3. On 30 June 1981, Father Jozo Zovko, parish priest of Medjugorje, told the seers that he would prefer the last three apparitions to take place in the parish church. The seers expressed anxiety that that might result in many of those attending the apparitions on the hill ceasing to come, but they eventually agreed. The following conversation is recorded on a tape stored in the archives of the bishopric of Mostar:

> **Zovko**: What are you going to say to the people?
> **Ivanka**: I could say to them that Our Lady has appeared to us at some other place....
> **Vicka**: ...and that she has told us that we will see her tomorrow in the church, but that others will not be able to see her.
> **Zovko**: All right, tell this to the people....[1]

Can one imagine St. Bernadette or the children of Fatima instructing Our Lady on where she should or should not appear? On 1 July, the apparition duly took place in the presbytery and was accompanied by Mass and the Rosary. During the Mass Father Jozo told the faithful: "At the end of Mass, the children who have met the *Gospa* will pray for you and your families."

Commenting on this statement, Father Rudo Franken states:

> This is incredible. Father Jozo guarantees the apparition is true. Did he not know that only a bishop is to give such a guarantee? Did he not know a deep investigation is required before such a guarantee can

---
1 Franken, 13.

be given? Jozo Zovko spoke without any restriction and this was the beginning of a mass movement.[2]

On 3 July, 1981, the date specified for the final apparition, Father Tadija Pavlović, pastor of a neighbouring parish, came to Medjugorje to help hear confessions. He was present in the presbytery when what was to be the final apparition took place. There were, in fact, two apparitions, one lasting ten minutes and one five minutes. All six seers affirmed that the apparition had told them that this would be her last appearance. Father Pavlović was shocked when he learned from one of his parishioners that there had been further apparitions on 4 and 5 July. Never again has he gone to Medjugorje to celebrate Mass or hear confessions.[3]

According to the seers the apparition had a change of mind concerning her final appearance, and decided to visit them each day. Two years later, in 1983, Vicka was asked by a Father Janko Bubalo why the apparitions had continued after 3 July, 1981. She replied: "Really, I can't remember any of this. If someone [i.e. one of the seers] has said this, then it must have been intended to ensure that we were left alone."[4] On other occasions Vicka seems to have had no problem with her memory: "I remember very well asking her: Our Lady, for how long will you stay with us? She answered: As long as you wish, my angels. Imagine, as long as we wish! That means: forever. We did not have the courage to tell her."[5]

When asked the same question on another occasion, the apparition replied: "Have you had enough of me already?"[6] Can one imagine Our Lady saying this? According to Britain's National Medjugorje Centre:

> The visionaries are able to see, and even touch the Virgin during the apparitions. They can converse with her, but are oblivious of noise, light, and pain—as numerous scientific tests have proved. Exhaustive psychiatric investigation has also shown them to be

---

[2] Franken, 18.   [3] Ibid., 55.   [4] Ibid.
[5] Ibid., 56.   [6] Ibid.

The First 'Apparitions'

normal in every way. Mary stands a few feet away upon a small cloud. Her presence is preceded by a brilliant light. The visionaries describe her as beautiful beyond words, radiant with holiness. She looks no more than nineteen, with dark hair and blue eyes. She usually wears a grey dress with a white veil down to her feet, and a crown of 12 stars.

The Virgin's conversations with the children express motherly tenderness and love, and she has assumed the role of both mother and teacher, guiding them in prayer, and advising and directing them in their lives.[7]

This very sentimentalised image of Our Lady would appear to have been concocted on the basis of well-known pictures of the Immaculate Conception reproduced on the type of holy cards to which those of a peasant background in Herzegovina would have access. The claim that while witnessing an apparition the seers are oblivious to the outside world, and the description they give of Our Lady, correspond very closely with what is claimed at Garabandal.[8] The self-styled, and now very rich, "seers" claim to have witnessed thousands of apparitions of Our Lady. The six of them claimed initially to have a daily apparition. Why Our Lady needed to appear to six people every day to

---

[7] Children of Medjugorje, PO Box 29, Inverness, IV1 2FT. This is the address for all references to Britain's National Medjugorje Centre.

[8] When the vision appeared, the girls fell instantaneously on their knees, striking the sharp rocks with a loud noise that was frightening, yet they showed no signs of injury. The expression on their faces was suddenly transformed. Their look became extraordinarily beautiful, sweet, one of profound mysticism. There are no words that can properly describe the change. They were completely absorbed in their rapture, unaware of anyone or any material thing around them except for each other. They did not react to pricks, burns or blows. All attempts to distract them failed. Powerful beams of strong light were focussed on them, yet their eyes did not even flicker, blink or show any signs of discomfort. Quite the contrary, their eyes remained wide open, expressing a look of intense joy.

The Virgin is dressed in a white robe with a blue mantle and a crown of golden stars. Her hands are slender. There is a brown scapular on her right arm, except when she carries the Child Jesus in her arms. Her hair, deep nut-brown, is parted in the centre. Her face is long, with a fine nose. Her mouth is very pretty with lips a bit thin. She looks like a girl of eighteen. She is rather tall. There is no voice like hers. No woman is just like her, either in the voice or the face or anything else. (See http://www.garabandal.org/)

deliver her message was never explained. Even on the occasions when all six purported to have gone into ecstasy together, each received a different message. The six "seers" claimed that each of them would be entrusted with ten secrets, and that once a "seer" had received ten secrets the apparitions would be reduced to one a year plus extra appearances on special occasions.

During the course of this book, I will not on every occasion refer to "alleged" apparitions, "the alleged seers", or to the fact that they "claim" to have seen Our Lady or to have received messages from her. It would become tedious to use these terms on almost every page. But the fact that I will not be using such terms does not indicate in any way that I believe there is the slightest possibility that the individuals involved are genuine seers, or that even one of them has had an apparition of Our Lady on a single occasion, or that Our Lady has conveyed a message to one of them on a single occasion, even by an inner locution. Thus, when I state below that Vicka "has received nine of the ten secrets and still receives apparitions daily", this must not be taken as implying I believe that she has received a single secret or experienced a single apparition. I will put "apparitions" in parentheses only when quoting a source that has done so, such as the Congregation for the Doctrine of the Faith, which invariably puts the word in parentheses. Like the two bishops of Mostar-Duvno during the period of the Medjugorje phenomenon, I am convinced that all the apparitions and all the messages have been fabricated by the seers. Claims have been made that the seers have indeed had apparitions, but that they are of satanic origin, as seems to have been the case at Palmar de Troya. I am sure that this is not the case, and agree with the judgement expressed by Monsignor Žanić, bishop of the diocese of Mostar-Duvno, in a letter to Father Hugh Thwaites, SJ, dated 17 August, 1987: "I am sure that Our Lady does not appear. No miracles. The "Messages" cannot be of our Virgin. They are the fruit of a fabrication, fraud and disobedience to the Church. It is about big money and personal interest too." This judgement is shared by the successor of Bishop Žanić, Bishop Ratko Perić.

3
The Charismatic Connection

IN 1967 THE CATHOLIC CHARISMATIC RENEWAL was founded in Pittsburgh by two Catholic professors from the University of Notre Dame who had received what they termed "baptism of the spirit" through the laying on of hands by Protestant Pentecostalists. There is no basis in Catholic theology for this so-called "baptism of the spirit," which amounts to an eighth sacrament. We receive and become temples of the Holy Spirit when we are baptised.

Father René Laurentin, the principal propagandist for Medjugorje, is one of the original members of the charismatic movement, which he believes to be of great importance for the future of the Catholic Church. There has been a close connection between Medjugorje and the charismatic movement from its very inception. Many of the best-known members of the movement have given their complete support to the authenticity of the Medjugorje apparitions during which, as a *quid pro quo*, it is purported that Our Lady has endorsed their movement. It is claimed that on 25 July, 1982, she said: "Pray for the sick! Fast for the sick! Lay your hands on them! Administer them charismatic anointings with oil! Any layman can do it!" Father Franken asks whether this does not suggest that a layman can administer the sacrament of the anointing of the sick, which is reserved for priests.[1]

On the three days 23, 24, 25 August, 1983, charismatic services were held at Medjugorje and all six seers and a number of priests and nuns of the parish received the "baptism of the spirit". Some had received it on previous occasions. Father Emilio Tardif taught the faithful to prophesy, to speak in tongues, and to sing.[2] As mentioned above, the two locutionists, Jelena Vasilj and Marijana Vasilj, have established a

---

1 Franken, 49. 2 Ibid.

prayer group which the Virgin leads through them. Our Lady is also said to lead another prayer group which she directs through Ivan Dragicević and Marija Pavlović. The seers claim that prayer groups on the Medjugorje model should be established in every parish in the world:

> In every church community, and therefore also in every parish, prayer groups should have a mediating, assisting, and uniting task. Pilgrims should integrate in parish life at home and offer assistance, even in cases where parish priests do not yet accept the events of Medjugorje and the message of Our Lady.[3]

---

3 Ibid., 52.

4

A Preposterous Proliferation

A CONVINCING REASON FOR QUESTIONING THE events at Medjugorje is that they are so strikingly unlike all previous Marian apparitions. Which other apparitions have gone on almost daily for 23 years with no sign of coming to an end, and have involved tens of thousands of messages, most of which are notable only for their banality?

Bishop Ratko Perić, the present bishop of Mostar-Duvno, has calculated that the number of alleged apparitions had reached a total of 31,860 by December, 2002.[1] This total alone deprives Medjugorje of any credibility when set beside the number of appearances made by Our Lady in apparitions approved by the Church as authentic. The words spoken by Our Lady in all these approved apparitions could be recorded in the exercise book of a six-year-old child, and leave most the pages blank. When asked why Our Lady found it necessary to appear on thousands of occasions, a phenomenon unprecedented in the history of the Church, Vicka replied: "If she had come for only ten or twenty times and then would have disappeared forever, no one in these hasty times would have remembered for long that she has appeared. Who would still have believed she really had come?" Father Franken comments:

> Now compare Medjugorje to Lourdes. How many times did Mary appear in Lourdes? How many years have passed since she last appeared in Lourdes? Still, every year millions of pilgrims from all over the world visit Lourdes. So Vicka's argument does not stand ground.[2]

Medjugorje is following a pattern quite different from that of earlier (and approved) apparitions—Lourdes, La Salette, Pontmain, Fatima or Beauraing, for example. In his

---

1 *Crkva na Kamenu*, December 2002, 13.   2 Franken, 24.

encyclopaedic study of Marian apparitions in the modern world, Donal Foley explains:

> The various Marian apparitions are classed as "private" revelations, in that the public revelation of the Church was completed during Apostolic times, and is now closed. All that the Church has done since then is to develop and clarify those public truths, and Catholics are bound to believe them as truths of the Faith. Private revelations, though, including the approved Marian apparitions, are given to an individual or group for their own good or that of others; Catholics are not obliged to believe in them, and they do not add to the sum total of public revelation, as the Catechism of the Catholic Church (67) makes clear: "Throughout the ages, there have been so-called "private" revelations, some of which have been recognized by the authority of the Church. They do not belong, however, to the deposit of faith. It is not their role to improve or complete Christ's definitive Revelation, but to help live more fully by it in a certain period of history. Guided by the Magisterium of the Church, the *sensus fidelium* knows how to discern and welcome in these revelations whatever constitutes an authentic call of Christ or His saints to the Church."
>
> There is always the danger of illusion or deception in visions or apparitions, and that is why the Church, in the person of the local bishop initially, has always been reluctant to accept them without a great deal of scrutiny.... The decision as to the authenticity of an apparition rests in the first place with the local bishop, who is the "Pope" of his own diocese. If, after sufficient study, there is solid evidence to support the apparition, in terms of the facts surrounding it and the activities of the seer or seers, and also regarding such matters as miraculous healings, then the bishop is empowered to issue some form of edict declaring the authenticity of a particular apparition....
>
> In sum, then, the Church has consistently taken a very cautious attitude towards Marian apparitions, with only a very small minority of such reported

events being accepted. Episcopal approval is the first step in such acceptance, but other factors such as general Church approval, expressed in the building of a basilica, for example, or a papal visit, are also necessary if an apparition is to be fully acknowledged.[3]

Episcopal approval is the first step in the acceptance of an apparition as authentic, and no apparition has been recognised by the Church without such approval. As regards the factor of a papal visit, it is very significant that during his visit to Croatia in 1994 and to Sarajevo in 1997, Pope John Paul II did not even mention Medjugorje, let alone pay it a visit, much to the dismay of its proponents (see 10-11 September, 1994, 12-13 April, 1997).

The pretentious pseudo-science deployed to authenticate the "ecstasies" of the "visionaries" (including the use of an electroscope to measure the intensity of *"spiritual energy"* developed during apparitions) can only be described as grotesque.

---

[3] Foley, 104-106.

5

Credibility of the Messages

THE MEDJUGORJE MESSAGES ARE ALMOST INVARIably of the utmost banality and could be put together by any ten-year-old familiar with a few traditional Catholic prayers and devotions, and a minimal knowledge of doctrine. A typical message published in the 6 October, 1996, issue of *The Catholic Times* (England) reads:

> Dear Children,
> Today I invite you to offer your crosses and suffering for my intentions. Little children, I am your mother and I wish to help you by seeking for you grace from God. Little children, offer your sufferings as a gift from God so they become a most beautiful flower of joy. That is why, little children, pray that you may understand that suffering can become joy and the cross the way of joy.
> Thank you for having responded to my call.

One might note that it is normal to offer the prayers, sufferings, and joys of each day for the intentions of Our Lord through the Immaculate Heart of Mary, and not for the intentions of Our Lady.

> I wish to give you messages in a way unprecedented in history.[1]

One can hardly deny that by the "apparition" making thousands of appearances whenever called upon by one of the seers, these messages are certainly unprecedented in history!

> By praying you have helped me realize my plans. I shall implore my Son that all my plans will be realized.[2]

> Dear children, without you I cannot help the world.[3]

---

1 Franken, 36.   2 Ibid.   3 Ibid.

Does this mean that the intercession of our most gracious advocate depends entirely on the seers of Medjugorje?

> I shall leave behind a sign for the infidels.

This is an interesting development, because, as will be shown below, the promised sign was originally intended to prove the veracity of the apparitions to the faithful.

> Dear children, I ask all of you to live and change all negativity within you, so that everything will become positive and living.[4]

This message seems to have come straight from a New Age manual.

Some of the messages are of very dubious orthodoxy. On 1 October, 1981, the apparition announced: "To God all religions are the same" using the Croatian word *iste*. In a more detailed statement, the apparition insists that all religions are equal:

> There is but one God for all people, but people have conjured up several religions. My Son is the one Mediator and Saviour of all people, but, as I see it, people get on well if they live their own religion well, if they follow their conscience.

Is Our Lady saying here that the Catholic religion was conjured up by men? How can a religion founded by the Incarnation of God the Son be put on the same plane as religions conjured up by men?

---

4 Ibid., 37.

6

Secrets

EACH SEER HAS A SECRET DESTINED FOR A PARticular group. Vicka Ivanković and Jakov Colo for the sick, Ivan Dragicević for the young and for priests, Marija Pavlović for the souls in purgatory, and Ivanka Ivanković for families.[1] They claim that they cannot reveal the nature of these secrets by the very fact of their being secret, but information concerning them has been included in a leaflet published by Britain's National Medjugorje Centre. It states that Mary has promised to leave a visible sign at the place of the apparitions for all mankind to see, but before the appearance of this visible sign there will be three warnings to the world in the form of events upon the earth. Mirjana will be their witness. Three days before one of these warnings she will give advance notice of it to a priest of her choice. This testimony will be a confirmation of the apparitions and an incentive to the conversion of the world.

After the warnings the visible sign will appear as a testimony to the authenticity of the apparitions and to call men back to the Faith. The ninth and tenth secrets refer to a chastisement for the sin of the world. The chastisement is inevitable. It can be mitigated by prayer and penance but it cannot be prevented. Those who remain alive after the visible sign will have little time for conversion, which is why the *Gospa* requests conversion and reconciliation as a matter of urgency. According to Mirjana we are very close to these events. These secrets have evidently been fabricated by the seers and bear a striking similarity to the messages of other apparitions, approved ones such as Fatima, and unapproved ones such as Garabandal, e.g. the prophecies of great and coming chastisements.[2]

---

1 R. Laurentin, *La Vergine appare a Medjugorje?* (Brescia, 1984), 44.
2 Conchita, one of the seers of Garabandal, claims that Our Lady has promised a great miracle in Garabandal so that all may believe the apparitions

7

4 SEPTEMBER, 1981

The Sign

ON 4 SEPTEMBER, 1981, IVAN DRAGICEVIĆ WAS promised that a sign would appear at the end of the apparitions. Our Lady contradicted herself by assuring Vicka that she would continue to appear after giving the sign.[1] Vicka Ivanković states that the sign will be given on Mount Podbrdo (part of Mount Crnica), where she first appeared. At one moment it will not be there and at the next moment it will. Everyone who visits Medjugorje will be able to see it. It will be a great basilica in honour of the apparitions. The seer most involved in the prediction of a sign is Ivan Dragicević. His predictions will be examined in more detail below. Mirjana assures us:

> The sign will be big. On Mount Podbrdo, on the very spot of the first apparition, it will be visible on earth. Not in the sky. All of a sudden it will be there and everyone visiting Medjugorje will see it. It will be long lasting and no one will be able to destroy it.[2]

---

and be obedient to the message. "As the punishment which we deserve for the sins of the world is great, the miracle must also be a great one, for the world needs it." There will remain a permanent sign at "The Pines" as a proof of Our Lady's tremendous love for all her children. Conchita has been granted permission by Our Lady to announce the date of the miracle eight days in advance. Before *The miracle* takes place Our Lady has said that all mankind will receive a warning from heaven. The day of *The miracle* may be the last opportunity given us by God and may be also Our Lady's last effort to save the world from the punishment already threatened. See www.garabandal.org.

1 Franken, 19.   2 Ibid., 21.

8

The Position of Bishop Pavao Žanić

MONSIGNOR PAVAO ŽANIĆ, THE BISHOP OF Mostar-Duvno, Herzegovina, the diocese in which Medjugorje is found, was initially well disposed towards the seers and the apparitions. He did his best to shield the children from the communist police, who feared that the apparitions could arouse opposition to the regime. As will be made clear below, he changed his mind when it became apparent that the seers were lying when they told him on thirteen occasions that Our Lady had supported two disobedient Franciscan priests in their opposition to him. Bishop Žanić's own account of the incident will be provided later in this book.

The attitude of the then-communist government of Yugoslavia to the Medjugorje phenomenon was transformed into an attitude of enthusiastic co-operation once it became clear that the pilgrims provided an extremely lucrative source of foreign currency. The bishops and clergy of the former Yugoslavia had every reason to be predisposed in favour of Medjugorje. If the visions were authentic, they would have been a tremendous asset to the Church in a country with so many atheists and adherents of non-Catholic religions who might have been convinced by them of the truth of the Catholic religion. In addition, the income from the pilgrimages would not only have benefited their poor country, but it would also have provided badly needed financial help for the Church. Bishop Žanić in particular, who had a great devotion to Our Lady, and had led pilgrimages to Lourdes, would have been delighted to have a Lourdes in his diocese, but soon concluded that the Medjugorje phenomenon was the "fruit of fabrication and fraud" (see May, 1990).

Only one Croatian bishop, Archbishop Franic of Split, a charismatic, expressed belief in the apparitions, and not one of the one hundred diocesan clergy in Herzegovina accepts them as authentic. Only two members of the fifteen-man commission which examined the events at Medjugorje accepted the authenticity of the apparitions (and they were both Franciscans). The Franciscans themselves are divided on the matter. Some of the most influential among them support the position of Bishops Žanić and Perić. Supporters of the authenticity of the apparitions have been unable to suggest any credible ulterior motive to explain the rejection of their authenticity by the clergy of every rank outside the Franciscan Order in the former Yugoslavia.

My object in this study is simply to show that the case against the authenticity of the Medjugorje apparitions is unanswerable, a viewpoint which has been kept from most Catholics due to the vast publicity campaign in favour of their authenticity conducted in the mainstream Catholic media, which derives considerable financial benefits from Medjugorje advertising. Advertisements for literature critical of the apparitions have been refused by the British Catholic press, including one for an extremely important statement by Monsignor Ratko Perić, the present bishop of Mostar, which is included here as Appendix I. It is not without significance that Catholic journals which have not shown the least interest in the Fatima message are enthusiastic in their support of Medjugorje. I happen to know that the late Hamish Fraser believed that Medjugorje was a means being utilised by Satan to subvert the message of Fatima.[1]

---

1 Hamish Fraser, a convert from Communism, and editor of the journal *Approaches* (Scotland) until his death in 1986, was one of the world's greatest authorities on Fatima.

9
An Immoral Priest Defended

BEFORE PROVIDING DOCUMENTATION TO PROVE the falsity of the alleged apparitions, I will give just two examples of the degree of credibility which should be given to the self-styled seers of Medjugorje. The first incident is documented in the 1990 statement by Bishop Žanić that is printed in full under the date May, 1990. It concerns a Franciscan priest who was dispensed from his vows and expelled from the Franciscan Order by a direct command of Pope John Paul II. Father Ivica Vego seduced a nun, Sister Leopolda, and when she became pregnant, they both left the religious life and began to live together near Medjugorje, where their child was born. They now have two children. But before that, Father Vego refused to accept his expulsion and continued to celebrate Mass, administer the sacraments, and pass the time with his mistress.

Why mention such a distasteful event? The reason is that the seers claimed that Our Lady appeared to them on thirteen occasions stating that Father Vego was innocent, that he was as entitled to celebrate Mass as any other priest, and that the bishop was harsh! Any reader with a *sensus catholicus* will need to read no further to realise the full extent of the mendacity of the seers, a mendacity which cannot be excused simply on the grounds that they have been manipulated by their Franciscan mentors. What credibility can be given to those who claim that the Mother of God told them repeatedly that an immoral priest, expelled from his order on the instructions of the Holy Father himself, was innocent, and that the bishop, who had taken the only course open to him, was the guilty party! And how does a supposedly reputable theologian such as Father René Laurentin, who has made a great deal of money from books on Medjugorje, react when

An Immoral Priest Defended

confronted with such facts? Bishop Žanić gave us the answer. Laurentin begged him not to publish details of the incident. Bishop Žanić stated that this has been Laurentin's consistent position—to hide the truth and defend falsehood. Despite the fact that the truth about Father Ivica Vego can no longer be denied, his prayer book is still sold in Medjugorje and beyond in hundreds of thousands of copies!

Propagandists for Medjugorje still insist that Ivica Vego is the innocent party and the bishop the guilty one. Their "proof" is that Our Lady is supposed to have told Vicka that this was the case, and that where they were concerned, any statement by Vicka was a self-evident truth. In a pro-Medjugorje booklet published in 1991, Our Lady is alleged to have spoken as follows to Vicka on 3 January, 1982:

> Ivica is not guilty. Have him keep the faith even if he is expelled. I do not cease to repeat, "peace, peace, peace," and in the meantime agitation increases. He is not guilty [Our Lady repeated this three times]. The bishop does not keep order. That is why he is responsible. The justice you have not seen will come back.[1]

---

[1] *Bishop Žanić—What Went Wrong?* (Saint James Publishing, Birmingham, Alabama), 5.

10
Fraud on Film

THE FORMER FATHER VEGO PLAYED A PROMINENT part in the second incident. The "seers" and their Franciscan manipulators have consistently maintained that during their "ecstasies" they are immobile and without communication with the outside world. On 14 January, 1985, a French cameraman named Jean-Louis Martin wished to test this claim while the "visionaries" were purporting to be in ecstasy in St. James' Church. He made a stabbing movement towards the eyes of Vicka Ivanković with his fingers. Vicka gave a start and jerked her head backwards. Fortunately, the entire incident was filmed, and I possess a videocassette that shows the incident in slow motion. The girl left the room and returned a few minutes later accompanied by no less a person than her old friend Ivica Vego, who was wearing a very smart blue overcoat. Vego was very much in command and did most of the explaining. (The fact that after his expulsion from the order he is still so actively involved with the visionaries is of no little significance.) The hastily fabricated explanation that Vego instructed Vicka to give went as follows:

> When I arrived in the chapel I saw Jean-Louis, I saw all the people, but when the ecstasy began, I saw nothing except the Virgin Mary who had the Infant Jesus in her arms, and at that time I saw that the Infant Jesus would fall on the floor so I made a gesture to catch the Infant Jesus because He should not fall on the floor.

There could hardly be a more evident case of outright lying. It is inconceivable that during an apparition of Our Lady with the Child Jesus, the child could possibly slip. If, *per impossibile*, that did happen, it is stretching coincidence beyond the bounds of credibility to be asked to believe that it happened at the precise moment that the journalist made the movement towards Vicka's eyes. Finally, if she had been speaking the truth she would have moved forward—towards the apparition—and not backwards!

One might add, almost as an afterthought, that if Our Lady had truly appeared at Medjugorje on more than 31,000 occasions by the end of 2002, a claim which in itself defies credibility, she did not bother to warn the Croatian people of the coming onslaught which they would have to undergo from fanatically anti-Catholic Serbia.

11

The Herzegovina Question

WHILE READING THIS BOOK ONE MUST KEEP IN mind that Herzegovina has been the scene of a longstanding and bitter dispute between the Franciscan Order and the diocese, a problem referred to as the "Herzegovina Question." During the Turkish occupation of Bosnia-Herzegovina, the Franciscans remained to care for the Catholic people together with several diocesan priests and priests from the parishes of the diocese of Trebinje.[1] They were admired for their courage and devotion even by the Turks. Since 1968 there has been a bitter dispute between the Franciscans and the diocese, the former refusing to hand over parishes to diocesan priests even when ordered to do so by the Holy See (see May, 1990, no. 23). The principal significance of the Medjugorje phenomenon is the extent to which it has been used as a very effective weapon by the Franciscans in their dispute with the diocese, and a lucrative source of income that provides the finances necessary to maintain them in their state of disobedience.

---

1 This diocese has been administered by the diocese of Mostar-Duvno since 1890.

12

25 MARCH, 1985
A Letter from Bishop Žanić to Father Tomislav Pervan

Father Pervan was the parish priest of Medjugorje from 1984–1988, and then became the Provincial of the Franciscan Province of Herzegovina.

REVEREND FATHER TOMISLAV,

Most certainly the pastoral personnel (clergy) of the Medjugorje parish know about the latest developments and the circumstances of the letter of the "visionary" Ivan Dragicević on the sign that he described on 9 May, 1982, during his stay in the seminary in Visoko. With a copy of that letter, we are also supplying you with a copy of the minutes of the last meeting of the commission on the events of Medjugorje held in Mostar on 7 March, 1985, on the occasion of the opening of Ivan Dragicević's letter. This letter contains the described sign which would occur in order to confirm the "apparitions" of the Madonna in Medjugorje. Last year, in a conversation with [members of] the investigating commission, Ivan Dragicević declared that the sign we speak of will be the Madonna's shrine and that the sign will appear suddenly one morning.

Even before this, the bishop had come to the firm conclusion that the apparitions of the Madonna in Medjugorje are not a reality. Meanwhile, in 1982, the bishop's office had formed the commission to investigate the events and to study the case thoroughly. Because of it, the bishop's office has refrained from making any official statement on the real state of affairs. However, several times through letters, the bishop's office expressed its desire, and even demanded, that the propaganda stop because of the disobedience of the pastoral personnel and the "visionaries." This was a futile attempt. I present the documents which have been sent to you, and the subject of each one of them:

- 13 December, 1981 (N 977): attitude toward the events in Medjugorje;
- 12 April, 1983 (N 241): letter to the parish priest, instructions to be followed;
- Invitations for meetings: 31 March, 1983 (N 297);
- 27 September, 1983 (N 982); 19 July, 1984 (N 777).

Following a two-day session, the commission on the events of Medjugorje declared that the pastoral personnel and the seers in Medjugorje are requested to abstain from any public statement or declaration to the press about the contents of the visions and the alleged miraculous cures.

At our meeting, held in the chancery office in Mostar on 31 October, 1984, I demanded that Medjugorje's occurrences "be toned down and eliminated little by little."

In the meantime, matters remain as they were, and a great disgrace is expected to befall the Church. Now, without any delay, after all this, I demand from you that you remove the "visionaries" from public display and put an end to their "visions" in the parish church. They have had "visions" in Mostar, and earlier in Sarajevo, Visoko and Dubrovnik. Let them now have them at their homes: people say that they had them at their homes during 1981. In ten days, the new statue of the *Gospa* in front of the main altar ought to be discreetly removed late one evening and replaced by the old one. You must stop talking about apparitions and also cease publicizing messages. The devotions that grew out of the "apparitions" and their messages must be eliminated, sales of souvenirs and printed material which propagate the "apparitions" must also stop. The faithful can go to the sacrament of reconciliation and attend Mass. I do not allow the other priests, especially Fathers Jozo Zovko, Tomislav Vlašić and Ljudevit Rupčić, to celebrate Mass for the faithful or to preach.

A Letter from Bishop Žanić to Father Tomislav Pervan   **33**

The "visionaries" must give you whatever they wrote, especially what pertains to the so called "Biography of the Madonna." No excuse that "that's a secret" can justify them from not handing over that material to you. Since there was so much public talk about their diaries and their other writings, and since all this had a great influence on the events of Medjugorje, thus all these documents and [written] materials fall under the supervision of the ordinary and become subject to the investigation of the phenomenon of Medjugorje.

We do hope that you will execute what we demand from you in this letter. With greetings and a prayerful wish for God's blessing.

Monsignor Pavao Žanić
Bishop of Mostar-Duvno and Apostolic
Administrator of Trebinje-Mrkanj

13

23 FEBRUARY, 1987

Communiqué of the Yugoslav Bishops Concerning the Facts of Medjugorje

Verbatim from L'Osservatore Romano, *English Edition, 23 February, 1987.*

WE PUBLISH BELOW THE TEXT OF A COMMUNIQUÉ published in the official bulletin of the diocese of Zagreb, signed by His Eminence Cardinal Franjo Kuharić, President of the Yugoslav Episcopal Conference, and Most Rev. Pavao Žanić, Bishop of Mostar-Duvno, concerning the facts of Medjugorje.

In conformity with the canonical norms concerning the discernment of alleged apparitions and private revelations, the diocesan commission instituted for this purpose by the bishop of Mostar, ordinary of the place, has conducted an inquiry into the events of Medjugorje. In the course of the investigation, it emerged that the events went far beyond the diocese in question. Consequently, on the basis of the above-mentioned norms it seemed fitting to continue the investigation on the level of the episcopal conference with the institution of a new commission for that purpose.

The Congregation for the Doctrine of the Faith was informed. It expressed appreciation for the work carried out under the responsibility of the local ordinary, and it encouraged the continuance of the work at the national episcopal level.

The episcopal conference, therefore, is establishing a commission to continue the investigation of the events at Medjugorje. While awaiting the results of the commission's investigation and the Church's judgement, pastors and faithful should observe an attitude of prudence customary in such situations.

Therefore, it is not permissible to organise pilgrimages and other manifestations motivated by the supernatural character attributed to the facts of Medjugorje.

Legitimate devotion to Our Lady, recommended by the Church, must conform to the directives of the Magisterium and especially those contained in the Apostolic Exhortation *Mariali Cultus* of 2 February, 1974 (cf. AAS, 66, 1974, 113-168).

Zagreb, 29 January, 1987,
Pavao Žanić, Bishop of Mostar,
Franjo Card. Kuharić,
President of Yugoslav Episcopal Conference

14

25 JULY, 1987

Declaration of the Bishop of Mostar Concerning Medjugorje

After a version of this declaration, translated into English not from the original Croatian but from an Italian translation, had been circulating for some time, the bishop asked Father Hugh Thwaites, an English Jesuit, to have an accurate translation made from the original Croatian. The task was undertaken by my wife, Marija, who is Croatian, and my son Adrian, who has a Cambridge degree in Serbo-Croatian.

BROTHERS AND SISTERS,

Today in Medjugorje, on the occasion of administering the sacrament of confirmation, you are perhaps expecting me to say a few words concerning those events about which the whole world is talking. The Church must concern herself with them, and whatever is of concern to the Church, she refers to particular individuals and commissions. You know that at this moment the subject is being discussed by the commission that was convened by the Conference of Bishops of Yugoslavia, because the Church cannot expose her credibility lightly before the twentieth-century world which seeks to discredit and criticise her, so that it can say: "There you are—there is Jesus Christ for you."

I can assure you that I prayed, studied, and kept silent for six years. Others have prayed too, and I thank them for it. In every Holy Mass that I have said Medjugorje was present in my intentions. In my daily Rosary I prayed to Our Lord, and to the Holy Ghost, to give me light from God. This has helped me to form a firm and certain conviction concerning everything that I have heard, read or experienced. There is a great deal of praying and fasting going on here (in Medjugorje), but it is in the belief that all the events are truly supernatural. However, to preach falsehood to the faithful concerning God, Jesus, and Our Lady—that merits the depths of hell.

In all my work, prayers, and studies I had one aim before me—to discern the truth. With this aim, as early as 1982, I formed a four-member commission which later, with the help of some bishops and fathers provincial, I expanded to fifteen members drawn from nine theological centres from seven dioceses and four provinces, and two leading psychiatrists who were enabled to consult their colleagues. They worked for three years. The Holy See was informed about their work, and the events. This commission of the Conference of Bishops of Yugoslavia continues to concern itself with the same problem.

However, there were impatient people who went ahead, before the judgement of the Church, and declared that miracles and supernatural events were taking place. They preached on private revelations from the altar, something which is not permitted until the Church declares such revelations to be authentic. That is why the various authorities demanded that pilgrimages should not be organised, that the Church's judgement should be awaited. This was first done on 24 March, 1984, when the commission on Medjugorje warned against it, but, unfortunately, without effect. Then, in October of the same year, the Conference of Bishops declared that there should be no more officially organised pilgrimages to Medjugorje. By "officially organised" is meant those who gather or come in a group. That had no effect either. Then the Congregation for the Doctrine of the Faith in Rome, on 23 May, 1985, sent a letter to the Conference of Italian Bishops asking them to try to reduce the number of organised pilgrimages, and likewise to minimise all forms of propaganda. That, too, bore no fruit.

Finally, when the second commission was formed, Cardinal Franjo Kuharić and the Bishop of Mostar, in the name of the Conference of Bishops of Yugoslavia, declared publicly on 29 January, 1987: "For this reason it is forbidden to organise pilgrimages or other manifestations motivated by the supernatural character attributed to the events in Medjugorje." This pronouncement came from the highest level in the Church and must not be ignored as if it were of no significance. Ever since the first news appeared concerning the unusual events in this diocese, the bishop's office followed the reports carefully, and collected everything that could serve in the search for truth. The bishop allowed the seers and religious involved full freedom, and even defended them from political and press attacks. We taped all the conversations, collected chronicles and diaries, letters and documents. The commission of our professors of theology and physicians studied all this for three years. The three-year work of the commission concluded as follows: two members voted in favour of the truth and supernatural nature of the apparitions. One member abstained from voting. One accepted that something had happened at the beginning. Eleven voted that there had been no apparitions—*non constat de supernaturalitate*.[1]

I am firmly convinced that all the members of the commission worked conscientiously and examined everything which could have aided their search for truth. The Church cannot risk her credibility, and often, in similar cases, she has studied events like these carefully and rebuked groups who gathered in places where it had been established that the events were not supernatural. Let us remember Garabandal in Spain, San Damiano in Italy, and dozens of similar places in the past few years. The seers at Garabandal claimed that Our Lady promised a great sign for the whole world. Twenty-five years have passed since then, and still there is no sign. If Our Lady had left a sign, it would be clear to all what this is about.

---

1 There are three possible verdicts on claims of supernatural apparitions: *Constat de supernaturalitate*, which constitutes recognition of the supernatural character of the events in question; *non constat de supernaturalitate* denotes that there is no evidence of the supernatural character of the events while not ruling out the possibility that such evidence could be forthcoming; and *constat de non supernaturalitate*, a final negative judgement by ecclesiastical authority that there is definitely no supernatural character attached to the events in question.

It was said that Our Lady started to appear at Podbrdo on Mount Crnica. When the police stopped people going there, she appeared in people's homes, on fences, in fields, in vineyards, and tobacco fields. She appeared in the church, on the altar, in the sacristy, in the choir-loft, on the roof, in the belltower, on the roads, on the road to Cerno, in a car, on a bus, in schools, at several places in Mostar and Sarajevo, in monasteries in Zagreb, in Varazdin, in Switzerland, in Italy, then again at Podbrdo, in Krizevac, in the parish, in the presbytery and so on. This does not list even half the number of locations where apparitions were alleged to have taken place, so that a sober man who venerates Our Lady must ask: "My Lady, what are they making of you?"

By divine law I am the pastor in this diocese, the teacher of the Faith, and the judge in questions concerning the Faith. The events in Medjugorje have caused strife and division in the Church—some people believing, others not believing—because there are those who have refused to submit themselves to the authority of the Church. Because the recommendations and decisions of the above-mentioned authorities, commissions, congregations of the bishops' conference, had no effect, I, the bishop of Mostar, answerable before God for discipline in this diocese, repeat and confirm earlier decisions of ecclesiastical bodies, and I forbid pilgrimages to come here and attribute a supernatural character to these events before the Commission of the Bishops' Conference completes its work.

I turn to you, O Immaculate Virgin and Mother, Mother of God, and Mother of the Church, Mother of the faithful who seek, pray to, and love you. I, your servant, the bishop of Mostar, turn to you, and before the whole world declare my deep and constant faith in all the privileges God bestowed upon you according to which you are the first and most excellent of His creatures. I express my profound and unswerving faith in your intercession before Almighty God for all the needs of your children in this vale of tears.

I declare my profound and constant faith in your love towards us sinners, that love to which you have testified by your apparitions and assistance. I myself have led pilgrimages to Lourdes. It is precisely with the strength of this faith that I, your servant, the bishop of Mostar, before the great multitudes who have called upon you, discern and accept your great sign which after six years, has become clear and certain. No special sign is necessary for me, but it was necessary for those who believed in a falsehood. The sign you have given is that for six years you remained silent continually whenever they prophesied that there would be an apparition on the mountain which would be permanent and for all to see. "It will be soon, quite soon, just be patient a little longer." They were saying this as early as 1981. Then they claimed that it would be on the feast of the Immaculate Conception, then at Christmas, then for the New Year and so on.

Thank you, Blessed Lady, for manifesting by your six-year silence whether or not you have spoken here, whether or not you had appeared or given messages, revealed secrets, or promised a special sign. Most holy Virgin, Mother of Christ and our Mother, intercede for peace in this restless region of the Church, the diocese of Mostar. Intercede especially for this village, this parish where your holy name has been mentioned countless times in messages. Accept, most holy Virgin, in reparation, the sincere prayers of those devout souls who are far from fanaticism and disobedience within the Church. Help us all to come to the real truth. Beloved, humble, and obedient Maiden of God, help Medjugorje to follow with a firm step the shepherd of the Church on earth, so that we all may glorify you and thank you in truth and love. Amen.

✠ *Pavao Žanić*
Bishop of Mostar

15

20 JANUARY, 1988

Letter to Mrs Marija Davies from the Bishop of Mostar

DEAR MRS DAVIES,

Thank you very much for getting in touch with me. Thank you especially for the translation of my statement about Medjugorje, and thank you for taking the correct attitude over this great source of confusion. God knows how this will all end—not well, you can be sure of that. The Church is divided. Factions are at war in the name of the Queen of Peace. I, who saw the beginning of this falsehood, of this lie, have before my very eyes a great deal about which it is impossible to write, or to describe, for various reasons. A huge amount of money is involved, and so the propaganda has no bounds. In my office there are some fifty books about Medjugorje, a vast number of cassettes, newspapers, and magazines, and new material is arriving all the time, and yet the position I have taken hurts them. For an average Catholic the first question to ask is: "What does the ordinary [bishop] of the place think about this matter?" The position that I have taken brings many people to their senses. Of course, the fanaticism of some is incorrigible, and no argument avails in their cases.

Archbishop Franic has caused me dreadful problems, although the mere fact that he thinks something does not mean that it must be true. One of the first questions asked by the sectaries of Medjugorje is: "How is it that Archbishop Franic believes?" I, for my part, say to them that there are thirty-five bishops in Yugoslavia, and that he is the only one who believes, so that argument is worthless. For them, however, it is enough that one archbishop believes.

I am firmly convinced that no responsible person will dare to defend the apparitions. The contrary arguments are too strong. It is only necessary to be aware of them.

Thank you once more for your work, and for the confidence that you have shown in me.

I give you and your husband my pastoral blessing.

✠ *Pavao Žanić*

16

11 JULY, 1988

Marija Pavlović Contradicts Herself

AS BISHOP ŽANIĆ MAKES CLEAR (MAY, 1990, PART 15), Marija Pavlović has proved beyond any possibility of doubt that no confidence whatsoever can be placed in her veracity—"Marija has consciously spoken falsehoods." In 1987, Father Tomislav Vlašić, the Svengali figure who has been the principal manipulator of the alleged seers, and was no longer a member of the Franciscan community in Herzegovina, established a bizarre community in Parma, Italy, with an enigmatic German lady named Agnes Heupel who claimed to have been cured of an illness at Medjugorje. The community had the rather long title of "Queen of Peace, wholly Thine; to Jesus through Mary" (*Kraljico Mira, potpuno tvoji po Mariji k Isusu*). In this community, guided by Vlašić and Heupel, young men and women lived together (which, Bishop Žanić adds, is something unheard of in the history of the Church).

Like his fellow Franciscan Father Vego, Father Vlašić had also made a nun pregnant.[1] When their child was born at the beginning of 1977, he did not leave the order to marry the woman named Mada (formerly Sister Rufina), but begged her not to name him as the father, assuring her that if she kept the matter secret she would be like Mary, and God would bless her![2] He advised Mada to lie, and even composed a story for her:

> I think it's best to say that you met someone passing by and he gave you a false name, and he told you he

---

1 The full details of this scandalous event can be found in E. Michael Jones, *Medjugorje: The Untold Story* (Fidelity Press, 206 Marquette Avenue, South Bend, IN 46617, USA).   2 Ibid., 85.

wants to marry you. Later he left and did not call and you got pregnant. It's best to say that you don't know him, because they won't bother you then and it would be better for the child later.[3]

This was the priest who was virtually the spiritual director of the Medjugorje seers! Mada complied with his wishes initially, but later, feeling abandoned, revealed the whole story to Bishop Žanić. As he did in the case of Father Vego, Father Laurentin resorted to a cover-up. He evidently felt that the credibility of the seers could be endangered if the immorality of their spiritual director became known, and fabricated a story that a Franciscan named Pehar, who had left the order and gone to live in the U. S., was the father of the child. His evident presumption was that no one would be able to find Pehar, but he was mistaken. The former priest, now laicised and married, was located and made it clear that by no possible stretch of the imagination could he have been the father of Mada's child. He had no hesitation in stating categorically that Laurentin was lying.[4]

The founding of the Vlašić/Heupel community was a cause of scandal even to some devotees of Medjugorje. Vlašić decided that his critics would be silenced if it could be shown that he had acted in obedience to a command from Our Lady. Marija Pavlović was a member of the community from February, 1988, until July of the same year. It was here that she met her future husband, Paolo Lunetti. In response to a request by Vlašić for an endorsement of his community by Our Lady, Marija duly "revealed" the fact that it had been established at Our Lady's express command. In July 1988 great consternation was caused among the Medjugorists when Pavlović swore before the Blessed Sacrament that her previous statement had been false and that the Vlašić/Heupel community was in no way endorsed by Our Lady. Even Father Laurentin would find it hard to cover up the fact that Pavlović must have been lying on at least one occasion. The full text of the 11 July, 1988, retraction follows:

---

3   Ibid.   4   Ibid., 91.

I feel morally bound to make the following statements before God, Our Lady, and the Church of Jesus Christ:

(1) The message of the text *An Invitation to the Marian Year* and the deposition which bears my signature is that I brought Our Lady's answer to Brother Tomislav Vlašić's question. That answer was supposedly: "This is God's plan." In other words, it follows from these texts that I transmitted to Brother Tomislav Vlašić Our Lady's confirmation and express approval of this work and of the programme set in motion in Italy with the Medjugorje prayer group.

(2) I now declare that I never asked Our Lady for any confirmation whatsoever of this work begun by Brother Tomislav Vlašić and Agnes Heupel. I never expressly asked Our Lady whether I should take part in this work and I never received from Our Lady any instruction connected with the group, apart from her instruction that each of us should be free to make a choice for his or her own life.

(3) From the texts and depositions which bear my signature it appears that Our Lady suggested that the community and the programme of Brother Tomislav Vlašić and Agnes Heupel are God's way for myself and the others. I now repeat that I never received from Our Lady nor gave Brother Vlašić or anybody else such a statement or instruction from Our Lady.

(4) My first statement in its published form in Croatian and Italian does not correspond to the truth. I personally had no desire to make any written statement. Brother Tomislav Vlašić advised me, stressing the point again and again, that I, as a seer, ought to write a deposition, which the world expected.

(5) I must, moreover, declare that the contents of the letter as set out and my having signed it give rise to a number of questions. For the time being, I can give to all possible questions only this one answer, which I give, I repeat, before God, Our Lady, and the Church of Jesus Christ: everything which might be understood as a confirmation and approval of this work of Brother Tomislav Vlašić and Agnes Heupel by

Our Lady through myself is absolutely untrue and no less untrue is the idea that I spontaneously conceived the wish to write down that deposition.

(6) I consider myself morally bound to repeat the following statements before God, Our Lady and the Church: After seven years of daily visions, after my most intimate experience of Our Lady's kindness and wisdom, in the light of all that I can remember of Our Lady's advice and of Our Lady's answers to the questions which I personally put to her, I can say publicly that the idea that heaven's plan and the message of Our Lady to the world at Medjugorje have as a holy consequence and a process desired by Our Lady this work and the programme begun in Italy by Brother Tomislav Vlašić and Agnes Heupel is unsustainable. It must, however, also be said that the daily apparitions are continuing.

I sign this declaration before the Holy Sacrament, and destine it for all those devoted to the "Work" of Our Lady in Medjugorje.

Marija Pavlović,
11 July 1988

Before leaving the subject of lying, it should be noted that Father Ivo Sivrić, OFM (who was born in Medjugorje), reveals that two Franciscans, who were members of the bishop's first investigative commission, had detected "thirteen apparent cases of deliberate and conscious lying" on the part of the alleged visionaries.[5]

The Community "Queen of Peace, wholly Thine; to Jesus through Mary", is still directed by Father Tomislav Vlašić, who insists that he is not the founder of the community, for the true founder is the Holy Spirit Who inspires people to respond to His call. The entire history of salvation, he explains, is marked by the Spirit's intervention, just as are the apparitions of Our Lady at Medjugorje.[6]

---

5 Ivo Sivric, *The Hidden Face of Medjugorje* (Editions Psilog, 1989, CP 300, Saint-François-du-Lac, Quebec, Canada, J0C 1M0), 14.
6 To contact the Community: lamamira@genie.it

17

31 MARCH, 1989

Visions in Alabama?

Excerpt from "Letter from London", by Michael Davies, The Remnant, 31 March, 1989.

I HAVE EXCERPTED FROM SOME CUTTINGS, UNFORtunately not dated, concerning a recent visit to Alabama, U.S.A., by Marija Pavlović, one of the so-called seers of Medjugorje. Miss Pavlović was in Alabama for fifty-three days, and readers will certainly be wondering whether she had any visions during her visit. Miss Pavlović claims that she did. How many, you may be wondering? Fifty-three of course! One a day. She had come to Birmingham to donate one of her kidneys to her brother in an operation performed at the University Hospital, and she deserves our admiration for this fine gesture. During the operation, while unconscious under an anaesthetic, she claims to have had a vision—which must be a first in the history of apparitions.

During her stay, Miss Pavlović stayed with a Mr. Terry Colafrancesco—who, it appears, works full time for a non-profit organisation called *Caritas*, which he established in 1986 to promote Medjugorje: "Since then he has let his business, Country Landscaping, go dormant." Mr. Colafrancesco purchased a 90-acre field adjacent to his property for $400,000. In that field there is a pine tree. Mr. Colafrancesco mowed a path from his home to the tree, mowed around the tree, and placed a crucifix and a Madonna on the site. He asked Miss Pavlović to have a vision under the tree, and she duly obliged.

It is somewhat remarkable that Mr. Colafrancesco had been able in advance to distribute information about the date and time that Miss Pavlović would have her vision under the pine tree on his newly acquired property. Thousands of pilgrims are now visiting the field, much to the delight of the Alabama Bureau of Tourism and Travel. The Shelby County Sheriff's Deputy, a gentleman by the name of Gene Hamby, predicted, while directing a steady stream of cars to the field, "It's just beginning."

A Mr. Cyril Auboyneau, Miss Pavlović's translator, confirmed that Colafrancesco asked for a vision in the field: "Terry wanted a vision in the field under that tree—he prayed about that. So, we asked Marija to ask Our Lady if she would appear in the field on Thanksgiving Day. Our Lady said she would appear in the field."

Well, what can one say? I am astounded that anyone with a modicum of intelligence can give one second's credence to anything connected with Medjugorje, apart from the statements of Bishop Žanić.

18

MAY 1990

The Truth about Medjugorje

A Statement by Monsignor Pavao Žanić,
Bishop of Mostar-Duvno

1) **THE TRUTH** REGARDING THE EVENTS IN MEDjugorje is being sought out by a commission of the Bishops' Conference of Yugoslavia (BKJ). Their work is progressing slowly. Therefore, with this statement I wish to help the commission in coming to a decision as soon as possible. Propaganda in favour of Medjugorje is being rushed in order to place the Church and the world before a *fait accompli*. This has been the intention of the defenders of Medjugorje from the beginning. It must be admitted that they have succeeded, because the other side is either working too slowly or remaining silent. For these reasons, and due to the motivation that I have been given from many from all over the world who realise that the truth has been trampled upon, I have decided to make another statement according to my duty and my conscience, and help the commission. With this statement I wish to awaken the consciences of those who defend Medjugorje. Their path is simple, wide and downhill all the way, while mine is difficult, thorny and uphill. The Church and Our Lady have no need of falsehoods. Jesus says: "The truth will make you free" (Jn 8:32). "I am the way and the truth and the life" (Jn 14:6). "For this I was born, and for this I have come into the world to bear witness to the truth. Every one who is of the truth, hears my voice" (Jn 18:37). For a short description of the falsehoods about Medjugorje we would need two hundred pages, but for now all I will give is this short summary without a scientific approach. I am somewhat uneasy because of the fact that in some statements my name is in the forefront, yet

from the beginning of the "apparitions" I have been in the centre of the events due to my episcopal position and duties. I am sorry as well for having to mention some "unpleasant things," but without them the arguments lose their strength. However, the most unpleasant things will not be mentioned.

2) **A characteristic attitude:** Marina B., a tourist guide for Atlas Travel, brought a priest from Panama to my office in August 1989. His name: Presbitero Rodriguez Teofilo, pastor of Nuestra Senora de Lourdes. With him came journalist Carmen Capriles, Gerente General of the IATA agency, and Averrida Alberto Navarro, Apartado 1344 Zona 7, Panama. Marina presented herself as a tour guide, translator for English and a convert of Medjugorje. The priest asked me the reasons that I do not believe in the "apparitions". I told him that I have at least twenty reasons not to believe, of which only one is necessary for those who are sober and well instructed in the Faith to come to the conclusion that the apparitions are not of the supernatural. He asked me to please tell him at least one reason. I told him about the case of the ex-Franciscan priest Ivica Vego. Due to his disobedience, by an order of our Holy Father the Pope, he was expelled from the Franciscan religious order by his General, dispensed from his vows, and suspended *a divinis*. He did not obey this order and he continued to celebrate Mass, administer the sacraments and pass the time with his mistress. It is unpleasant to write about this, yet it is necessary in order to see of whom Our Lady is speaking. According to the diary of Vicka and the statements of the "seers", Our Lady mentioned thirteen times that he is innocent and that the bishop is wrong. When his mistress, Sister Leopolda, a nun, became pregnant, both of them left Medjugorje and the religious life and began to live together near Medjugorje where their child was born. Now they have two children. His prayer book is still sold in Medjugorje and beyond in hundreds of thousands of copies.

I asked Marina to translate this into English. Marina cannot be blamed for having fallen into a community which is concealing the truth. She spontaneously responded according to the practice in Medjugorje: "Do we have to tell them these ugly things?" I responded by saying that if you had not held back and covered these "ugly events" these people from Panama would have found out earlier and they would not have had to travel to Medjugorje for nothing. It is an injustice and a sin to hide this truth; even though it be unpleasant, it must be said.

3) **The Marian theologian** René Laurentin behaves in the same manner. He came to visit me around Christmas 1983, and I offered him dinner. He asked me why I did not believe in the apparitions. I told him that according to the diary of Vicka and the words of the other "seers", this "Lady" has been speaking against the bishop. Laurentin quickly responded: "Don't publish that, because there are many pilgrims and converts there." I was scandalised by this statement of this well-known Mariologist! Unfortunately, that has remained Laurentin's position: to hide the truth and defend falsehoods. He has written around ten books on the topic of Medjugorje and in almost all of them, the truth and Bishop Žanić are under fire. He knows well what people like to hear. Therefore, it was relatively easy for him to find those who believe him. "*A veritate quidem auditum avertent, ad fabulas autem convertentur*"—"They will turn away from listening to the truth and wander into myths" (2 Tim 4:4). The "seers" and defenders of Medjugorje, led by Laurentin, from the very outset have seen that the modern believer in a communist country very quickly believes in everything "miraculous", in apparent miraculous healings and apparent messages from "Our Lady".

4) **The main players** on which Medjugorje rests are retired Archbishop F. Franic, Father René Laurentin, Father L. Rupčić, OFM, Father Amorth, Father Rastrelli, S. J., and some Franciscans and charismatics from all over the world. Many books have been quickly published, as well as articles, brochures, films and souvenirs. On the move are tourist agencies and pilgrimages, as well as prayer books written by two Franciscans, Vego and Prusina, who were expelled from the Franciscan Order,[1]

---

[1] Two Franciscan chaplains in Mostar, Ivan Prusina and Ivica Vego, who later left the order, were expelled from the order, dispensed from their vows, and

published in many languages in 600,000 copies, fanatical prayer groups that are inspired by the alleged messages of Our Lady and the greatest motivator of all—money. No one even mentions anything which throws doubt on the "apparitions". The bishop has been warning everyone, but the "machinery" has been breaking forward. There have been fifty miraculous healings mentioned, then one hundred and fifty, two hundred, three hundred, and so on. Laurentin chose fifty-six dossiers and sent them to the "Bureau Medical de Lourdes". Dr. Mangiapan responded in their bulletin in April, 1986, that these dossiers had no practical value, and they could not be used or considered as serious proofs of the apparitions in Medjugorje. Much has been written about the healing of Diane Basile. I sent the dossier to Dr. Mangiapan, who studied the case and then took the position: *"opinion plus que reservée"*. It is a case of sclerosis multiplex. More will be written about this later in a book.

5) **The credibility** of the "seers"—Mirjana Dragicević. One month after the beginning of the "apparitions" I went to Medjugorje to question the "seers". I asked each of them to take an oath on the cross and demanded that they must speak the truth. (This conversation and the oath were recorded on tape.) The first one was Mirjana: "We went to look for our sheep when at once...." (The associate pastor in the parish interrupted and told me that they actually went out to smoke, a fact they hid from their parents.) "Wait a minute, Mirjana, you're under oath. Did you go out to look for your sheep?" She put her hand over her mouth: "Forgive me, we went out to smoke." She then showed me the watch on which the "miracle" occurred because the hands of the watch had gone haywire. I took the watch to a watch expert who said that it had certainly fallen and become

---

suspended *a divinis* in accordance with the instruction from the Holy See dated 11 December 1980. Father Onorio Pontoglio, Vicar General and Procurator of the Order, made an announcement concerning their dismissal on behalf of the order on 29 January 1982. As a result of a procedural error in the process against them the sentence was annulled, but without calling into question the facts on which the sentence has been based. In the case of Vego the annulment is irrelevant as he has married his mistress and is hence no longer a Franciscan. See Bishop Ratko Perić, *Ogledalo Pravde*, 64. Prusina now lives in Germany and is not permitted to exercise his priesthood in Herzegovina.

The Truth about Medjugorje 53

disordered. After bringing the watch back to her I told her not to mention that a miracle occurred. Yet, on cassettes taped later on, she went on to speak of how a miracle occurred with the watch and that initially they had gone out to search for their sheep. Later on, she claimed that Our Lady stated that all faiths were equal. To what extent can we believe Mirjana?

6) **Vicka Ivanković** has been the main "seer" from the beginning, and through her the creator of Medjugorje, Father Tomislav Vlašić, OFM, has launched the main portion of falsehoods regarding Medjugorje. He presented himself to the Pope in a letter dated 13 May, 1984, as follows: "I am Father Tomislav Vlašić, the one according to Divine Providence who guides the seers of Medjugorje." It would have been better for him to have withdrawn into the desert and remained silent, because his past speaks enough about him. Vicka spoke and wrote much, and in so doing she fell into many contradictions. Professor Nikola Bulat, a member of the first commission, questioned her and wrote a sixty-page study on her. He numbered all the illogicalities and falsehoods of her diary. Here I will mention only the bloody handkerchief. Word spread around that there was a certain taxi driver who came across a man who was bloody all over. This man gave the taxi driver a bloodied handkerchief and he told him: "Throw this in the river." The driver went on and came across a woman in black. She stopped him and asked him to give her a handkerchief. He gave her his own, but she said: "Not that one but the bloody handkerchief." He gave her the handkerchief she wanted and she then said: "If you had thrown it into the river the end of the world would have occurred now." Vicka Ivanković wrote in her diary that they asked Our Lady if this event was true and she said that it was, and along with this, "That man covered with blood was my son Jesus, and I (Our Lady) was that woman in black."

What kind of theology is this? From this it appears that Jesus wants to destroy the world if a handkerchief is thrown into a river, and it is Our Lady who saves the world!

7) **On the 14th of January 1982**, Vicka, Marija and little Jakov came to visit me. Vicka began to speak quite nervously

because she was speaking falsehoods. She said: "Our Lady sent us to you to tell you that you are too harsh with the Franciscans...." In what way? "We don't know!" Two Franciscan chaplains in Mostar, Ivica Vego and Ivan Prusina, whom the bishop sought to remove from Mostar because of disorder and disobedience towards the faithful of the newly established cathedral parish in Mostar, defended themselves before their superiors by saying that they would not leave Mostar because Our Lady, through Vicka, told them not to leave. This was mentioned to me by a member of the Franciscan Provincial council. I asked Vicka at our meeting: "Did Our Lady mention anything about the Mostar chaplains, Vego and Prusina?" "She did not, we don't know them," responded all three. Our conversation lasted 30 minutes and I taped all of it. I brought up the question of the chaplains of Mostar several times and they always responded: "We don't know them." Later on, I found from Vicka's diary that they knew the chaplains very well. It was clear to me that they were lying, yet I did not want to mention this to them in order to maintain their confidence during our conversations.

8) **On the 4th of April, 1982**, Vicka and Jakov came to visit me, "sent by Our Lady." The chaplains of Mostar, Father Vego and Father Prusina, were expelled from the Franciscan Order in January of that year by the superiors of their order. Many followers and "Our Lady" defended the expelled chaplains. During our conversation Vicka very excitedly began: "The last time we were with you we didn't tell you everything and for this reason Our Lady scolded us. We spoke of many things and therefore we forgot...." "What did you forget?" Our Lady told us to tell you that those chaplains Vego and Prusina are priests and therefore they can celebrate Mass just as other priests." "Wait a minute. Did Our Lady tell you this before our last meeting?" "Yes, that's why she sent us to you. Last time I spoke of many other things and I forgot to mention this." During that previous meeting I asked her directly several times if Our Lady mentioned anything about the two chaplains. It was clear to me that Vicka was lying and

this was proof enough for me not to trust her statements. Marija and Jakov also participated in this lie.

9) **Towards the end of January 1983**, Father Grafenauer, a Slovenian Jesuit priest, came to me with the intention of searching out the phenomenon of Medjugorje. He listened to twenty cassettes and after having listened to them he said that he would not go to Medjugorje because he concluded that Our Lady was not there. Upon my insistence he went to Medjugorje and after a few days he came back as a "convert" of Father Vlašić. He brought some documents, threw them on the table and said: "Here's what Our Lady wishes to tell you!" I understood this as a plot to overthrow the bishop with the help of Our Lady. The documents he brought were a compilation of Vicka's diary, the parish chronicle, and handwritten documents. For this reason, it is difficult to establish where they were first written. Vicka and those who defend Medjugorje hid this from the bishop for more than a year.[2]

10) **Vicka** never denied that Our Lady said these things or that she wrote these things down in her diary. The assurance and authenticity of this statement can be best confirmed by a cassette taped by Father Grafenauer during his talks with Vicka and Marija. He left taped copies of the cassette in the parish of Medjugorje, with the bishop and also with the bishops' conference in Zagreb. The cassette should be heard!

A CONVERSATION WITH VICKA

Graf: The bishop has the duty to judge whether or not this is Our Lady.

Vicka: He can judge as he wants, but I know it's Our Lady.

Graf: The Church says of those who are confident in themselves, that this itself is a sign that Our Lady is not in question here.

Vicka: Let those who are doubtful remain doubtful, I'm not.

Graf: This is not a good thing... you once told the bishop that he should pay more attention to Our Lady than to the Pope.

---

2 The relevant extracts from Vicka's diary are provided in Appendix III.

Vicka: Yes, I did.

Graf: This means that the bishop should listen to you more than to the Pope.

Vicka: No, not me.

Graf: But the bishop doesn't know what the phenomenon is and perhaps it is not Our Lady.

Vicka: Yes, it is Our Lady.

Graf: You told the bishop that he was to blame and that those two (Vego and Prusina) were innocent and that they could perform their priestly duties.

Vicka: Yes, I did.

Graf: Can they hear confessions? Did Our Lady mention this?

Vicka: Yes.

Graf: If Our Lady said this and the Pope says that they cannot…

Vicka: The Pope can say what he wants. I'm telling it as it is!

Graf: See, this is how one can come to the conclusion that this is not Our Lady… when the Pope says no, they cannot celebrate Mass, and they cannot hear confessions, and then on the other hand, Our Lady says they can do both. This cannot be!

Vicka: I know what is right (what Our Lady said).

Graf: This cannot be true. I would put my hand into fire to testify that this is not Our Lady speaking. When a person has a greater gift there also exists a greater danger that the devil could be at work upon this person.

What a degrading humiliation of Our Lady! From these statements she is destroying obedience in the Church, obedience to the bishop, to the heads of the Order of Friars Minor, and to the Holy Father. She is defending Vego!

11) **The apparition in Cerno.** Cerno is a village not far away from Medjugorje. The eighth day after the beginning of the apparitions in Medjugorje there was an "apparition" near Cerno. The "seers" told Father Jozo Zovko, the pastor of Medjugorje at the time, of this happening the evening of the event.

They mentioned that Our Lady said four or five times that she would appear three more days, that is, on July 1, 2, and 3.

The Truth about Medjugorje 57

This was taped on cassette publicised by Father Ivo Sivrić OFM. The cassette was reproduced. A few years later Father Janko Bubalo published a book entitled: *A Thousand Meetings with Our Lady*. This is a book of conversations with Vicka. Vicka does not mention this event, therefore Father Bubalo asked whether or not Our Lady said "only three more days." Vicka responded that she does not remember!

It is evident that Vicka is speaking falsehoods and that Our Lady cannot say that which Vicka is saying. Vicka is fabricating these statements. Should this remain unknown to the rest of the world? Evil (such as speaking falsehoods about Our Lady) must not be done in order to obtain a good (such as pilgrimages, prayers, etc.)

12) **"Seer" Marija Pavlović.** Here is a written account of the taped conversation between Father Grafenauer and Marija:

Graf: Did Our Lady say that the bishop is to blame?
Marija: Yes.
Graf: Did she say that Vego and Prusina were not to blame?
Marija: Yes.
Graf: When Our Lady says that the bishop is to blame this immediately appears suspicious and we could conclude that... this is not Our Lady speaking. The seers are apparently... spreading word around that the bishop is to blame.
Marija: Our Lady told us this.
Graf: This is causing revolt in Herzegovina and these are not good fruits. People will be angry with the bishop and will defame his reputation. How can Our Lady do such things? The Church knows... well that Our Lady is good and that she would never do such things.
Marija: Our Lady told us this.

Archbishop F. Franic, Father Laurentin and many others know all this, yet they remain silent. What kind of theology can accept these statements by Our Lady through the declarations of the "seers" that their teacher, pastor and liturgist—the bishop, who has legally received his duty from Christ through the Church—has no love of God in his heart, that he is declared a sinner throughout the world, that he should convert and that prayers will be said in Medjugorje for this intention? There were even statements made that Jesus Himself would pray for the bishop so that he would believe and then take better action in favour of the events in Medjugorje. To say that the bishop is to wait for Our Lady's judgement is an absurdity. It is an offence against Our Lady, Mother of the Church. God knows that I am not without sin, and that Our Lady could criticise me, yet God alone is the judge. I have never been reprimanded or warned by the Holy See for my episcopal service.

13) **The creator of Medjugorje**, Father Tomislav Vlašić, amongst other things, has published and distributed in many languages a seventeen-page booklet titled *A Calling in the Marian Year*, Milan, 25 March, 1988. This regards the founding of a prayer group for young men and women (from Medjugorje) who would live together at Parma in Italy, something unheard of in the history of the Church. They would be the ones who would save the world. Our Lady apparently gave Father Vlašić and Agnes Heupel (a German woman supposedly healed in Medjugorje) the inspiration to establish and to lead this community together in a manner similar to Saints Francis and Clare, as described by Vlašić. In order for this action to succeed, Father Vlašić asked Marija Pavlović to add "her witnessing" on three pages. She is a member of this community, and on 21 April 1988 she wrote: "*Sento il bisogno...*" ("I feel the need").

> As can be concluded, Our Lady has given a set program to this community of the "Queen of Peace" and she leads this community through Father Vlašić and Agnes, who give messages to the community. I have been in the community for a month and a half. I have apparitions and Our Lady leads me in the mystery of suffering, which is the foundation of this community. I must write down everything and publish this once Our Lady tells me to. I have understood God's plan which He began through Mary in the parish of Medjugorje.

This quotation is taken from pages fifteen and sixteen of Father Vlašić's text. The defenders of Medjugorje quickly understood that this community of young men and women living, sleeping, working and praying together in the same house would eventually destroy itself and Medjugorje. Therefore, they sent their Provincial, Father Jozo Vasilj, to Parma. He went together with the Bishop of Parma, Monsignor B. Cochi and Father T. Vlašić to the Congregation in Rome. They were told there that the Church could not allow such a community to exist, and Father Vlašić was ordered to dissolve the community and to return to Herzegovina. Vlašić did not obey immediately, yet he returned later. This is what was explained to me by Father Jozo Vasilj regarding the community.

14) **The same Marija Pavlović** made another public declaration on 11 July, 1988. The declaration was printed on a single sheet of paper and distributed in the same manner as the statement of 21 April, 1988 (referred to in paragraph 13). In this statement she retracted her claim that Our Lady had given her approval to the Vlašić/Heupel community in Parma. She explained that Father Vlašić had pressured her into making this statement, which did not correspond to the truth. (The full text of this statement was cited in May, 1990.)

15) **Marija does not deny** that she made her first statement. Father Vlašić sought statements from her many times, and this obviously turns out to be manipulating one of the "seers". So, we can conclude that Marija has consciously spoken falsehoods on either the first or second occasion. She has lied, and this she attributes to Our Lady. It is evident that she (Marija) is a toy in Father Vlašić's hands. This was clear to me even earlier, yet up till now I didn't have material proof to back this up. Father Vlašić has manipulated all the "seers" in the same fashion.[3] Under this type of manipulation Marija saw how Our Lady cried when someone mentioned the bishop at a prayer meeting: "From Our Lady's eye flowed forth a great tear. The tear ran down her face and disappeared into a cloud under her feet. Our Lady began to cry and she ascended to

---

3   A German photographer named Walter Fuerhoff had witnessed Marija Pavlović in the company of Vlašić copying messages that he had written for her.

heaven crying" (22 August, 1984)—an obvious fabrication by Father Vlašić intended to frighten the bishop.

Why don't the defenders of Medjugorje mention these two statements of Marija? Must these "ugly" things be hidden from the world because there are many "conversions" in Medjugorje? Father Laurentin writes in his book *Dernières Nouvelles 3*, on page twenty-seven, that a certain monsignor asked Marija to pray for a message from Our Lady for his priests. Marija answered: "Our Lady said that they should read Laurentin's book and spread it around!"

It is a terrible sin to attribute one's own lies to Our Lady. When the world learns of this, who will believe them anymore? They have been discredited. No one can destroy this material evidence. It will be reproduced and spread by word of mouth. I know well that there are many who disregard such material. They accept the events of Medjugorje irrationally, with great emotion and with personal interests. They are blind, but these documents will remain a part of the history of the Church and of Mariology.

16) **The "seer" Ivan Dragicević**. Regarding the "great sign", Vicka mentions this thirteen times in the diaries, it is mentioned 14 times in the Parish chronicle, fifty-two times on the cassettes, and on numerous occasions in talks with the bishop. In the spring of 1982, I asked the "seers" to write everything they knew about the sign without making the "secret" public. The way I suggested they do it was to write down information on paper in duplicate. It would be sealed in an envelope. One copy would remain with them and one with the bishop. Then, when the "sign" occurred, we would open the envelopes and see whether or not the "sign" had been predicted. Father Tomislav Vlašić, pastor of Medjugorje at the time, told the "seers" to say that Our Lady had told them not to write anything down for anybody, and so they did not. Ivan Dragicević was in the Franciscan minor seminary at Visoko, Bosnia at that time and he wasn't informed of this on time. Two members of the first commission, Dr. M. Zovkic and Dr. Z. Puljić (now bishop of Dubrovnik), went to visit Ivan in Visoko. They gave

him a sheet of paper that was somewhat greenish in colour with questions typed out on it. Ivan wrote down the content of the "sign", dated the document and signed it in their presence without a word or any sign of fear. A few years later, Father Laurentin wrote that Ivan told him personally that he wrote absolutely nothing down on that sheet of paper and that he tricked the two members of the commission. On 7 March, 1985, three members of the commission went to ask Ivan if what Laurentin wrote was true. Ivan said it was true, and that they could freely go ahead and open the envelope in the chancery office because in it they would find only a white sheet of paper. They came back to Mostar where the commission was having a meeting and before all the members, they opened the envelope. In the envelope on a greenish sheet of paper they found written the content of the sign:

> Our Lady said that she would leave a sign. The content of this sign I reveal to your trust. The sign is that there will be a great shrine in Medjugorje in honour of my apparitions, a shrine to my image. When will this occur? The sign will occur in June.
>
> Dated: 9 May, 1982.   Seer: Ivan Dragicević.

After having heard this lie, the members of the first Commission wanted to end all further work, yet they stayed on. Within a few days of this event Father Slavko Barbarić, OFM, took the "seers" somewhere and instructed them all, including Ivan, to write a declaration that Ivan had not disclosed the sign!

Ivan sent messages from Our Lady to the bishop. On 24 April, 1984, Our Lady said the following regarding the bishop: "My son Jesus is praying for him so that he [the bishop] would believe and therefore take better action in favour of Medjugorje." She added: "How would he react if my Son were to appear on earth? Would he then believe?" Regarding the commission, Our Lady said only the following: "Pray, pray, pray! Think over and live the messages I have given and you will see why I have come."

17) **According to Ivan**:

> Tell the bishop that I seek a quick conversion from him towards the happenings in Medjugorje before it is too late. May he accept these events with plenty of love, understanding and great responsibility. I want him to avoid creating conflicts between priests and to stop publicising their negative behaviour. The Holy Father has given all bishops the duty to fulfil certain tasks in their respective dioceses. Among these, the parishes in Herzegovina. For this reason, I seek his conversion towards these events. I am sending my second-last warning. If what I seek does not come about, my judgement and the judgement of my Son await the bishop. This means that he has not found the way to my Son, Jesus." Our Lady told me to give you this message.
>
> With greetings,
> Ivan Dragicević,
> Medjugorje. Bijakovici, 21 June, 1983

Father Tomislav Vlašić brought this document to me, which he more than likely wrote himself in a moment of exaltation.

18) **Ivan kept his own diary** of the apparitions for a couple of years. This has not been made public as Vicka's has not; nor have the writings of the others. These are original fonts of the events, yet they are full of naive statements, clear falsehoods and absurdities. They are good proof of the fact that the "seers" do not see Our Lady or receive messages from her. These messages were written by someone else and were given to Ivan for him to sign as his own. When Father Grafenauer brought excerpts from Vicka's diary to me I later asked Vicka to bring her diary to me. She wrote to me on 7 May, 1983: "I have found out that excerpts from my diary are being distributed...." This was a very important point that the commission accepted as a good argument that the diary had been written by Vicka herself or that she considered it her own. Later on, Father T. Vlašić also came to this conclusion, and therefore in 1984 he declared before the Commission and myself that Vicka did not write that letter to me but rather that a Franciscan did (probably Vlašić himself) and that he

gave it to her to sign! There are many similar examples of manipulation, but none have such clear-cut evidence as this.

19) **Secrets and secrecy.** From the beginning of the "apparitions", in order to evade the detection of discrepancies in their accounts the "seers" have obviously been instructed to claim that "Our Lady" speaks differently to each of them. When the "secrets" were fabricated, each was to have his/her own (sixty in total) and no one was to reveal them to anyone. Mirjana and Ivanka received a letter from Our Lady that nobody was to read. In the beginning there were no moments of ecstasy or avoiding of the community. They admitted that they were consulted; they asked "Our Lady" if they could write down the content of the "great sign" on paper and seal it in an envelope. "Our Lady" responded: "No!" Ivan, though, wrote down the sign, and later on said (in a statement that has been taped as well) that "Our Lady" had not scolded him for doing so. The secrets were to be given to a priest (a Franciscan). Why were they not given to the commission, the bishop, or to the Pope? In the first months they often said that the "great sign" would come: very soon, quickly, and so....

When the first year ended, they changed their tone. Vicka wrote "Our Lady's life," for a year and a half, and this is a great secret which shall be published "when Our Lady permits." The commission asked for this diary about Our Lady, yet "Our Lady" did not comply with their demand. Can the commission just see the diary without taking it or opening it? No, it cannot! This turns out to be a plot to make fools out of all those who are naive enough to wait for this sign until the end of the world. I have already declared earlier, and now I repeat the same declaration, that if Our Lady leaves a sign which the "seers" are speaking of, I'll make a pilgrimage from Mostar to Medjugorje (thirty km) on my knees and beg the Franciscans and the "seers" for forgiveness.

20) **Slander against the bishop.** "The bishop also believed in the beginning." This is not true! While the communists were persecuting the Franciscans, the "seers," and the pilgrims, I defended all of them; thus, I did not change my mind

"because of threats by the Republic commission or because the diocesan priests sought this from me." This is simply fabricated slander. While I was publicly defending the imprisoned Franciscans, Father Jozo Zovko said during the investigations that the bishop was a "wolf" and a "hypocrite". These are the exact words written down in his sentence. Zovko's lawyer, N. N., asked through a colleague what I had done to Zovko to deserve such heavy accusations. Father T. Vlašić often put "Our Lady's" words into the mouths of the "seers", such as "Our Lady's" affirmation that Satan (in this case the bishop) was out to destroy her plan. He wrote this more clearly in a letter to friends in the Vatican. I complained about this accusation—that he had called the bishop Satan, in front of Vlašić and his Provincial. He did not deny my objection, but rather justified his words by saying that he wrote them while under the influence of extreme emotion. A person can say something while under the influence of emotion, but this cannot be written down and translated into foreign languages.

21) **By their fruits.** The most common argument of the defenders of Medjugorje is that the fruits of the events in Medjugorje prove that Our Lady is appearing there. Those who know a little more than the pilgrims who come to Medjugorje say: The fruits of the staunchest defenders of Medjugorje show that they themselves do not believe in the apparitions. If all the "ugly things" could be made public then surely the answer would be clearly negative to everyone. Yet Fathers Laurentin, Rupčić, Vlašić, Barbarić and others meticulously hide the truth. If the defenders of Medjugorje come across someone who is sceptical of the apparitions, they quickly isolate this person, accuse him of something or declare him mad (Jean Louis Martin). The majority of the pious public has naively fallen victim to the great propaganda, the talk of the apparitions and of healings. These people themselves have become the greatest propaganda for the events. They do not even stop to think that the truth has been hidden by deliberate falsehoods. They are unaware that not even one miraculous healing has occurred that could have been

verified by competent experts and institutions such as the *Bureau Medical de Lourdes*. No one knows of anyone healed from Herzegovina. Everyone knows that little Daniel, old Jozo Vasilj, Venka Brajcic and others cited in the first books about Medjugorje were not healed.

22) **Promises of healings** are characteristic of the events. When they don't occur as promised, then they are denied because they were never taped or written down on paper. There have been many promises that have ended tragically. What interests us is whether or not "Our Lady" is giving these promises, or whether or not they are thought up by the "seers". The tragic end of Marko Blazevic as described by the retired archbishop of Belgrade, Monsignor Turk, says much regarding "promises" of healing. The archbishop wrote on 22 May, 1984, that he was received as a patient of the cardiology clinic at the Belgrade hospital. He was given the bed that was previously occupied by Marko Blazevic of Buna, near Mostar, who was to go in for an operation. Mr. Blazevic told the archbishop and many other patients, doctors and hospital staff that Our Lady had promised, through the "seers", that the operation would succeed. A nun who assisted in the operation, wrote to me later that Blazevic's wife and his daughter spoke to her with a fanatical type of faith in "Our Lady's promise." A certain doctor was also convinced by this promise. The patient did not wake up after the operation. During the operation, a group of patients prayed fervently outside the doors of the operating room. Many spoke of this incident, which left many very disappointed and ashamed before atheists and people of other faiths. Father Vlašić, in his typical fashion of hiding the truth, succeeded in convincing the daughter of the late Mr. Blazevic to go to the bishop to tell him that Our Lady only told them to pray, not that she promised them that the operation would succeed. I told her not to make a liar out of her late father or liars of the others to whom he spoke.

23) **The Franciscan and diocesan clergy.** The relations between the Franciscan and diocesan clergy regarding pastoral duties in the parishes of Herzegovina were established

by a decision of the Holy See in 1899 at the suggestion of the Franciscans themselves and then Bishop Paskal Buconjic, OFM. According to this decision the parishes were to be divided equally into two groups of fifty per cent of the faithful (between the Franciscan and diocesan clergy). Since there were no diocesan clergy at the time, the parishes that rightfully belonged to them were, in 1923, left to the Franciscans *ad nutum S. Sedes*. Bishop Čule, the first diocesan bishop of Mostar, was sentenced in 1948 to eleven years and six months in jail (by the communist regime). He served eight and a half years of this sentence before being released.

After his jail term the number of diocesan clergy began to rise. In 1968, the Holy See ordered the Franciscans to hand over five parishes to the diocesan clergy. They barely gave two parishes. In 1975, after many years of talks and consultations, a Decree of the Holy See was issued regarding the division of parishes in Herzegovina (*Romanis Pontificibus* of 6 June 1975). The Franciscans publicly and collectively denounced this decree even though they administered to over eighty per cent of the faithful in the diocese of Mostar. In 1976, due to disobedience, the hierarchy of the Franciscan province, along with the provincial Sialic, lost their authority. Since then, the province has been without its independence, and the general of the order has ruled directly over the province *ad instar*. Another penalty was that in 1979 the Franciscans from Herzegovina were not allowed to participate in the election of the general. The first point mentioned by the new general of the order to his brothers in Herzegovina called for "the development or creation of obedience to, and co-operation with the bishop in Herzegovina." Disobedience prevails today as before, and "Our Lady" from the beginning has been defending disobedient Franciscans. Vicka writes in her diary of the apparitions that Our Lady said that the bishop was to blame for all the disorder in Herzegovina (see App. II). This is repeated many times.

The Franciscans themselves are divided. The Franciscan opposition that defends Medjugorje succeeded in toppling their own *ad instar* superiors who had developed good relations with the bishop, and they installed a group that defended Medjugorje. The new provincial *ad instar*, Father Jozo Vasilj, did not succeed in creating peace and order amongst his brothers so he escaped to the missions in Zaire and will not come back! (Fruits?) He has been replaced by the vice-provincial, and the general has called for obedience from all or else the province shall be abolished. "It is time that everyone takes their own personal responsibility before judicial sanctions are made or the province is abolished" (*Acta Ordinis F. M. fasc.* 1/89). The province will not receive its own hierarchy until the decree (*Romanis pontificibus*) is implemented. Three visitors of the OFM who came to the province in 1988 said that there was not one Franciscan in the province who was in favour of complying with the decree. This opinion is exaggerated yet still important.

24) **This is only a portion** of the "good fruits" of the events. The pilgrims, though, know only that the bishop "hates the Franciscans." There are a good number of Franciscans in the province who co-operate well with the bishop and these Franciscans do not believe in the apparitions either. Some of them have never set foot in Medjugorje.

A number of good Franciscans have begged me to write something so that, together, we could start a battle against the lies of Medjugorje, because they believe that "God will punish us Franciscans severely because we have spread lies and falsehoods throughout the world and made money from them."

Of the one hundred diocesan priests in the dioceses of Herzegovina, not one believes in the apparitions. Of the forty-two bishops of Yugoslavia (ordinaries, auxiliaries and retired), only one has been outspoken in declaring his belief and has defended the events. Of the fifteen members of the first commission, which was formed by the bishop of Mostar with the help of the bishops and provincials from Yugoslavia, eleven of the members said that there was nothing supernatural in the events of Medjugorje, two (Franciscans) claimed that the apparitions were authentic, one member said that there was something *in nucleo* (in the beginning) and one abstained. Contrary to what has been spread by the defenders of Medjugorje, the Holy See has never asked for, seen, or passed a judgement on the three-year work of the commission. Neither did the Holy See abandon the bishop.

25) **From the beginning** of the events I warned the Franciscans that they must wait for the judgement of the Church, so that together we could search for the truth. The leaders of the events, though, had as their aim to bring the masses as soon as possible to Medjugorje, obtain a lot of money for propaganda and use Our Lady for their battle against the bishop. They fabricated miracles regarding the sun. Many pilgrims damaged their eyes from staring into the sun. They cited fifty, one hundred and fifty, two hundred, and three hundred healings and they spoke of all sorts of things seeing that the faithful believed everything they said, especially when Archbishop F. Franic and Father Laurentin were there to back them up. The faithful in Medjugorje look upon the events as they are instructed, as is the case in all other places of apparitions, be they true or false. The marvelling and excitement here has been regarded at times as leading to great blindness and fanaticism.

26) **The Italians know well** the "story" of Gigliole Ebe Giorgini, the foundress of the false order of "Pia Opera di Gesu Misericordioso." Separated and remarried civilly, she spent time doing quackery. She gathered young women for her order and received and earned great amounts of money. She had two priests in her service and many houses. She led a double life and had false stigmata that she made herself. Her "sisters" followed her fanatically, calling her Mamma Ebe. She had male vocations as well, but some who left her later on declared that she led an immoral life. She had many jewels and gold, two yachts, thirty-two furs, etc. Many in the Church objected to her way of life, while others fanatically defended her, citing good fruits. She even received praise from two bishops. Twice during the night police raided her room in the motherhouse and they found her in bed with one of her seminarians. A scandal broke out and twice she was sentenced to many years in prison along with a Franciscan who was her confessor. The press wrote for years about this

scandal. An illicit film was made as well, yet her followers fanatically and blindly defended her even when the order fell apart. According to them, she was a saint who attracted many vocations; this was argument enough for many that she was obviously inspired by God! Religious blindness is extremely hard to cure. Fanaticism brought the beginning of heresies in the Church, today it is the foundation of sects.

The Protestant pastor Jim Jones developed a great charitable organisation in southern Chicago, gathering great sums of money and many fanatical followers to his sect. In order to be freer in their work, about one thousand of them went to Guyana, South America where they established "Jonestown" as their new home. They established a dictatorship and fanatical obedience to their "Messiah". Much was written about terrible things that went on, about the immorality of Jones and how some tried to escape the community but were caught and killed. Then they were without money. Rumours spread that the American army would intervene, so Jones ordered them to retreat to the jungle. Seeing no way out, he called on everyone to give up their lives in order to travel to eternity. Over nine hundred of them came with cups to a huge pot in order to drink poison and then fall dead. What gave them the strength to commit suicide? Fanaticism! Yet when the Christian faithful hear of apparitions and miracles, they easily accept these events as facts without being at all critical of the events. They are then caught up in their blindness and fanaticism. Whatever is spoken is believed automatically, such as the claim that ordinary rosaries in Medjugorje turn to gold! And people actually believe this!

27) **This blindness** towards the events in Medjugorje has also caught some priests and bishops. Many priests from Italy (such as Amorth, Restrelli and others) could easily have heard that the bishop, the commission, the bishops of Yugoslavia, a portion of the Franciscans and all the diocesan priests do not believe in the events. Yet they avoided the truth, even though I received everyone who inquired about the events and gave them my time. I'm particularly surprised at the lack of

collegiality by some bishops. Nobody has to accept my judgement, but everyone is obligated by conscience to study well the events of Medjugorje before taking a position, especially if that person has a position of authority in the Church, as bishops do.

What have they done to you, Our Lady! For nine years they have been dragging you along as a tourist attraction. They have been speaking with you whenever it pleased them, as if you were a bank teller. They have fabricated messages, and they say that you come and appear there, but beyond their own arguments they have nothing to prove that what they say is true. The whole world is in expectation of a "great sign" and the naive still wait and believe. Unfortunately, this false sensation will bring great disgrace and scandal upon the Church. Those who lead the events are not converting even though the threat of the abolition of the province by the general hangs over them.

This is only a small compilation of that which I would like to write about. I hope that I will have the opportunity to expand further, with precise documentation, and publish a book on these events.

28) **There are many prayers** and pious activities in Medjugorje. Some say that there have been conversions as well. I have received indeed many truly touching letters, and I feel sorry for those who will sooner or later be disappointed. But there have also been fanaticism, superstition and misinformation in the events of Medjugorje. I have received many rude accusations in the mail that I cannot mention, all in the name of the "Queen of Peace". That which is positive in these events cannot justify the falsehoods and lies that have been spread in order to win the world over for God. Jesus said: "I have come into the world to give witness to the truth" (Jn 18:37). The Church would easily be able to attract the masses if it dropped the sixth commandment, if divorce were allowed, if it let everyone believe and do what he wanted. But, Jesus died on the Cross for the truth, and the martyrs gave up their lives for the truth. St. Paul writes to his faithful: "If anyone

preaches to you a gospel besides that which you have received, let him be anathema" (Gal. 1:9). Today, many prayer groups all over the world pray from Father Ivica Vego's prayer book and meditate over the supposed messages of Our Lady as if these things were more important than the Bible and the teaching Magisterium of the Church. I do believe, despite these events, that Our Lady shall beg the necessary graces for the Church in order for it to live Christ's truth.

I know that there will probably be many sincerely pious souls who will misunderstand me and consider me an enemy of Our Lady. I have been to Lourdes many times and to other shrines of apparitions that the Church has recognised. What I am doing is defending the truth, defending the Church, and I pray to God that I be able to give up my life for this.

29) **Those who have written** about Medjugorje have sold their books well and have made great profits. Unfortunately, those who have written critically have not fared as well because they have come across an organised boycott. For the other side of the story, people should read:

Gramaglia, P.A. *L'Equivoco di Medjugorje, Apparizioni Mariane o Fenomeni di Medianita?* Claudiana, Toronto, Canada, 1987.
Jones, E. Michael. *Medjugorje: The Untold Story*. Fidelity Press, 206 Marquette Avenue, South Bend, IN, 1994.
Sivrić, Dr. Ivo, OFM. *The Hidden Side of Medjugorje*. Editions Psilog, 1989, CP 300, Saint-François-du-Lac, Quebec, Canada, J0C 1M0. (514) 568-3036. Dr. Sivrić is a Franciscan born in Medjugorje and now living in St. Louis, Missouri.

✠ *Pavao Žanić*
Bishop of Mostar

19

13 JUNE, 1990

The Irish Bishops' Conference Statement

THE IRISH BISHOPS' CONFERENCE ISSUED A FIVE-point statement on the subject of Medjugorje. Point four stated, "Until the Church gives its decision no one is entitled, on behalf of the Church, to presume a favourable judgement regarding the apparitions in Medjugorje. That is why the Church does not approve of pilgrimages and other manifestations organised on the presumption that a supernatural character can be attributed to the facts of Medjugorje."

20
1991
Alleged Miracles at Medjugorje

BISHOP ŽANIĆ HAS BEEN CITED AS DENYING THAT even one miraculous healing has taken place at Medjugorje that would be accepted as authentic by such an institute as the Bureau Medical de Lourdes, which, indeed, passed a negative verdict on fifty-six dossiers sent to it from Medjugorje. Nevertheless, claims of four hundred or more miraculous healings are cited in Medjugorje propaganda. In the 1991 Australian television documentary, Terry Willesee, a well-known Australian reporter, went to considerable trouble to find evidence to confirm the authenticity of even one of these cures. When pressed, Father Slavko Barbarić, OFM, who has been actively involved with the Medjugorje events since the early years, admitted that only ten of the alleged four hundred cures had been thoroughly checked—and what he meant by thoroughly checked is far different from what the Bureau Medical de Lourdes would mean. The reporter was told of a woman who had been cured instantaneously of cancer, but when he asked for proof none was forthcoming. He was offered the chance to meet a cripple, a native of Medjugorje, who had been miraculously cured and could now walk. He went to the man's home to record the miracle on film, only to find that the man could not even stand up. He had, however, a little movement in his left leg.

There is ample evidence of promised cures that did not materialize. In 1981, a child from Grude suffering from leukaemia, was promised an unconditional and certain cure but died before the end of the year. In 1983 the doctor of a young girl suffering from cancer advised an operation and the removal of her breast. She consulted the "seers" at Medjugorje, who spoke to the Virgin—who replied that there was no need for an operation. The girl died on 24 December that year after agonizing pain.

Miracles of the sun are an everyday occurrence at Medjugorje. Many of the pilgrims stare at the sun, convinced that it is not harming their vision. It is hardly surprising that the sun appears to spin or pulsate. Willesee wished to film a solar phenomenon that he was assured was taking place. When the film was played back the sun appeared to be pulsating. His hopes of having filmed a miracle were dashed when his cameraman told him that it was simply a reaction of the iris of the camera.

I have heard the personal testimony of someone who was present when a lady began screaming at the top of her voice: "A miracle! A miracle!" The miracle consisted of the fact that she could see an image of the Host on the back of a man in front of her who was wearing a black leather jacket. This, of course, is exactly what would happen to anyone who stares at a bright light and then looks at something black.

The most widely cited Medjugorje "miracle" is that of rosaries turning to gold. There is not a single documented case of any rosary turning to gold there. What has happened is that in some cases silver-coloured links on rosaries have changed to a goldish colour. This has happened at the sites of other alleged apparitions, such as Bayside in New York. The official explanation is that this is a miracle performed by Our Lady, but those with real love for the Mother of God know that she would not engage in such cheap conjuring tricks. An obvious explanation is that it could be the work of Satan, seeking to delude faithful Catholics into putting their faith in spurious apparitions.

21

The Medjugorje Industry

IN A LETTER TO FATHER HUGH THWAITES DATED 17 August, 1987, which has already been cited, Bishop Žanić stated bluntly that the alleged apparitions were "the fruit of a fabrication, fraud, and disobedience to the Church. It is about big money and personal interest too." When he wrote this letter in 1987 the good bishop could scarcely have imagined the extent to which what can only be described as the Medjugorje industry would have expanded by 1993. The 1991 Australian documentary on Medjugorje showed the great material prosperity the "apparitions" have brought to what was a previously impoverished area (which most of the men had had to leave to find employment). Everyone in the area is now employed and many have become immensely wealthy by the standards of Herzegovina. Everyone with a spare room lets it out to pilgrims and in many cases houses have been expanded by knocking down external walls to provide more rooms to let. Medjugorje is now crammed with souvenir shops, restaurants, and pizza parlours. If any of the "seers" were ever to admit that the whole story had been a fraud from the beginning they would almost certainly be lynched by their families, friends, and neighbours, who have made a fortune from the "apparitions". Bishop Žanić has no doubt that "the greatest motivator of all"—money—is what inspires the "seers" and their manipulators, but it seems probable that more money is being made from Medjugorje in other countries than in Herzegovina itself. It must now be considered primarily as a multi-million-dollar business operation, particularly in the United States. The amount of money made by travel operators would be impossible to calculate, and many of the so-called Medjugorje centres are, in reality, quasi travel agencies.

An insight into the extent to which financial gain predominates in Medjugorje is made clear in an article by the sociologist Max Bax in the June 1993 issue of *Amsterdams Sociologisch Tidschrift*. It concerned what could be described fairly as a dirty little war between different Catholic families engaged in the pilgrimage industry in Medjugorje. One family had reached the stage of almost exercising a monopoly in this industry, and two other families decided to change this situation. Open war broke out. Of the three thousand inhabitants of Medjugorje one hundred and forty were killed, sixty disappeared, and six hundred fled the village, finding their homes destroyed when they returned. The two formerly less successful families now operate the pilgrimage and tourist industry within Medjugorje. (In this context the word "clan" would be more accurate than "family", since extended families in Herzegovina can number dozens or even hundreds.) This has all been concealed from the outside world because it does not correspond to the image of a community dedicated to the Queen of Peace.

22
MAY–JUNE 1993

Sacrificial Giving

DOCUMENTATION HAS ALREADY BEEN PROVIDED on the manner in which a certain Terry Colafrancesco paid for Marija Pavlović to bring her brother to Birmingham, Alabama for a kidney transplant in 1989, and in return asked for an apparition on land he had purchased, which immediately became a lucrative pilgrimage centre. In 1986 he had founded an organisation named *Caritas* to promote the Medjugorje messages.

Colafrancesco's organisation has expanded considerably, and in 1993 he was appealing for more than one and a half million dollars to build a "Medjugorje Tabernacle". On page fifteen of his May-June 1993 newsletter, which has a circulation of one hundred and fifty thousand, he described the proposed tabernacle as follows

> The "Tabernacle of Our Lady's Messages" is a 32,000-square-foot building that will house the six different ministries at *Caritas*. It will have three floors, all dedicated 100 per cent to Our Lady of Medjugorje. Through this tabernacle will flow the messages of Our Lady through the printing, producing and shipping of newsletters, tapes, booklets, textbooks, flyers, researching the messages and researching history, etc., all over the United States as well as into sixty-five foreign countries.

In order to build his tabernacle Mr. Colafrancesco would like $1,600,000. He requests his readers to "pray to the Holy Spirit" before reading his fund-raising appeal—a tactic that bears an uncanny, or perhaps not so uncanny, resemblance to techniques employed by Protestant TV evangelists who spread a gospel composed almost entirely of admonitions to make sacrificial donations. Mr. Colafrancesco warned his readers that the building of the tabernacle would be "in jeopardy" unless many of them were moved to help. Those who might be in doubt about donating were told to pray to Our Lady, since he has heard from many people who "after prayer felt Our Lady urging them to do so." Satan, he warns us, would do anything to persuade Catholics not to donate to the tabernacle. "We know times are difficult for many of you, but they are going to get more difficult and Our Lady's plan is what will reverse that in the long run. We are at a point in construction where decisions have to be made to proceed to the next steps and we need your response immediately. The people of this nation and the world need the security of Our Lady, not savings."

The alleged tens of thousands of messages of Our Lady that are to be housed in Mr. Colafrancesco's tabernacle are almost invariably truisms of such utter banality that any ten-year-old could compose them:

> Dear children. Today I invite you to live in humility all the messages which I am giving you. Do not become arrogant living the messages and saying, "I am living the messages." If you shall bear and live the messages in your heart, everyone will feel it so that words, which serve those who do not obey, will not be necessary. For you, dear children, it is necessary to live and witness by your lives. Thank you for having responded to my call.

> Dear children. Thank you for dedicating all your hard work to God even now when He is testing you through the grapes you are picking. Be assured, dear children, that He loves you and therefore He tests you. You just always offer up all your burdens to God and do not be anxious. Thank you for having responded to my call.

Can one seriously imagine the Mother of God appearing on earth four to six times a day if she has nothing more profound than this to say?

CELESTIAL BOOK REVIEWS

Mr. Colafrancesco sells the first two volumes of the *Poem of the Man God* at $35.00 each. Sales appear to have been adversely affected by Cardinal Joseph Ratzinger's admonition that the book should not be read, and Colafrancesco therefore consulted Marija Pavlović, whom he describes as "a close personal friend". Miss Pavlović demonstrated her friendship yet again with a promptness equal to that which she had displayed in arranging the Thanksgiving Day apparition for her benefactor. She used her direct line to heaven to consult Our Lady concerning the book, and was assured that we were free to read it. I understand that Our Lady's actual words were: "It makes for good reading." Mr. Colafrancesco assures us that there is "no question that she spoke to Our Lady". Conclusive proof has already been provided to prove that Pavlović is a self-confessed liar (see 11 July, 1988).

"REMARKABLE THINGS" AND "MIRACLES"

Mr. Colafrancesco claims that Our Lady speaks directly to his *Caritas* community through her daily messages. Each morning they read a randomly chosen message, which results in "remarkable things". The following "remarkable thing" concerned a retreat for children in "the Field" (note the upper case "F"):

> An area Catholic grade school had planned a retreat day at *Caritas* and the Field (the site of Our Lady's apparition to visionary Marija Pavlović in November 1988). Several hundred children from kindergarten through the eighth grade joined the *Caritas* community and staff for our daily rosary as well as assisting at a Mass they had planned for the Field. That day at morning prayer, before the students arrived, we opened up the following message: 29 April, 1983,—Concerning a group of young people as they leave for their pilgrimage: "I wish that you pray throughout your trip and that you glorify God. There you will be able to meet other young people. Convey the messages which I have given you. Do not hesitate to speak to them about it."

Not only does the *Caritas* community experience "remarkable things", but it also cites what it claims are "miracles" at Medjugorje. An account of a "Eucharistic Miracle" appeared in the May-June 1993 newsletter. A non-Catholic lady accompanied a *Caritas* pilgrimage from Birmingham to Medjugorje. Pilgrimages to Medjugorje have, of course, been forbidden by the bishop, the lawful authority in the diocese, as well as by the Congregation for the Doctrine of the Faith, and so every organised pilgrimage there constitutes an act of disobedience to lawful authority. This Protestant lady was annoyed that she could not receive Holy Communion. Non-Catholics are permitted to receive Catholic Holy Communion only on very rare occasions with specific permission after a number of stringent conditions have been fulfilled. But it would appear, Our Lady was more concerned at the displeasure of the Protestant than with adherence to the law of the Church, and so she arranged for the lady to receive Communion in circumstances that Mr. Colafrancesco describes as miraculous:

> When distribution for Communion came, the first priest off the altar came toward the group leader. He and the others around him expected to be given the Eucharist, but instead the priest walked through the crowd which opened up. The leader, as well as the group, watched stunned as everyone was passed by while the priest walked directly to the spot where the woman was sitting in the pew. He held up the Eucharist for her to receive. The leader and the group and she herself stared in disbelief at what they were seeing. Though it was but a moment, it seemed the hesitation lasted for minutes. While she sat there and Jesus in the Eucharist was held up before her, she hesitated at first, not being sure, then wilfully [sic] received Him. Everyone around her who was not weeping were [sic] fighting back their [sic] tears because all knew the priest could not have seen her until he was before her, much less known that she was not a Catholic. Only a few months later, the pilgrim who did not want to become a Catholic, received the Holy Eucharist a second time — as a new Catholic.

23

1993

Millions Are Deluded

WHAT IS MOST ALARMING ABOUT THE MEDJUgorje phenomenon is the number of Catholics who have been deluded into believing it. It would be a serious matter if a few thousand or even a few hundred Catholics were wasting their time and their money, and giving their credence and their cash to a fraud that detracts from the dignity of Our Lady, presenting her as possibly the most garrulous woman in history. But millions of people have now visited Medjugorje and are supporting the ever-expanding Medjugorje industry. Every month *Twin Circle* and the *National Catholic Register* publish what amounts to a Medjugorje colour supplement with a monthly message such as the following for August, 1993:

> Dear children, I want you to understand that I am your Mother; that I want to help you and call you to prayer. Only by prayer can you understand and accept my messages and practise them in your life. Read Sacred Scripture; live it and pray to understand the signs of the time. This is a special time; therefore, I am with you to draw you close to my heart and the heart of my Son, Jesus. Dear little children, I want you to be the children of the light and not of the darkness. Therefore, live what I am telling you. Thank you for having responded to my call.

These supplements list no fewer than one hundred and seventy-seven Medjugorje Centres throughout the U.S., which include, of course, *Caritas* of Birmingham together with Medjugorje Information centres, Peace centres, Resource centres, Message centres, Ventures, centres for Love, centres for Peace (many of these), Messengers of Peace, Queen of Peace, Hearts for Peace, Pilgrims for Peace Video Ministry, Mary's Touch by

Mail, Friends, Coalitions, and Book Centres. There is no little irony in the fact that the area in Bosnia where Our Lady is alleged to have appeared with the title of "Queen of Peace" was a centre of one of the most vicious wars of this century, of which she gave not the least warning in tens of thousands of messages.

There are now many Medjugorje newsletters serving the needs of the industry, including the *Medjugorje News*, which is circulated throughout Canada. It reports in its issue Number 5 in 1993 that twenty thousand people came to hear the "seer" Ivan Dragicević when he came to Marmora in Ontario, where Our Lady is also alleged to appear to children and adults of various ethnic backgrounds, including a member of the Macedonian Orthodox Church. It is claimed that angels and deceased members of families appear there and converse! The literature that circulates among Medjugorje devotees lists literally hundreds of apparitions of Our Lady allegedly taking place throughout the world, including twenty-five in Ireland alone. News of every new apparition is greeted with uncritical enthusiasm by many thousands of devotees. One can only say that whatever all this represents, it is not Catholicism.

The appearance of Ivan Dragicević in Ontario indicated the policy of the Medjugorje "seers", during the war in Bosnia. Gullible Catholics could not bring their cash to Medjugorje, and so the "seers" left Medjugorje to collect the cash from them, and are still doing so. One can refer with complete accuracy to a Medjugorje "road show". It has even reached Kent, the county in England where I live. The Autumn 1993 issue of *The Children of Medjugorje* (published in Scotland) recounts the appearance of Ivan Dragicević at "The Medjugorje Ecumenical Day of Prayer" on 28 August, 1993, at the Carmelite Priory at Aylesford in Kent. The people came expecting an apparition. This is what we read:

> The Mother of Jesus appeared (on 28 August) in "an indescribable light, wearing a grey dress with a white veil over her dark hair", according to the visionary, 27-year-old Ivan Dragicević. Her eyes are blue and

she has rosy cheeks, he told the gathering of 5,000 Christians.... Ivan said that Mary "was joyful and prayed over all of us with outstretched hands. She blessed us all."

Dragicević added that Our Lady "then prayed for peace in a special way for a long time." The Virgin gave no special message, having given one for the world only three days before in Medjugorje. She simply said, "Go in peace, my dear children", before departing in the light of a shining cross. Ivan's script could well have been written by Walt Disney! The report was accompanied by a picture of Ivan wearing what appear to be pyjamas and kneeling by a radiator, looking extremely pious.

A similar event took place at Aylesford in August, 1996, and an enthusiastic report in the 8 September *Universe* (which derives considerable revenue from Medjugorje advertising) stated that seven thousand gathered there to hear Father Slavko Barbarić and, of course, Ivan Dragicević. Seventy-five Catholic clergy were present, and in keeping with the ecumenical ethos of the messages, thirty Protestant ministers. Once again, the people came expecting a "miraculous apparition" and, as always, Ivan had no problem in providing it:

> As dusk fell, the Blessed Mother appeared to Ivan and afterwards Ivan told those assembled that the Mother of God had appeared to him joyful [sic]: she had brought a private message to Ivan and afterwards she had extended her hands and prayed over the crowd for a long period of time. Ivan said that he had asked the Blessed Mother to pray and intercede for everybody. The Blessed Mother prayed then left in a brilliant light. After the final blessing everyone left in a joyful mood.

In view of the large collection that had been taken up Ivan must have been in a particularly joyful mood.

24

24 JULY, 1993

A New Bishop of Mostar

BISHOP ŽANIĆ RESIGNED AS BISHOP OF MOSTAR in 1993 and was replaced by Monsignor Ratko Perić, his coadjutor bishop, on 24 July, 1993. Bishop Perić had spent ten years in Rome as rector of the Pontifical Croatian College, and was consecrated as coadjutor bishop on 14 September 1992. Rumours have been circulated that Bishop Žanić was forced to resign by the Pope, who did not approve of his intransigent opposition to the veracity of the Medjugorje apparitions. "The bishop of Mostar, Monsignor Žanić, was removed from his post and removed from the commission of enquiry and totally discredited," said one source. These claims constitute the type of malicious and totally unsubstantiated calumnies that we have come to expect from the Medjugorje industry. Where there is money to be made basic standards of decency can quickly be forgotten.

The truth is that Bishop Žanić, who was born on 20 May, 1918, offered his resignation in 1993 after reaching the statutory age of retirement, and was replaced by Bishop Perić, who is just as opposed to the authenticity of the alleged apparitions as was his predecessor. On 5 February, 1996, during a private audience with Cardinal Ratzinger, I mentioned the claim that Bishop Žanić had been "removed from his post". His Eminence was visibly shocked that such a disgraceful allegation could have been made, and he assured me that the bishop had resigned not simply because he had reached the statutory age, but also because he was very tired. In addition to the stress caused by the Medjugorje scandal, the war in Bosnia had caused him great hardship. Bishop Žanić's residence was destroyed and for a time he had been forced to leave his diocese.

Bishop Perić is, if anything, more adamant concerning the falsity of the alleged apparitions than was Bishop Žanić. In the

October, 1993, issue of his diocesan journal *Crkva n Kamenu* (The Church on the Rock), Bishop Perić directed an open letter to St. Francis of Assisi in which he complained to the saint that his spiritual sons, the Bosnian Franciscans, were disobedient. The same issue contains a long interview with the new bishop in which he makes it clear that he believes the alleged apparitions to be devoid of any credibility.

A partial translation of the interview appeared in the February, 1994, issue of *Fidelity*. Bishop Perić testified that his predecessor had been open to the veracity of the apparitions in the beginning. He pointed out that Bishop Žanić would evidently have been predisposed to believe in the alleged apparitions. He continued:

> What bishop wouldn't be delighted that the Virgin Mary should be appearing in his diocese? Especially Monsignor Žanić, a very Marian bishop, who as a priest and later as a bishop made eleven pilgrimages to various Marian shrines all over Europe: Lourdes, Fatima, Syracuse, etc. And then for the *Gospa* (Our Lady) to have mercy on him and begin to "appear" in his own backyard as if to bring an end to all his wanderings all over Europe.
>
> But after a few months, when he heard the small fibs and large lies, insincerities, inexactitudes, and all sorts of fabricated stories from those who claimed that the *Gospa* was appearing to them, he became totally convinced that it was not a matter of supernatural apparitions of the *Gospa*. Then he started to bring out the truth and to expose the falsehoods. The greatest satisfaction of his ten years of hard work was when the bishops of Yugoslavia at their spring meeting at Zadar on 10 April, 1991, dutifully declared: "On the basis of studies conducted so far it cannot be affirmed that supernatural apparitions and revelations are occurring." *This is an exceptionally clear ecclesiastical ruling, and is a rebuttal of the claims of all those who claim to have seen the Gospa everywhere and at any time since 1981* [emphasis added].

> The verdict of the bishops' conference is for me an authoritative instruction, responsive and binding unless another kind of verdict is brought. But until now there has been no other (ecclesiastical) judgement.... If, after serious, solid, and professional investigation, our bishops' conference had the courage to declare that Medjugorje's apparitions were not supernatural, in spite of massive stories and convictions to the contrary, then that is a sign that the Church, even in the 20th century, "upholds the truth and keeps it safe" (1 Tim. 3:15). I affirm this unequivocally.

In 1995, Bishop Perić published a book, *The Seat of Wisdom*, which contains an important chapter entitled "Criteria for Discerning Apparitions", appended here as Appendix I. It is an invaluable source of reference not simply where Medjugorje is concerned, but also as a means of exposing the falsity of the hundreds of spurious apparitions proliferating throughout the world. The bishop cites a series of criteria put forward by Professor R. Fisichella of the Gregorian University in Rome. "One must also recall," writes Professor Fisichella, "that apparitions are always something 'extraordinary', rare, and this is an important element for their discernment. If apparitions were to occur on a daily basis in the life of a believer, or if they were to continue for years, this would obviously create serious problems for the theology of faith."

Bishop Perić cites a series of positions made public by the diocesan chancery, which have been conveyed to the Holy See, and which are still maintained today. On the so-called fruits he states:

> The fruits which are so often mentioned, are not proof that they result from "supernatural apparitions or revelations" of the Madonna, but insomuch as they are authentically Christian, they can be understood as a product of the regular workings of the grace of God, through faith in God and the intercession of Mary, the Mother of Christ, and through the Holy Sacraments present in the Catholic Church. Not to mention anything at all about the negative fruits.

A New Bishop of Mostar

Bishop Perić warns:

> In some of the statements made by the so-called seers of Medjugorje published in the last 14 years, there are such contradictions, falsehoods and banalities, which cannot be attributed at all to our heavenly Mother *Sedes Sapientiae*—Seat of Wisdom, since there does not exist even a minimal guarantee of credibility. On the basis of such statements and the events tied to the statements: it cannot be affirmed that these matters concern "supernatural apparitions or revelations", of the Madonna or others. The talk of a "great sign", of "ten secrets", which Our Lady conveyed to the children, resembles the scare tactics which are typical of non-Catholic communities and not the sound teachings of the Catholic Church.

The bishop made clear in this 1995 statement that Medjugorje was not a Catholic shrine, and that pilgrimages there were forbidden:

> Neither the diocesan bishop as the head of the local diocese of Mostar-Duvno, nor any other competent authority has ever officially declared the parish church of St. James the Apostle in Medjugorje as a "Marian shrine" and no "cult" of the Madonna based upon so-called apparitions has ever been proclaimed. Due to these discrepancies, the local bishop has repeatedly forbidden anyone from preaching or speaking in churches on the supernatural nature of these so-called "apparitions and revelations", and he has asked that no official pilgrimages be organized, be they at the level of parishes, dioceses or generally in the name of the Church. These and similar warnings were made by our former bishops' conference and the Holy See. Whoever acts to the contrary, is directly going against the official statements of the Church, which even after 14 years of so-called apparitions and widespread propaganda, still remains valid in the Church.

25

OCTOBER, 1993

An Interview with the Bishop of Mostar (excerpts)

In October, 1993, an interview with Monsignor Ratko Perić, Bishop of Mostar and successor to the recently retired Pavao Žanić was published in Crkva na Kamenu *("The Church on the Rock"), the newspaper of the Diocese of Mostar-Duvno. The conversation covered a variety of topics, including the reported apparitions at Medjugorje, and was conducted by Father Ante Tonca Komadina, STD, the paper's editor.*

Father Komadina: You have a parish in your diocese that is known all over the world, one in which the Blessed Virgin Mary is supposed to have been appearing for over twelve years. What is your opinion of the Medjugorje movement?

Bp. Perić: Medjugorje was already "phenomenal" in the last century. Father Petar Bakula, OFM, noted in a book he wrote in 1867 that people were even then claiming to see a very strong and pinkish light in and around Medjugorje. So, the "phenomenon of light" did not start to fascinate people for the first time in 1981. I have followed the happenings in Medjugorje carefully. I tried to be of help to Bishop Žanić as a secretary, when he used to come to Rome and to submit his reports all about the events to the Holy See. I maintain that Bishop Žanić took a wise stand in the context of such circumstances. In the beginning he was open to accepting the phenomenon....

Fr. Komadina: Just recently a statement of Monsignor Žanić was misrepresented in the March, 1993, issue of *Glas Mira*, as if the bishop had uttered it last night. *Glas Mira* ["The Voice of Peace"], a pro-Medjugorje Franciscan newspaper published in Medjugorje, quoted the following statement of Bishop Žanić:

An Interview with the Bishop of Mostar (excerpts) 89

"Everything indicates that the children are not lying. However, the most difficult question remains: Did the visionaries have subjective, supernatural experiences?" [*Glas Mira* not only implied that this statement had just been made by Bishop Žanić, but also failed to mention that Monsignor Žanić had in fact said those words over twelve years earlier, during the first few months of the "apparitions".—MD.]

Bp. Perić: Perhaps misinformation is another of Medjugorje's phenomena. But let us go back to Bishop Žanić. The whole thing had so caught his interest that he became involved in questioning the visionaries himself and closely followed the happenings in Medjugorje. What bishop wouldn't be delighted that the Blessed Virgin Mary would be appearing in his diocese? Especially Monsignor Žanić, a very Marian bishop, who as a priest and later as a bishop made eleven pilgrimages to various Marian shrines all over Europe: Lourdes, Fatima, Syracuse, etc. And then for the *Gospa* to have mercy on him and begin to "appear" in his own backyard as if to bring an end to all his wanderings all over Europe. But after a few months, when he heard the small fibs and large lies, insincerities, inexactitudes, and all sorts of fabricated stories from those who claimed that the *Gospa* was appearing to them, he became totally convinced that it was not a matter of supernatural apparitions of the *Gospa*. Then he started to bring out the truth and to expose the falsehoods. The greatest satisfaction of his ten years of hard work was when the bishops of Yugoslavia, at their spring meeting at Zadar on 10 April, 1991, dutifully declared: "On the basis of studies it cannot be affirmed that supernatural apparitions and revelations are occurring." This is an exceptionally clear ecclesiastical ruling, and is a rebuttal of the claims of all those who claim to have seen the *Gospa* everywhere and at any time since the year of 1981.

The verdict of the bishops' conference is for me an authoritative instruction, responsive, and binding unless another kind of verdict is brought. But until now there has been no other (ecclesiastical) judgment. In the same declaration the bishops said that a healthy devotion to the Blessed Virgin Mary necessarily must be in accordance with the teachings of the Catholic Church and set about publishing proper liturgical-pastoral directives to that effect. [Bishop Perić repeats here almost exactly what he stated under the date 24 July, 1993.] The commission also promised to follow and investigate the happenings in Medjugorje. I know that the liturgical-pastoral committee met in Mostar in June, 1991, but that no document was released. In the fall of 1991, the Serbian aggression began in the Croatian regions of Eastern Herzegovina, and in the spring of 1992 the Serbs attacked the entire region of Bosnia-Herzegovina. It has become impossible for the commission to meet anymore.

Fr. Komadina: Aren't you delighted by the fact that the world has finally heard of us Croatian Catholics, even if only through Medjugorje?

Bp. Perić: I am delighted for each locality in the world wherever the grace of God is at work, as it was in the Acts of the Apostles when Barnabas was speaking of his visit to Antioch. But my "joy" with regard to Medjugorje is disturbed by several facts. For instance, there have been claims for over twelve years of daily "apparitions." If none of these several thousand "apparitions" have been recognized by the bishops as supernatural, then there is something very rebellious about the Medjugorje "phenomenon" that I cannot responsibly embrace in faith.

Fr. Komadina: It is said that even promoters of Medjugorje maintain that everything would go up in smoke if the apparitions stopped.

Bp. Perić: The official Church recognized only a few of the many reported apparitions at Lourdes, and 135 years later it is still active. If someone in Medjugorje is forcing "apparitions," he is probably looking more for quantity than quality.

Fr. Komadina: At present, allegedly, the *Gospa* is appearing every 25th of the month, and is giving the usual messages for fasting and penance. We read these messages in the secular newspapers. A few days ago (12 September, 1993) we read how one of the "visionaries" who used to transmit urgent messages of fasting and penance recently got married, of how she was planning to spend her honeymoon on Cote d'Azur

An Interview with the Bishop of Mostar (excerpts)   91

[the Riviera] and of how she was going to live in a six-story building in Monza, Italy!

Bp. Perić: The reports of monthly "apparitions" sound more like propaganda than responsible journalism. The Madonna does not deserve this kind of propaganda! Prayer, peace, fasting and penance are the core of the Christian message, and have been such since the very first appearance of Christ right up to the present. The Church ceaselessly preaches this message and tries to put it into practice. In this sense nothing new is contained in the Medjugorje messages.

Fr. Komadina: What do you think about Medjugorje's "healings" and "miracles"?

Bp. Perić: Notice that we do not hear so much about miracles today as we did earlier. I asked Father Ivan Landeka that he—as a pastor—give me a report on the present situation in Medjugorje, which he did in June of this year. It ran to six pages. He did not mention the "miracles" at all. Conversions are possible everywhere, and some are bound to happen in Medjugorje. But this is not proof that the "apparitions" are supernatural.

Fr. Komadina: Finally, what is your stand on Medjugorje?

Bp. Perić: The Church recommends prayer, fasting, penance, reconciliation, and conversion to each of its members. I do not want to forbid anyone to go wherever he wants to pray to God. But I cannot approve that from the altar of the church in Medjugorje the priests themselves advertise "pilgrimages to the place of apparitions," despite the fact that they have simply not been recognized as supernatural by the Church. If, after serious, solid, and professional investigation, our bishops' conference had the courage to declare that Medjugorje's "apparitions" were not supernatural, in spite of massive stories and convictions to the contrary, then that is a sign that the Church, even in the twentieth century, "upholds the truth and keeps it safe" (1 Tim. 3:15). I affirm this unequivocally, and I answer it publicly to all those who have written either anonymous or signed letters to me with contrary advice.

26

10–11 SEPTEMBER, 1994

The Pope Visits Croatia

PROPONENTS OF MEDJUGORJE ARE CONSTANTLY circulating statements favouring the apparitions allegedly made by the Holy Father in private conversations. If His Holiness has indeed made these statements, which seems highly improbable, they have no doctrinal status since they were made in private conversation; but, if the Pope does believe in the apparitions, it seems strange that as the successor to Bishop Žanić, he appointed Bishop Ratko Perić, who is, if anything, even more opposed to the authenticity of the apparitions than was his predecessor. Despite his appointment of Bishop Perić, proponents of Medjugorje still attempt to present the Holy Father as a supporter of the alleged apparitions. It is stranger still that if, which God forbid, the Holy Father believed that the Mother of God had appeared at Medjugorje on thousands of occasions under the title "Queen of Peace", he did not once mention that when he visited Croatia on a mission of peace on 10-11 September, 1994. Nor did he mention Medjugorje in any of the addresses he prepared for his proposed visit to Sarajevo, which was cancelled at short notice. This can be verified by reading these addresses in *L'Osservatore Romano*. The same was also the case during his visit to Sarajevo on 12-13 April, 1997.

A truly pathetic attempt was made to indicate that the Holy Father did indeed accept the authenticity of the apparitions. The Christmas 1994 edition of Scotland's *The Children of Medjugorje* informs us that a group of Medjugorje adepts was present with a Medjugorje banner at one of the Pope's Masses in Croatia, and that "this earned them a big blessing from the Pope, to whom they were quite close."

This is not simply a gratuitous but a ludicrous claim. I was able to watch the Holy Father's principal Mass in Croatia on

The Pope Visits Croatia 93

television, and, when it was over, he turned to bless each portion of the vast congregation as he always does. It was thus inevitable that he would give a blessing in the direction of the Medjugorje banner, but there can be no basis for claiming that it was directed at that banner or that this particular papal blessing was a "big" one. As far as I know, though I am open to correction, papal blessings are not classed in such categories as enormous, very big, big, standard, small, and very small.

The banner argument is typical of the means adopted by proponents of Medjugorje businesses to defend their indefensible claims. An incident is related in a glossy booklet entitled *Medjugorje and the Church* that is clearly intended to establish papal approval for the alleged apparitions. A young lady named Maryjo was present at a papal audience with rosaries that "had been blessed by the *Gospa* during an apparition". A guard whom she asked to give them to the Pope refused, but "at the sound of the word 'Medjugorje' the Pope turned around and a radiant smile lit up his face. 'Medjugorje?' he asked. Then he came back slowly towards Maryjo. Tears filled his eyes as he delicately took the rosaries in his one free hand, and said in English: 'Do everything you can to protect Medjugorje!'"

While moving away the Pope was seen by Maryjo to kiss the *Gospa*'s rosaries and press them against his heart! (P. O. Box 1110, Notre Dame, Indiana 46556, 1995, 30) It is very significant that although the Holy Father did not mention Medjugorje during his Croatian visit he did send a special greeting to Bishop Perić and the "totally discredited" Bishop Žanić.

Mention has already been made of the fact that if the Holy Father really believed in the authenticity of the apparitions, he would surely not have appointed a new bishop who has stated publicly that they are devoid of authenticity. Nor, as has been alleged, was Bishop Žanić removed from the Commission investigating the apparitions. The first investigation into the alleged apparitions was, as is normal in such cases, carried out by a diocesan commission appointed by him. Its verdict was that nothing supernatural was taking place at Medjugorje. In view of the worldwide publicity surrounding Medjugorje a second commission was appointed by the then Yugoslavian bishops' commission. The conclusions of this commission were made public in the name of the bishops' conference on 10 April, 1991. The commission declared with virtual unanimity: "The bishops have followed events at Medjugorje in contact with the local bishop, the local diocesan commission, and the special commission of the conference. On the basis of research it cannot be affirmed that the events are supernatural apparitions or revelations."

Previous editions of this book have been described by devotees of Medjugorje as "stale hearsay". That this statement is not simply "stale hearsay" was confirmed by the then Yugoslav Bishops' Conference on 10 April, 1991. This was revealed by Monsignor Ratko Perić in a very important statement published in the 9 November, 1994 issue of *L'Osservatore Romano* (page 7):

> The official position of the episcopal conference, 10 April, 1991, distinguishes the pastoral work of the Bishop and priests concerned from the content of the alleged "apparitions". The episcopal declaration states: "On the basis of investigations to date, it is impossible to confirm that we are here dealing with apparitions and supernatural revelations". The alleged apparitions create great confusion and division, and not only in the local Church. We are therefore waiting for the Holy See to exert its powers to restore and strengthen the unity of this particular Church.

Further arguments used to refute earlier editions of my book were claims that the Pope had sent large autographed portraits of himself to each of the visionaries and that he had said: "If I could have my own way I would be a parish priest, and that in the church of St. James (Medjugorje)." These statements are completely false, as can be confirmed by writing to the Secretariat of State at the Vatican. Those who have done so with respect to similar fabrications emanating from the Medjugorje industry in recent years have been informed that there was no truth in them. No such allegation emanating from any branch of the Medjugorje industry should be given the least credence unless it can be backed up by a letter from the Vatican, on Vatican stationery, with a protocol number to provide verification.

The 29 July, 1990, issue of *Mary's People*, a *National Catholic Register* supplement on apparitions, quoted the Pope as saying: "Let the people go to Medjugorje if they convert, pray, confess, do penance." An enquiry regarding the same alleged comment had been made to the Vatican in 1988, and the reply received from the then apostolic pro-nuncio, Archbishop Pio Laghi, read: "The statement you cite as a quotation from the Holy Father has never been published or officially verified. Although there have been observations made about Medjugorje attributed to the Holy Father or other officials of the Holy See, none of these have been acknowledged as authentic."

On 28 July, 1998, Cardinal Ratzinger wrote to a correspondent confirming that statements attributed to the Pope and to him in favour of Medjugorje had been "freely invented". I possess a photocopy of this letter.

Joseph Cardinal Ratzinger,
I-00120 Citta Del Vaticano,
22 Juli 1998

Herrn ....
00069 Trevignano Romano (RM)

Dear Mr. —

First of all, I have to apologize for answering your kind letter from 27th May only today. The burden (i.e., work load) of the last few weeks has been so heavy that I had to postpone my private correspondence again and again so that only now, as my vacation is about to begin, I can at last try to answer the more important letters.

I thank you very much for sending me the memorandum by Claus Peter Clausen, whom in fact I know as the author of the *Schwarze Briefe* (Black Letters). I can only say that the statements attributed to the Holy Father and me are freely invented.

With my best wishes for your manyfold activities,
Josef Ratzinger

It is more than probable that the Holy Father was referring to Medjugorje in a speech reported in the 18 September, 1996, edition of *L'Osservatore Romano* when he stated:

> Some members of the People of God are not rooted firmly enough in the faith so that the sects, with their deceptive proselytism, mislead them to separate themselves from true communion in Christ. Within the Church community, the multiplication of supposed "apparitions" or "visions" is sowing confusion and reveals a certain lack of a solid basis to the faith and Christian life among her members.

27

11 OCTOBER, 1994

Synod Intervention by Monsignor Ratko Perić

*Bishop of Mostar-Duvno,
Administrator of Trebinje and Mrkan,
Bosnia-Herzegovina*

1. THE CATHOLIC CHURCH HAS BEEN PRESENT IN Bosnia-Herzegovina for more than a millennium. In 1991, the population of 4,250,000 includes 830,000 Catholics (four dioceses, 272 parishes) with 360 diocesan and about 630 Franciscan priests, members of the two provinces. Many priests do pastoral work abroad. There are four provinces of women's religious congregations, with 690 sisters, many of whom are abroad. The spiritual and pastoral work carried out by religious in this Church has been invaluable, both in the past and today. During the present war, the Church has suffered the cruellest blows: more than 400,000 Catholics have been evicted; 150 parishes have no normal access; more than 200 ecclesiastical buildings have been destroyed or damaged. It is a sad fact that this war seems endless. We express our particular gratitude to the Holy Father for his interventions to promote peace.

2. There are also some intra-ecclesial problems. The ordinary ecclesiastical hierarchy with the resident bishops and diocesan clergy was restored in 1881. Having heard the opinion of the bishops and religious superiors, the Holy See assigned a certain number of parishes *ad liberam collationem Episcopi* which had been administered until that time by the well-deserving Friars Minor. However, when the time came to make over the parishes in question to the diocese of Mostar, the obedience professed was put to a hard trial. The religious community, once rewarded by the Holy See with many

privileges for its apostolate, today has to receive warnings for its rigidity.

3. In addition to this is the phenomenon of Medjugorje, a parish administered by the religious mentioned. The official position of the episcopal conference, 10 April, 1991, distinguishes the pastoral work of the bishop and the priests concerned from the content of the alleged "apparitions". The episcopal declaration states: "On the basis of investigations to date, it is impossible to confirm that we are dealing with apparitions and supernatural revelations." The alleged apparitions create great confusion and division, and not only in the local Church. We are, therefore, waiting for the Holy See to exert its powers to restore and strengthen the unity of this particular Church.

28

17 JUNE, 1995

The Film Gospa

THE MEDJUGORJE FRAUD IS MAKING SO MUCH money for so many people, particularly in the United States, that the propaganda in its favour must almost inevitably swamp any attempt to make the truth known. Thousands or even tens of thousands of well-meaning Catholics will be deluded into accepting the veracity of Medjugorje by a Hollywood movie produced to promote it, called *Gospa*. Martin Sheen portrays Father Zovko, a Franciscan priest, and a young lady named Morgan Fairchild portrays a nun named Sister Fabiana.

One can hardly deny that she looks very charming in the religious habit. Miss Fairchild reveals that she has wanted "to do this kind of stuff for years" because, up to this point, she has always had "to do the sex stuff". The publicity blurb for the film presents as a miracle the fact that the church at Medjugorje has not been destroyed. It claims that three cluster bombs fell on or near the church but failed to explode. There are, however, no authenticated reports of bombs falling anywhere near the church.

Confidence tricksters can succeed only if their victims wish to be deluded, and there are undoubtedly great numbers of Catholics today who wish precisely that. They yearn desperately for some direct link to heaven, and embrace such purported links uncritically. They flock by the thousands to any location where the Medjugorje road show puts on a performance, and become ecstatic when the starring "visionary" is able to produce an apparition of Our Lady as easily as a conjurer produces a rabbit from a hat. I have received an account of a show co-starring Marija Pavlović, who is proved in this book to be a self-confessed liar, and Father Tomislav Vlašić, who seduced a nun and then denied the paternity of his child.

There were many tables at the show marketing Medjugorje products including one selling for one pound (£1) a time, slips of paper with a typewritten message received from Our Lady: "To the people of England. I am in your midst today so that I can be near all of you." Does this mean that Our Lady is not normally in the country that is her dowry?

There was great excitement when the two stars appeared. Miss Pavlović was gazed upon with awe as if a heavenly being herself, and soon people were flocking to her with petitions to take back to Medjugorje accompanied by generous sums of money. Marija gave an angelic smile to each donor. Father Vlašić took up a collection for "war relief in Bosnia" and received £3,000. Marija then gave the exciting news that the Mother of God was standing on the crucifix over the high altar and blessing everyone in a "motherly way." One elderly lady was so excited by this that she gave Miss Pavlović about £150 that she had saved to pay her city tax, asking the young lady to take a petition to Medjugorje for her. (As Our Lady was allegedly present in the church at that very moment it is hard to understand why the petition needed to be taken to Medjugorje to be presented to her.)

29

31 AUGUST, 1995

A Warning Concerning the Film Gospa

(The Wanderer)

THE CHANCERY OF THE DIOCESE OF MOSTAR IN Bosnia-Herzegovina has issued a warning about the movie *Gospa*, which stars Martin Sheen and purports to be about the alleged apparitions at Medjugorje. The announcement, dated 17 June, 1995, states that *Gospa* exploits the name of Mary, using it as "a commercial or to promote propaganda."

The statement also criticizes the movie for its "false presentation" of the previous bishop of Mostar, Monsignor Pavao Žanić, who is accused of being a collaborator with the communists, a charge which has "no basis in reality."

30

23 MARCH, 1996

CDF Letter to Bishop Taverdet

Sacred Congregation for the Doctrine of the Faith, Vatican City, 23 March, 1996, Prot. No. 154/81-01985.

YOUR EXCELLENCY,

In your letter of 14 February, 1996, you inquired what is the present position of the Church regarding the alleged "apparitions" in Medjugorje, and whether it is permitted to the Catholic faithful to go there for pilgrimage. In reference to that, it is my honour to make known to you that, regarding the authenticity of the "apparitions" in question, the bishops of the former Yugoslavia confirmed in their declaration of 10 April, 1991, published in Zadar:

> On the basis of investigation up till now it cannot be established that one is dealing with supernatural apparitions and revelations. However, the numerous gatherings of the faithful from different parts of the world, who are coming to Medjugorje prompted both by motives of belief and certain other motives, require the attention and pastoral care in the first place of the bishop of the diocese and of the other bishops with him so that in Medjugorje and everything related to it a healthy devotion toward the Blessed Virgin Mary would be promoted in conformity with the teaching of the Church. For that purpose, the bishops shall issue separate appropriate liturgical-pastoral directives. Likewise, by means of their Commission they shall further follow and investigate the total event in Medjugorje.

The result from this in what is precisely said is that official pilgrimages to Medjugorje, understood as a place of authentic Marian apparitions, are not permitted to be organized either on the parish or on the diocesan level, because that would be in contradiction to what the bishops of former Yugoslavia affirmed in their aforementioned declaration.

Kindly accept, your Excellency, an expression of my profoundly devoted affection!

✠ *Tarcisio Bertone*

31

16 JUNE, 1996

The Ban on Pilgrimages Reaffirmed

ON 16 JUNE, 1996, THE ANSA NEWS AGENCY reported that the Vatican had reaffirmed its prohibition of pilgrimages to the site of the alleged apparitions at Medjugorje. Bishop Leon Taverdet of Langres in France had asked the Holy See for a ruling on the status of Medjugorje. *The Catholic Times* in England reported in its 30 June, 1996, edition:

> The Vatican position, which also reflects that of local bishops in the former Yugoslav Republic was outlined in a letter by Archbishop Tarcisio Bertone, secretary of the Congregation for the Doctrine of the Faith. Archbishop Bertone cited a 1991 report by the Yugoslavian bishops which said that, after much study, it could not be confirmed that supernatural events were occurring at Medjugorje. From what was said, it followed that official pilgrimages to Medjugorje, understood as a place of authentic Marian apparitions, should not be organized, Archbishop Bertone said. Such pilgrimages would be in contradiction with what the local bishops had determined, he added.

32

4 DECEMBER, 1996

The Circulation of Texts of Alleged Private Revelations

THE 4 DECEMBER, 1996, ISSUE OF THE ENGLISH edition *L'Osservatore Romano* contained a declaration from the Congregation for the Doctrine of the Faith. The first part was a warning to the faithful against the writing and messages of Vassula Rydén. The second part clarified the correct procedure to be followed by those wishing to circulate alleged private revelations. It applies to Vassula Rydén, Medjugorje, and the hundreds of alleged seers throughout the world who claim to be receiving messages from heaven.

Regarding the circulation of texts of alleged private revelations,

> The Congregation states:
>
> 1) The interpretation given by some individuals to a declaration approved by Paul VI on 14 October, 1966, and promulgated on 15 November of that year, in virtue of which writings and messages resulting from alleged private revelations could be freely circulated in the Church is absolutely groundless. This decision actually referred to the "Abolition of the Index of Forbidden Books", and determined that—after the relevant censures were lifted—the moral obligation still remained of not circulating or reading those writings which endanger faith and morals.
>
> 2) It should be recalled, however, that with regard to the circulation of texts of alleged private revelations, canon 823 §1 of the current Code remains in force: "the pastors of the Church have the...right to demand that writings to be published by the Christian

faithful which touch upon faith or morals be submitted to their judgement".

3) Alleged supernatural revelations, and writings concerning them, are submitted in the first instance to the judgement of the diocesan bishop, and, in particular cases, to the judgement of the episcopal conference and the Congregation for the Doctrine of the Faith.

Despite the fact that the law of the Church has been made clear, the "seers" of Medjugorje have declined to submit their alleged revelations to the judgement of their diocesan bishop, Monsignor Ratko Perić. It has been claimed by Medjugorje propagandists that statements made by the bishop represent no more than his personal opinion. On the contrary, in the norms for examining alleged private revelations issued by the Congregation for the Doctrine of the Faith on 27 February, 1978, it is the diocesan bishop who in the first place has the authority to enquire into and pronounce upon such events. It is in precisely this capacity, as diocesan bishop, that Bishop Perić has made his pronouncements. These pronouncements conform exactly to the twenty-eight-point statement made by Bishop Žanić in May, 1990, in his capacity as diocesan bishop explaining why the alleged apparitions at Medjugorje were unworthy of credence, and the 10 April, 1991, declaration of the Yugoslav Episcopal Conference that it is not possible to affirm that any supernatural apparitions or revelations have taken place at Medjugorje.

33

25 JANUARY, 1997

Medjugorje: The State of the Question in 1997

An interview with Monsignor Ratko Perić, Bishop of Mostar, by Yves Chiron was published in the French journal Présent, 25 January, 1997. Monsieur Chiron was particularly anxious to obtain clarification from the bishop concerning the claim by propagandists for Medjugorje that superior authorities in the Church will overturn the verdict non constat de supernaturalitate *(that there is no evidence of any supernatural happenings at Medjugorje), which means that there have been no genuine apparitions. A lengthy extract from the interview conducted by Monsieur Chiron follows with his kind permission.*

Yves Chiron: The last official Church document concerning the events at Medjugorje is the declaration published at Zadar on 10 April, 1991, by the members of the Episcopal Conference of Yugoslavia. This declaration stated in particular: "On the basis of studies conducted so far it cannot be affirmed that supernatural apparitions and revelations are occurring." It is almost six years since this judgement was published; is it still valid?

Bishop Perić: The judgement of the Church is the same and it is still valid. There is no fact, argument, affirmation or miracle which proves that there is a case of "apparitions or supernatural revelations".

Yves Chiron: The same 1991 declaration required that at Medjugorje "a healthy devotion to the Virgin Mary should be promoted in accordance with the teaching of the Church." Certain authors have interpreted this requirement as a recognition of the cult of "Mary, Queen of Peace", the name under which the Holy Virgin is presented at Medjugorje. Can it therefore be said that at Medjugorje there has been a "recognition of the cult" as a preliminary to a recognition of the supernatural basis of the events at Medjugorje, or does this requirement of the conference at Zagreb simply represent a wish that uncontrolled and unrecognized liturgical practices and devotions should not develop at Medjugorje?

Bishop Perić: It can not be claimed in any way whatsoever that there has been a "recognition of the cult" or that the parish church at Medjugorje has been recognized as a Marian sanctuary on a diocesan, national or international level. This requirement of the conference for a "a healthy devotion to the Virgin Mary" represents no more than the wish that at Medjugorje, as in every other Catholic parish in the diocese of Mostar-Duvno, a Marian devotion in accordance with the teaching of the Church should be promoted (*Marialis cultus* [1974], *Redemptoris Mater* [1987], etc.).

Yves Chiron: Certain authors claim that the enquiry into the events at Medjugorje has been withdrawn from the competent authority—your own, in your capacity as bishop of Mostar—and that it has been reserved to the Holy See. Is this correct? Is one of the commissions of enquiry continuing a work of investigation and study?

Bishop Perić: I would be very happy if the Holy See would reserve to itself the enquiry on the events at Medjugorje, forming its own commission and arriving at a definitive judgement. It certainly has the authority to do so. But, right up till today, I have received no such request. In 1993 the Episcopal Conference of Yugoslavia was dissolved, and was replaced by a number of episcopal conferences of Croatia, Slovenia, Bosnia-Herzegovina, etc. The commission of enquiry into the events at Medjugorje of the Episcopal Conference of Bosnia-Herzegovina (which is composed of four bishops) has the authority to form a new commission eventually. I endeavour to visit the parish of Medjugorje on a regular basis. There are many disorders there. There are Franciscan priests there with no canonical mission, religious communities have been established without the permission of the diocesan bishop, ecclesiastical buildings have been erected without ecclesiastical approval, parishes are encouraged to organize official pilgrimages, etc. Medjugorje, considered as a location of presumed apparitions, does not promote peace and unity but creates confusion and division, and not simply in its own diocese. I stated this in October 1994 at the synod of bishops and in the presence of the Holy Father, and I repeat it today with the same responsibility.

Yves Chiron: Can we expect a solemn declaration on the events at Medjugorje, made either by you or by the Congregation for the Doctrine of the Faith?

Bishop Perić: We, the bishops of Bosnia-Herzegovina, are preoccupied with the consequences of the four years' war (1992–1995), and of the reconstruction of the life of the Church, and we do not see the need to form a new commission of enquiry and to make a new declaration concerning Medjugorje. For my part, I have included an article entitled "Criteria for Discerning Apparitions: Regarding the events at Medjugorje" in my most recent book, *Prijestolje Mudrosti* (*Seat of Wisdom*), published at Mostar in 1995, 266–286. I put forward ten points explaining the reasons that one cannot recognize the authenticity of Medjugorje. I am, moreover, very grateful to the Congregation for the Doctrine of the Faith for on two occasions having explained and implemented the affirmation of the episcopal conference of the ex-Yugoslavia. This was done in a letter to Monsignor Daloz, Archbishop of Besançon, on 4 July 1995, and in a letter to Monsignor Taverdet, Bishop of Langres, on 23 March, 1996. After having cited the declaration of the episcopal conference of the ex-Yugoslavia, the Congregation for the Doctrine of the Faith added: "From what has been said, it follows that official pilgrimages to Medjugorje, understood as a place of authentic Marian apparitions, should not be organized either on a parish or diocesan level, because this would be a contradiction of what has been affirmed by the bishops of the ex-Yugoslavia in their previously cited declaration."

34
12–13 APRIL, 1997

Medjugorje in the Light of the Pope's Visit to Sarajevo

The following commentary appeared on page 52 of Medjugorje: A Millennium Update *published in August 1999 by the UK Medjugorje Information Group, 14 Trensdale Avenue, Coventry, CV6 1AT.*

The Pope has come and gone from Sarajevo (12/13 April, 1997), and he did not visit Medjugorje as many had hoped he would due to the Pope's obvious goodwill toward the events in the parish of Medjugorje. We remember that the Croatian president, Dr. Franjo Tuđman, immediately preceding the Pope's coming to Sarajevo, testified before an assembly of politicians and priests that Pope John Paul II in their last conversation said that on the occasion of his visit to Sarajevo he wanted also to visit Medjugorje. The local bishop, Dr. Ratko Perić, was also present for this testimony and did not say a word at that.

What the Pope said behind the scenes to the assembled Church leaders in Sarajevo is not known and most likely will not be known. What is known is his question about who is the provincial of the Franciscan province in which the parish of Medjugorje is located. Also known is his mentioning the name of Medjugorje with a smile on the occasion of his arrival in Sarajevo, at the supper in the Catholic School of Theology and at his departure from Sarajevo. In general, no great stir came from all that.

Spirits were upset only after the usual papal general audience on the Wednesday immediately after the Sarajevo visit. According to reports of the news agencies, the Pope on that occasion said among other things: "In the course of the war pilgrimages of the faithful to the Marian shrine in Bosnia-Herzegovina did not stop as also not in other parts of the world, especially in Loreto, in order to request the Mother of Nations and the Queen of Peace to intervene in that suffering region." These words of the Pope were interpreted by many as his indirect recognition of the Medjugorje events.

THIS REPORT IS TYPICAL OF THE SHALLOW AND deceptive nature of those promoting the Medjugorje "apparitions". The first part concerning President Tuđman is based on a press bulletin issued by Father Miljenko Mića Stojić, parish priest at Medjugorje. There is, of course, no verifiable evidence of "the Pope's obvious goodwill toward the events in the parish of Medjugorje". The testimonies of Cardinal Ratzinger and the apostolic pro-nuncio to the U.S., Archbishop Pio Laghi, have been cited to this effect. As regards the claim by President Tuđman, that as well as visiting Sarajevo the Pope also wished to visit Medjugorje, Monsignor Perić has testified that during the preparations for the Pope's visit to Sarajevo, and in the course of many visits by the apostolic nuncio and delegates from the Holy See, there was never any mention of the Pope wishing to visit Medjugorje during his visit to Sarajevo. Had he wished to make such a visit his representatives would have made this clear and Medjugorje would certainly have been included in his itinerary. As for the statement by President Tuđman, Monsignor Perić writes: "I did not consider that a serious proposition, which is why I made no comment."

The fact that Medjugorje propagandists have to base their claims of papal support on a gratuitous assertion that he mentioned "the name of Medjugorje with a smile" makes clear the paucity of their case, just as does the claim that the Pope gave a "big blessing" in the direction of a Medjugorje banner during his 1994 visit to Croatia. The true significance of his 1994 visit, as explained above, is that he did not so much as mention Medjugorje in any of his addresses.

Grasping desperately at any possible straw which might indicate the Pope's approval of Medjugorje, the UK Medjugorje Information Group claims that a reference by the Pope to the Marian shrine in Bosnia-Herzegovina where Our Lady is venerated as the Queen of Peace was "interpreted by many as his indirect recognition of the Medjugorje events". This allegation is nonsensical. Medjugorje is not recognised by the Church as a shrine. There is, however, an official Marian shrine in Bosnia-Herzegovina, and Monsignor Perić has pointed out that it was to this shrine that the Holy Father was referring—the Marian Shrine "The Queen of Peace" in Hrasno, in the diocese of Trebinje. The Pope sent a telegram to Archbishop Francesco Monterisi, the apostolic nuncio in Bosnia-Herzegovina, which he read during a Mass which the nuncio celebrated on 11 May, 1997. The text was as follows:

> On the occasion of the twentieth anniversary of the Marian Shrine "The Queen of Peace" in Hrasno, the Holy Father, Pope John Paul II, sends greetings and best wishes to your Excellency and all those participating in this solemn celebration, and hopes that the solemn anniversary of this shrine, a true centre of Marian devotion for the whole diocese, will always be a place in which the peace of the Risen Christ shines out in the life of the Catholics of this region. It is the Holy Father's prayer that, with Our Lady's maternal intercession, He (the Risen Christ) will support the Catholics of Croatia in building a future of hope and peace worthy of their rich and proud Christian heritage which goes back some fourteen centuries. The Supreme Pontiff gladly bestows his particular apostolic benediction upon you the secular clergy, the religious, and all the faithful of the diocese of Trebinje.
> Signed:
> Angelo Cardinal Sodano,
> Secretary of State

35

13 APRIL, 1997

The Pope, Medjugorje, and the Provincial of the Herzegovina Franciscans

The following report also appeared on page 53 in Medjugorje— A Millennium Update.

The visit of Pope John Paul II to Bosnia-Herzegovina 12-13 April was a visit which many had hoped would end with a visit of the Pope to Medjugorje, since in several references he had expressed such a desire. Unfortunately, that did not happen. Nevertheless, the Pope did not forget Medjugorje.

At the Sarajevo airport on 12 April, the very first to await the Pope's arrival were the bishops and provincials of Bosnia-Herzegovina. When the provincial of the Sarajevo Province, Father Peter Andjelovic, as the first of the provincials approached the Pope to greet him, the Pope asked him the question, "Medjugorje?" He pointed to Dr. Father Tomislav Pervan, the provincial of Herzegovina, who said, "I am from Mostar and Medjugorje." The Pope nodded his head with satisfaction and twice repeated, "Medjugorje, Medjugorje." All TV viewers who watched the presentation of the Pope's arrival also saw it.

THE ALLEGED REFERENCES BY THE POPE TO MEDjugorje consist of no more than gratuitous assertions. Why, when he did not visit Medjugorje, or express any desire to visit Medjugorje in the preparations for the visit, mention the place immediately upon his arrival?

> While the Pope prayed with those gathered in the Sarajevo cathedral, he prayed twice referring to the Queen of Peace for Bosnia-Herzegovina. Many of those present interpreted it as having recourse to the Queen of Peace from Medjugorje.

It has already been explained that the Pope was referring to the Shrine of Our Lady of Peace in Hrasno.

> After supper in the Sarajevo Catholic School of Theology Father Tomislav took advantage of the occasion to personally present the Pope with the newest photo-monograph on Medjugorje, which the Franciscans who work in the parish of Medjugorje had sent to him. On that occasion he spoke to him briefly about Medjugorje. The Pope did not say anything, but by the expression on his face, he accepted both the former and the latter with satisfaction and interest.

We have yet another gratuitous statement intended to prove papal approval of Medjugorje–approval indicated by the alleged expression on his face!

> On the occasion of the Pope's departure from the Sarajevo airport, Father Tomislav Pervan, by way of greeting, said, "Holy Father, we are expecting you in Medjugorje." The Pope answered with a smile, "Medjugorje, Medjugorje," as was visible also on TV screens.

Yet another use of an alleged smile cannot overcome that fact that not even on one occasion has this Marian Pope John Paul, who is totally devoted to Our Lady (*Totus Tuus* is the motto for his pontificate), uttered a single word concerning Medjugorje in any public address.

36

22 JUNE, 1997

What Kind of "Fruits" are These?

A VERY IMPORTANT STATEMENT ON MEDJUGORJE was published by the Catholic Information Agency in Zagreb on 22 June, 1997, documenting the extent to which the Franciscans in Herzegovina were now beyond the control of the legitimate Church authorities. I was informed in Rome in 1996, at a very high level, that no progress was being made on the matter of Medjugorje because the Franciscans, who control the alleged seers, refuse any cooperation. It is hard to imagine how any Catholic could believe that Our Lady was involved with the litany of disobedience related by Don Ante Laburic, chancellor of the diocese of Mostar, who has summed up the situation perfectly by stating: "Medjugorje has become a place of religious disorder, disobedience, and anti-ecclesial activity." The full text of his statement follows.

> On 14 May, three bishops from Uganda came to visit Medjugorje and from there went to visit Bishop Ratko Perić of Mostar (their former classmate from Rome) in order to inquire about the local Church's position on the so-called events of Medjugorje. The undersigned was also present. The bishop gave his former classmates some documents, which clearly show that from 1981 to 1991, three qualified commissions in the service of the local bishop and the bishops' conference have investigated the events. Ten years ago, in 1987, Bishop Pavao Žanić, formally and officially declared that, in the parish of Medjugorje, the Madonna had not appeared to anyone. In 1991, the bishops' conference did not only declare that the apparitions were not authentic, but also stressed that: "It is impossible to confirm that the events involve supernatural apparitions or revelations at all." From 1981 onward,

"messages of peace" have been sent out to the world from Medjugorje. Yet in our local Church these messages include the following "fruits":

—The administration of the Franciscan province of Herzegovina, which was punished in 1976, has, from 1982, been given the further penalty of being at the level of *ad instar*, due to its unwillingness to implement the decisions of the Holy See regarding pastoral services in some of the parishes of the diocese of Mostar-Duvno.

—Many churches have been built by the Franciscans through the help of the faithful and the benefactors, which they blessed themselves, without even informing the local bishop, which goes against canon law and the charisma of St. Francis. A church in the parish, Ljuti Dolac, was blessed this way on 23 April of this year. In Medjugorje itself, many ecclesiastical buildings have been erected without any permission from the proper Church authorities.

—More than ten Franciscan priests do not have canonical faculties to hear confessions in the diocese of Herzegovina. Some due to their own fault, while others, due to the fault of their religious community which is not fulfilling the papal decree.

—More than forty Franciscans have not received the necessary faculties to work pastorally in Herzegovina, yet they do not even bother with the decisions of the legal Church authorities. Some of them are currently in Medjugorje.

—Many religious communities are living and working in the parish of Medjugorje without the permission of Church authorities, such as: "Beatitudes," "Kraljice mira, potpuno tvoji," "Cenacolo," "Oasi di pace," and "Franjevacke pomocnice svecenika." Hence, Medjugorje has become a place of religious disorder, disobedience and anti-ecclesiastical activity.

—Last year, some "Catholic faithful," with the knowledge of the Franciscans, built a brick wall over the entrance doors of the church in Čapljina and the cathedral's affiliated church in Miljkovici. Two Franciscans who are without canonical faculties for the parish

What Kind of "Fruits" are These?

of Čapljina are currently working in the enclosed church. Everything they are doing is unlawful and the marriages performed there are invalid!

—Some of the Franciscans in Mostar are ignoring the legally established cathedral church and the other four diocesan parishes in Mostar dedicated to the four evangelists, while they continue to organize religious services with the people on their own, against the specific decisions of the Holy See and the head of the Franciscan Order.

—The Provincial *ad instar* has, on many occasions, warned his brothers in writing, that serious measures of the Franciscans' General Administration are being considered for the entire province due to their disobedience.

—In Medjugorje, the periodical *Glas Mira* and "Press Bulletin" are published without the necessary permission from Church authorities. These same periodicals proclaim the "authenticity of the apparitions" and speak of the "shrine"—even though no responsible Church statement has ever claimed "authenticity" or proclaimed any "shrine."

—The counter-Church organization "Mir i dobro" (*Pax et bonum*) was allowed to borrow the shield and motto of the Franciscans, who have not distanced themselves from their group's illegal activities, even when this was asked of them.

—Hence, these are some of the "fruits" of those who are using Medjugorje to "sell shady peace" to the world, and who have hardened themselves in their disobedience towards the Holy See and the Franciscan charisma.

—On May 15, there appeared a dispatch from Medjugorje in *Slobodna Dalmacija*, regarding the Ugandan bishops, whereby the "seer," Ivan Dragicević, transmitted the Madonna's message, who on that occasion said that she was "very pleased that the bishops are in Medjugorje." Ivan had been in the seminary in Visoko during 1981-1982. The commission investigating the "apparitions" questioned him once in Visoko. On 9 May, 1982, he wrote: "A sign shall occur in June." Nothing happened in June!

—Later on, he was expelled from Visoko due to poor grades. He continued on in Dubrovnik from 1982-83. During his two-year stay in the seminary, he said that he was seeing the Madonna and that she told him that he would be a priest. Yet he was expelled from Dubrovnik for poor grades. In 1994, he found the former Miss Massachusetts, Loreen Murphy, whom he married in Boston (*Slobodna Dalmacija*, 9 November, 1994). On the day of the wedding, the groom "had an apparition" in Massachusetts. The Madonna seems to be following him around the world as with some of the other "seers" of Medjugorje. Now he presents the Blessed Virgin Mary as being "very pleased that bishops are in Medjugorje." This type of "message" is not only a clear advertisement for Medjugorje, but a simple invention aimed at making the naive "avert their ears from the truth and turn to extravagant tales" (2 Tim 4:4).

Don Ante Luburic, Chancellor,
Mostar, 16 May, 1997

37

NOVEMBER, 1997

Medjugorje Incredibilities

The article that follows, entitled "MEDJUGORSKE NEVJERODOS-TOJNOSTI" ("MEDJUGORJE INCREDIBILITIES"), was published in Crkva na Kamenu *(The Church on the Rock), the pastoral bulletin of the bishops of Herzegovina, Number 11, November 1997, page 3.*

WE WOULD LIKE TO PRESENT AN EXAMPLE OF how the so-called messages of the "Madonna" are being manipulated in the interests of the material aim of building an hotel in Medjugorje. One can understand easily that new structures must be built in this post-war period, including hotels, but that the approval of the Blessed Virgin is required for the project just does not register in a Christian mind. Our wish has always been to let the light shine in its splendour—*Splendor veritatis*. But if even the noblest aims are based upon falsehoods, they shall sooner or later be exposed and bring shame upon all involved.

The information that we are about to present comes with the permission of those who have responsiblity in the community (from the Netherlands, as mentioned below), and who have provided us with the written material. The persons involved are Father Slavko Barbarić, OFM, Vicka Ivanković, a "seer", a community from the Netherlands, and one of our local families, which we shall designate as NN.

A pastoral centre or hotel? What does it involve? At the beginning of 1995 a community from the Netherlands received a request for financial aid for a project involving the building of a pastoral centre in Medjugorje. A local family of ours, NN, which wanted to build the centre, is associated with the head of the Dutch community. The daughter of this family wrote a three-page letter, dated 16 March, 1995, in which she describes this pastoral centre in Medjugorje. In the letter she mentions that the first time they asked the Madonna (through Vicka), "last year in April, I believe it was the end of April, the answer was: 'It is not yet the right time. When the right time comes I will tell you'." The daughter then continues:

> My father says that he asked [Vicka] once again, and that the answer was roughly the same. The third time, on 2 December, 1994, Vicka came to see my father and said: "Last night, 1 December, I asked the Madonna for you, and this is written on a piece of paper." Vicka said exactly this: "I asked the Madonna last night for you and she said that you can slowly start building. Many greetings, and I am praying for you. Vicka."

After investigations, it was discovered that a hotel with about one hundred beds was being proposed, which would include a chapel and an inn for "pilgrims". The head of the abovementioned Dutch community wanted to borrow a large sum of German marks in order to begin the construction. The reason was that the "Madonna" wanted this hotel built.

In Mary's name. Since it appeared very strange and incredible that the Madonna was involved in hotel projects, the community sent a letter by fax to Father Slavko Barbarić, the spiritual director of the "seers", asking him in German: "Did Vicka, in Mary's name, tell [the NN family]: 'Now you can slowly start building'?" In the meantime, before Father Slavko could respond, the "seer" Vicka, probably suspecting that the community was reluctant to provide the loan, wrote a letter on 19 March, 1995. Here is the exact text of the letter, signed by Vicka in her own hand:

> Esteemed and honourable friend,
> I have already written to you through my friend NN and his family, and I now write to you again since perhaps you did not understand me correctly, and, moreover, I am somewhat surprised that you are seeking someone else's messages over and above the messages of the Madonna, the Mother of God. When

the Madonna, the Mother of God, approves and insists upon the commencement of the building works, then I do not understand why you have doubts and ask for any other messages and approval from ordinary people.

The Madonna, the Mother of God, has given her approval for the building works through me, and so if you believe in Medjugorje and the apparitions of the Madonna, the Mother of God, I do not understand why you have doubts.

I wish you from my heart a happy commencement of the building and mutual collaboration. Many greetings to you, and I am praying for you.

Vicka.

This is how a "seer of the Madonna" claims confidently that the Madonna requires the construction of an hotel with 100 beds.

Not in Mary's name. Father Slavko responded to the previous letter of the community on 28 March, 1995 (we now translate from German), that Vicka did not consult the Mother of God on this question, and that therefore her response could not be considered to be "in Mary's name": "My opinion, which I state clearly, is that it is wrong to question the seers about such matters, because there exists the danger that the opinion of the seers can be placed in the mouth of the Mother of God, which can happen, as has happened, 'in Mary's name'." This means that Father Slavko, not knowing of Vicka's letter, contradicts Vicka's claims, and denies that the Madonna has said anything to her regarding the construction of an hotel.

Why the falsehoods? The Dutch community then responded to Father Slavko the very next day, 29 March, with two questions. How is it that the seer Vicka states one thing to the Dutch community, and another to Father Slavko Barbarić? They ask Father Barbarić to explain these lies or inconsistencies of the "seer" Vicka to them.

One family's wish is represented by Vicka as the Madonna's. Father Slavko responded on 3 April, 1995, and he explains how everything had developed. He had spoken to Vicka and he describes what took place as follows:

My question was: why did she tell me that she did not ask her [the Madonna]; why did she lie to me? I spoke to Vicka in front of her parents, and she was rather afraid to confirm her answer before her father because he was already angry due to the insistence of the NN family. She has now apologized to me in writing, and says that she had not thought that it was all that important. She wrote: "It has happened this time, but it will not happen again." In order that you may understand Vicka's situation better, I should add that regarding the letter you received from Vicka and faxed to me, when I read the letter, I was certain that the text was not Vicka's, so I asked her, and this is how matters stood. She was getting ready to go to Rome and she did not have much time. Mr. NN and his son wrote the text and asked Vicka to sign it. She signed in a hurry, but only the last sentence can be attributed to Vicka. Vicka then began to cry and to apologize repeatedly because she knows what the consequences of this case of "lies" can be, because you yourself have asked if Medjugorje was "authentic".

Hence the "seer" Vicka signs what someone else has brought to her, and, while in a hurry before her journey to Rome, claims this to be a "message" of the Madonna. Would this same "seer" deliver truthful messages to the entire world, so that the world may believe in the lies of Medjugorje?

Two questions which reveal the lies. The community from the Netherlands then wrote to Father Slavko on 28 April, 1995, putting two questions to him. How is it that Vicka, who claims that the Blessed Virgin Mary has been "educating" her for fourteen years, is telling a lie for such an unimportant thing (fear of her father, but not of sin)? Should not the effect of the apparitions be a deeper prayer life (not necessarily mystical), which would restrain Vicka from this type of sin? Secondly, is it normal for the Madonna to respond to such questions? Does this not cast into doubt the authenticity of the apparitions?

Father Slavko disregards the lies and asks for money. Father Slavko answered this letter almost a year later on

14 February, 1996, in English. Note the manner in which he ignores the question of the lies and asks for money for the building of the hotel. He writes:

> Today the family NN, with whom you were in contact, came to the parish office. They were very concerned because you now hesitate to support this project. They told me that they have invested a large amount of money, and are now unable to continue construction because of this most recent action.
>
> When you asked me about Vicka's answer, I did not know that it was the same family whom I have known for a long period of time. They are an honest and trustworthy family. I am sorry that this misunderstanding between myself, Vicka, the family and yourself has taken place.
>
> After discussing the situation with them at length, and seeing all that is happening now with more pilgrims returning to Medjugorje, and with many local people beginning to build once more, I dare myself to ask you if you could possibly re-examine the entire situation and perhaps find the means to assist this family?

We do not know whether the community re-examined the entire situation, whether or not it accepted the Medjugorje manipulations along with the "Madonna's" approval of the project, or if it disregarded the confusion of Father Slavko and Vicka in order to hand over a large sum of deutschmarks simply because Vicka's and Father Slavko's "Madonna" said so.

All that we have written shows that the "apparitions" of Medjugorje are unauthentic, and that what is attributed to the "Madonna" is nothing less than an offence against the holiness of God and the Madonna.

38

11 NOVEMBER, 1997

The "Confirmation" in Čapljina and the "Charisma" of Medjugorje

The article which follows, "Capljinska 'Krizma' I Medugorska 'Karizma'" ("The 'Confirmation' in Čapljina and the 'Charisma' of Medjugorje"), by Monsignor Ratko Perić, Bishop of Mostar-Duvno, was published in Crkva na Kamenu *(The Church on the Rock), the pastoral bulletin of the Bishops of Herzegovina, Number 11, November, 1997, page 2.*

AN ANONYMOUS "BISHOP". THE NEWSPAPER *SLObodna Dalmacija*, 6 October, 1997, page 4, published an article written by three journalists revealing that on Sunday, 5 October, 1997, at the parish of Čapljina in the diocese of Mostar-Duvno, an anonymous so-called bishop, from an anonymous country, anonymous diocese, and of anonymous origin, conducted a "confirmation". It is said that he spoke German, and that a Franciscan who was acting unlawfully (as a parish priest) in Čapljina translated for him into Croatian. The hosts felt it unnecessary to introduce the illicit "minister of confirmation" to the faithful, nor did the illicit guest consider that politeness required him to introduce himself, except for the following: "I come to you from a distant yet beautiful country. My homeland is more than one thousand miles from your lovely country and your beautiful town" (as reported by *Slobodna Dalmacija*).

The holy sacraments are licitly and validly conferred by the competent ministers who are united to the Church according to the precepts of canon law, and who have a correct intention,

The "Confirmation" in Čapljina and the "Charisma" of Medjugorje 125

with the foreknowledge of the participants and the permission of the local bishop. Where there is force and deceit, there is no sacrament.[1] We always invite the candidates for confirmation to be courageous witnesses for Christ, yet here the "minister of confirmation" himself has been hidden behind a veil of anonymity and secrecy!

A hireling. To such shepherds Jesus would say: "Truly, truly, I say to you, he who does not enter the sheepfold by the door but climbs in by another way, that man is a thief and a robber" (Jn 10:1). The anonymous guest in Čapljina did not enter the Church through the main doors, because for fifteen months now a brick wall has been built up in front of them, blocking the entry of the legitimate pastors of the Church. This guest jumped in from the other side, rejecting every Christian tradition, all norms of courtesy, and ignoring the specific law of the Church. They say that he even carried the

---

1 On 30 December, 1997, I faxed Bishop Perić to ask him to clarify precisely what he meant by his statement, "Where there is force and deceit, there is no sacrament." I mentioned that provided that the anonymous bishop had used the correct matter and form with the intention of doing what the Church does the sacrament would certainly have been valid. Bishop Perić replied to me on the same day:

> "Where [there] is force and deceit, there is no sacrament." This derives from a fundamental axiom for the sacraments generally. Anyone who receives any sacrament through force or fraud receives no sacrament, whether it be holy orders or matrimony or confirmation or baptism. In the case of the "confirmations" [in Čapljina] if a bishop did in truth officiate, and there was neither force nor fraud, the sacrament was valid in itself, but illicit. This was not the situation that I had in mind. My belief all along has been that the individual officiating was no bishop at all, but some deceiver (perhaps a priest, perhaps not) dressed up in a bishop's vestments, but with no respect for the sacrament of confirmation or for the Holy Ghost. That the Franciscans will not give his name, and that no man alive knows who it was who administered the "confirmations" is surely less a rare than a unique case in the Church. I have sent certain questions to the Holy See, and am waiting for an answer. In such a situation, before I have the Holy See's answer, were some boy to ask me for permission to enter a seminary or some girl for permission to enter a convent, I would in conscience feel bound to confirm such a one *sub conditione*. As long ago as the summer of last year, the Franciscans publicly said that confirmation administered by a priest, even against the ordinary's express command, was nevertheless valid. I have given the answer to that.

symbols of the bishop's office, a mitre and a crosier, which no authentic bishop of the Catholic Church would ever do in the territory of another diocese without the express permission of the local bishop.

Irresponsible. If the person involved is truly a bishop of the Church, then surely he knows into what kind of illegal activity he has fallen with his illicit "good turn". Church law states that a bishop outside his diocese cannot administer the sacrament of confirmation "without the express or at least reasonably presumed consent of the local ordinary" (Canon 390). In this case the *Slobodna Dalmacija* (3 October, 1997, 15) reported specifically that the local ordinary did not grant permission for confirmation in the parish of Čapljina to any bishop or priest. A confirmation for the candidates of Caplijina was held in June of last year. There was a confirmation this year as well, also in June, and another is scheduled during the school year. The anonymous guest knows this norm of the Church. He even mentions the local bishop and his motives. "Your bishop has his reasons for not doing this, and I do not wish to pass judgement on this." On the other hand, the guest says about himself: "I wish to emphasize that I too have my reasons for being here today in Čapljina." It appears that he also spoke with Rome. "I also tried in Rome to contribute towards finding a happy solution to this situation, but as far as I know, my efforts have remained unsuccessful." The unlawful stranger does not mention with whom he spoke, what he suggested, and why his "efforts" have remained "unsuccessful". How can he then ignore the Holy See and do as he pleases in the areas of jurisdiction and the sacraments in another diocese and a different country?

"Spiritually Unhappy". However, the anonymous guest reveals a secret about himself. He mentions only one place that he has come from: Medjugorje! From his words one understands that he is a regular visitor to Medjugorje: "I came to your homeland for the first time exactly ten years ago. The reason for my visit at that time was the apparition of Our Lady at Medjugorje. Now I must tell you that each time I arrived home after visiting Medjugorje I felt happier and more at peace. But last year I arrived home feeling quite sad and spiritually unhappy. The real reason for my uneasiness and great sadness were these walled-up doors of your church in Čapljina. Even though this sign, written in five languages, speaks sufficiently for itself, I continued asking friends for more news on the situation" (*Slobodna Dalmacija*, 6 October, 1997).[2]

After this type of testimony and the actions of the "minister of confirmation", the Medjugorje fanatics should not be admonishing the local bishop of the importance of separating the problem of Medjugorje from the problem of Čapljina, the case of Medjugorje from the case of Herzegovina. This anonymous, irresponsible hireling, this "unhappy spirit", wishes to solve the case of Čapljina by coming from Medjugorje. He is coming to the aid of Franciscans who are unlawfully residing in Čapljina, who are disobeying the decrees of the Holy See, the decisions of the Franciscan Order, and the norms of the local Church, as mentioned in the declaration of the *ad instar* provincial, Father Tomislav Pervan, distancing himself from them. Now it is said that the anonymous "Monsignor" from Čapljina is also mentioned in the Canon of the Mass, is inspired by the spirit of Medjugorje first of all with "peace and happiness", and then with "sadness and great unhappiness", upon seeing that things are not going the way that he and those who invited him would like them to go, is now working against unity, peace, and order, against the laws and canons of God's Church. He is also abusing the sacrament of the Holy Spirit. Medjugorje transmitted the first "messages" fifteen years earlier, when in January, 1982, the so-called "Madonna", through one of the "seers", became involved in a question of the jurisdiction of the local Church by defending some disobedient Franciscan chaplains and rebuking the local

---

2 "The wall will be pulled down when those who built the church (the Franciscans) return." The Franciscans have evidently returned as they now occupy the church, and so what they mean presumably is that their *fait accompli* should be recognized and the church which should be administered by diocesan priests must be officially surrendered to them.

bishop Pavao Žanić for making a "rash decision". (The "seer" used a much coarser expression in her description!) And now Medjugorje has "spiritually inspired" an unlawful "minister of confirmation" who goes to Čapljina to destroy Church unity and to deceive hundreds of candidates for confirmation.

Canonical and non-canonical. On Sunday, 5 October, 1997, we were at Our Lady's National Shrine at Marija Bistrica. We took part in the ceremony for the appointment of a new military ordinary for the Republic of Croatia. Before this event nearly all the bishops participated in the solemn diocesan and episcopal celebrations in Pozega, Varazdin, and Zagreb Cathedral. Everyone was delighted to witness these events, conducted as they should be, with the papal decree being read aloud, the crosier handed over, and the Mass beginning with the new bishop presiding. Yet what would have happened if a certain priest, religious, or mayor of the city had jumped out of the crowd and grabbed the crosier from Archbishop Bozanic or Bishop Skvorcevic and said: "This is mine! This is my diocese!" Everyone would have remained breathless. The police would probably have had to intervene and the sick person would have been sent to a hospital. In Čapljina, the sick person had a mitre on his head during Mass — even during the Canon, if we are to believe the witnesses.

St. Paul once said to those whom he ordained: "I know that after my departure fierce wolves will come in among you, not sparing the flock; and from among your own selves will arise men speaking perverse things, to draw away the disciples after them. Therefore, be alert..." (Acts 20:29-31). "Wolves" from the outside and "heretics" from the inside. Hence it is impossible not to react to such abuse, scandal and lawlessness! I feel truly sorry for the Catholic faithful of Čapljina, especially those who are refugees, and the candidates for confirmation whose parents have constantly inquired: "Will there be a confirmation? Will it be licit and valid?" We instructed the Christian consciences to follow the norms of the Church. A few listened and these deserve credit. We have no other choice than to wait until the Peter of our days, by his supreme authority, restores order among the disorderly, and to pray that the Holy Spirit enlightens the paths and hearts of all.

Mostar, 7 October, 1997.
✠ *Ratko Perić*
Bishop of Mostar-Duvno

The identity of the anonymous "bishop" from "a distant yet beautiful country" who performed the illicit and invalid confirmations at Caplinja was eventually discovered and the entire squalid story is documented by Monsignor Luka Pavlović, vicar general of the diocese of Mostar-Duvno, under the date 28 May, 2001. The self-styled bishop was Srecko Franjo Novak, an apostate Croatian seminarian who joined the Old Catholic Church, was ordained to the diaconate, but not to the priesthood or episcopate. He claimed to have received Old Catholic ordination to both these orders but his Old Catholic superiors considered him unsuitable for these orders and refused to confer them. Monsignor Pavlović explains:

> Such are the facts of the matter regarding Novak as a pseudo-professor, deceptive doctor of theology, phoney-priest, bogus-bishop and spurious "successor of the apostles"—all this documented with his signature. From his signatures and the documents which others have received from him, we are convinced that we are dealing with not only a dismissed Catholic seminarian, an expelled Old Catholic deacon, but also with a scientific and ecclesiastical falsifier, whom the above-mentioned dismissed, and disobedient Franciscans of the province of Herzegovina have promoted to be their "bishop"! These sad events probably best describe how deep the disease of disobedience can go in the Church and concretely in the entire "Herzegovinian affair"!

39

26 DECEMBER, 1997

The Grievous Fate of the Truth

Under the title "Bolna Sudbina Istine" ("The Grievous Fate of the Truth"), a letter from Father Bože Radoš, OFM, appeared in the journal Horizont *on 26 December, 1997. It concerns the question of the confirmations at Čapljina, but in his abusive comments concerning Bishop Perić and the papal nuncios it is evident that the real issue is the decree* Romanis Pontificibus *of 6 June, 1975, in which Pope Paul VI instructs the Franciscans to hand over half their parishes to the diocese. The abusive language used by Father Radoš requires no comment. The Franciscans in Herzegovina have consistently used the alleged apparitions at Medjugorje as a weapon in their conflict with the diocese and as a lucrative source of income for their schismatic activities. They are at present building a cathedral-sized church in Mostar without the authorization of Bishop Perić.*

WHEN NUNCIO FRANCESCO MONTERISI AND NUNcio Giulio Einaudi, Cardinal Vinko Puljic and Bishop Ratko Perić speak of the truth, the truth bleeds, for with their lies they are ever preparing a new Calvary for the truth. By dint of substituting lies for the truth again and again, they have succeeded in convincing themselves that their lies are the truth. Put bluntly, they have fallen into the trap of their own lie. In the words of the psalmist: "The snare that they set in secret has caught them by the legs."

The facts, the very embodiment of the truth, demonstrate the following points. Nuncio Monterisi and Nuncio Einaudi bore witness to Christ's love to the Catholics of Croatia and of Bosnia and Herzegovina, a people to whom they were sent to be the Pope's representatives, by asking the Croatian Minister of Defence, Gojko Susak, to deploy the army against the faithful of the parish of Čapljina, regardless how many might be wounded or even killed. Whether the gentleman in question [i.e. Gojko Susak] would send troops against his countrymen, I know not, but this much I know for certain, that such a thing has nothing whatsoever to do with Christ's love.

Nuncio Monterisi may remember me from our meeting in Posusje. I told him on that occasion what it was that troubled my conscience, namely the lie in the first sentence of the decree *Romanis Pontificibus,* on account of which my brethren uttered their *non possumus* to that very decree in 1975. They fortified their *non possumus* by setting their signatures to it. It is not therefore a case of "the most recent turn that the open and lasting disobedience of the Franciscan province of Herzegovina with regard to the Holy See's decree *Romanis Pontificibus* of 6 June, 1975 has taken" (*Glas Koncila,* no. 49, page 2, 7 December, 1997), as he would have it, but rather a case of heroic resistance to the evil incarnate in the decree as a lie. The nuncio, thinking himself very high and mighty because of his title, clearly cares not a jot for men's consciences, which he mercilessly tramples underfoot, having replaced the Father of truth with the father of lies.

Bishop Ratko will remember, to the extent that this fact has not fallen victim to his distortions of the truth, that in conversation with him I expressed the view that the question of the parishes concerned me not at all, that I would leave that matter to him and to my provincial, and that I was troubled only by the unjustified attack on my priesthood. I have documentary proof that this is so. At the time I called upon God, asking Him to bear witness between us. Doubtless God will have the last word.

What they have said about the confirmations in Čapljina, they have said. The fact is that they were asked to be the ones through whom the Holy Ghost would come to Čapljina. Why did they not come? The answer must be either that what they wrote and what they think are two different things, or that they made no effort to prevent something that they saw as being wrong. Taking all things into consideration, it seems to me that they are seeking to deceive the people, while pretending to tell the truth.

Only a man who has puffed himself up with pride can maintain that the sacraments which Jesus confers through my hands are not valid. If they really believe and think so, why, they might spit upon the hosts consecrated at a Mass which I have celebrated without the least qualm. Well?

In Posusje, in Tomislavgrad and now in Čapljina, my only concern has been my pastoral work.

Be that as it may, it should be said for the sake of the truth that some in the ranks of the clergy are better at business, others at diplomatic manoeuvres, and yet others at, well, if the need arises, I shall give concrete proofs of what the third class are good at... than at being what they ostensibly are [i.e., priests].

That may all be considered usual and appropriate for those who have not distanced themselves sufficiently from this world, but let not such men then stand in the way of those who have the kingdom of heaven before their eyes, and who understand only the love of God.

Father Bože Radoš
Franciscan residing at Čapljina.

40

19 MARCH, 1998

Father Laurentin Visits Bishop Perić

The following communiqué was published by the Catholic Information Agency–Mostar (KIUM), March, 1998, pages 14–15. All the footnotes were compiled by Monsieur Christian Bhavsar.

ON 19 MARCH, 1998, BISHOP RATKO PERIĆ, WITH his secretary, received Father René Laurentin, who had asked for the audience, in the chancery in Mostar. Father Laurentin is a well-known French Mariologist, yet in our country he is better known as a propagator of the Medjugorje "apparitions", "miracles", and other phenomena. Laurentin has written numerous books and brochures on the topic (something every year), in which he propagates the authenticity of the "apparitions" and "messages" of Medjugorje to such an extent that, as he himself admits, he has lost much of the academic prestige that he once enjoyed as a serious Mariologist. The bishop mentioned to Laurentin that he used to avail himself of his books on Mariology while he taught the subject at the Theological School of Sarajevo, yet now he has some serious criticisms concerning Laurentin's writings on the Medjugorje "apparitions".

In a frank and open exchange of opinions, the bishop drew Laurentin's attention to many of his imprecise and incorrect conclusions concerning the events at Medjugorje. Here we present only a few of the subjects touched upon during the meeting.

In defending the "seer" Ivan, after his expulsion from both the high school and the Franciscan minor seminary in Dubrovnik as a result of academic failure (1983), Laurentin wrote in *Glas Koncila*, 7 May, 1984, that Ivan had experienced a "shock" due to the severe admonitions of the bishop and by hostile questions and mockery from his colleagues. When the superiors and the bishop of Dubrovnik reacted by affirming that none of this was true, Laurentin, instead of publicly apologizing, resorted to the unusual justification that his French text had not been translated well, that he was not referring to the bishop of Dubrovnik, but to the bishop of Mostar, and he even sent Bishop Pernek, the late bishop of Dubrovnik, an "original" text that was different from the one sent to *Glas Koncila*.[1] This was a morally inadmissible action.

It is also morally inadmissible that in one of his books of 1985, Laurentin wrote that one of the members of the diocesan commission for Medjugorje, Monsignor Nikola Bulat, STL, a priest of the Archdiocese of Split, now deceased, "is one of those who is fighting for the early resignation of Archbishop Franic so that Bishop Žanić could replace him". In 1986 Father Bulat stated that this is "objectively libellous", "because I never sought this nor do I know anyone else who sought it. Twice I asked Laurentin to correct this, yet to my knowledge he still has not done so."[2] Laurentin now says that he heard this from someone. Bishop Perić told him that truth should be founded not on hearsay but on authentic sources.

Laurentin appears naive in believing and writing in December, 1984, that the "seer" Vicka, who had been asked earlier about the existence of a personal diary, told him: "There is no secret diary with anything written against the bishop."[3] Bishop Perić then showed Laurentin Vicka's "diary," which contains many passages hostile to Bishop Žanić; for example: "The Madonna answered that Bishop Žanić is the one most to blame for this entire disorder."[4] A particularly superficial

---

[1] Documents filed in the diocesan curia of Mostar.
[2] N. Bulat, *Neopouzdanost izvora o dogadjajima u Medugorju*. A document typed in 1985, 24. Document filed in the diocesan curia of Mostar.
[3] Laurentin, op. cit., 40.
[4] Vicka Ivanković, Diary entry for 19 December 1981 to 29 September 1982: "Gospa je rekla, da je ove nerede najkrivlji biskup Zanic" (19 December, 1981). See Appendix III.

passage appears in one of Laurentin's books of 1985, where one reads that a pilgrim to Medjugorje sent a message to him saying that the Madonna was very pleased with his writing on Medjugorje. The "Madonna" of Medjugorje stated precisely the following: "Let priests read Laurentin's book and propagate it."[5] These are no longer "messages" of the Madonna, but an abuse of her name for a commercial purpose, which certainly does a disservice to the Blessed Virgin Mary. Despite all his polite distancing, Father Laurentin reveals his superficiality by mentioning this episode in his book. It is particularly sad and comical to see how Father Laurentin is involving himself in the disobedience to the Pope of some local Franciscans, and yet how ignorant he is of their disobedience to the papal decree of 1975 that ordered the Franciscans to hand over eight parishes to the bishop of the diocese. In his fervour for Medjugorje, and his naivety towards the Franciscans, he wrote in 1985: "From Medjugorje, the Franciscans have gone as far as to write to their general and to Cardinal Ratzinger in order to ask how to proceed. I believe this to be a true miracle of Medjugorje." If, according to Laurentin, the "miracles" of Medjugorje amount to no more than this, then nobody is revealing the reality of Medjugorje more clearly than he is.

Laurentin is aware of the fact that last year the Franciscan general curia in Rome forbade the Franciscan province of Herzegovina to accept more novices due to its unbelievable disobedience. And this comes twelve years after he proclaimed the fact that they had written to Rome to be "a true miracle of Medjugorje".

Laurentin wrote, incorrectly, in 1997, that Bishop Perić told Father Jozo Zovko that he was "excommunicated". Father Jozo Zovko had, in fact, been deprived of his canonical faculties to hear confessions, but despite his suspension he continued to hear confessions and thus involved himself in an *ipso facto* suspension.

---

5   R. Laurentin, *Dernières Nouvelles de Medjugorje* (March, 1985). Complément no. 3, OEIL, 27.

Laurentin also wrote incorrectly in 1997 that the Holy Father in returning from Sarajevo in that year, authorized "a part of his retinue" to visit Medjugorje.[6] Curious journalists and ambassadors do not form part of the Pope's retinue. Nor did the Pope authorize such a pilgrimage.

During the two-hour discussion, which, in a careful and documented manner, had the objective of bringing to light a number of falsehoods concerning Medjugorje, the bishop asked the 81-year-old Laurentin to begin writing his retractions on Medjugorje so that the real truth on this controversial issue could be brought to light. By ceasing to write on the "phenomenon" of Medjugorje in his current fashion he would render the Church a great service. Father Laurentin, the controversial supporter of the "apparitions" of Medjugorje and the accompanying events, said that a new book would be published in June this year, and that he would try to take note of the corrections. Next year he will consider putting an end to his writings on Medjugorje.

At the conclusion of the meeting Bishop Perić and Father Laurentin exchanged some of their books.

KIUM
Mostar, 20 March, 1998,
Rev. Zeljko Majic

---

[6] R. Laurentin, "Tempête sur Medjugorje" in *Chrétiens Magazine*, no. 103, 34. "The Pope did not insist, but during his visit to Sarajevo, he authorized a part of his entourage to leave him during the journey in order to make a public pilgrimage to Medjugorje: eleven personalities including bishops, and ambassadors, together with Vatican journalists."

41

22 MARCH, 1998

Father Laurentin Writes to Bishop Perić

YOUR EXCELLENCY,

I thank you for having received me. I was happy to meet you and to be better informed of your point of view.

I had considered this request for a meeting to be private and not to be the object of a public bulletin published by a press agency.

It is a matter for regret that this communiqué was published. Besides which our conversation was in Italian (a language in which I am not fluent as you are in French), and the translation into other languages (Croatian and English) presented many problems. I do not recognize what I said in many of the nuances of your text. It would be regrettable to initiate a polemic when I am trying to proceed towards the silence which you hope for in the coming year.

Please accept, your Excellency, the expression of my religious respect and of my best wishes for you and for your diocese where so many races and conversions flourish.

René Laurentin,
La solitude, Grand Bourg,
Rue du Général San Martin,
B. P. 808,
91001 EVRY CEDEX,
France.

42

23 MARCH, 1998

The Franciscan Rebellion in Herzegovina: Rome Acts

Congregation for the Religious
Prot. No. 32343/97.

HOLY FATHER, THE PROCURATOR GENERAL OF THE OFM beseeches your Holiness to confirm the decree for the dismissal from the aforesaid order of Fra. Petar Barbarić, pronounced on 2 March, 1993, by the general minister for the reasons mentioned previously.

The Congregation for the Religious,[1] having carefully considered the matters set out above,[2] confirms the aforesaid decree for the dismissal from the aforesaid order of Fra. Boniface Petar Barbarić as requested, in conformity with the provisions of canons 696/700 of the Code of Canon Law on the grounds of his unauthorized absence [that is to say, from the house of his order], all the consequences prescribed by canons 701 and 702 of the Code of Canon Law moreover ensuing.

Contrariis quibuslibet non obstantibus, ili.
Vatican City, 23 March, 1998

O. D. Di Odoardo CP,   Jesus Torres CMF,
Principal of the Section   Undersecretary

Copy conformed to the original, Father Antonio Riccio.

---

1 *Congregatio pro Institutis Vitae Consecratae et Societatibus Vitae Apostolicae.*
2 Documentation previously supplied to the Pope.

Congregation for Religious
Prot. No. 32344/97

Holy Father, the procurator general of the OFM beseeches your Holiness to confirm the decree for the dismissal from the aforesaid order of Fra Bože Radoš pronounced on 2 March, 1993, by the general minister for the reasons mentioned previously.

The Congregation for Religious, having carefully considered the matters set out below, confirms the aforesaid decree for the dismissal from the aforesaid order of Fra Bože Radoš as requested, in conformity with the provisions of canons 696/700 of the Code of Canon Law on the grounds of his unauthorized absence, all the consequences prescribed by canons 701 and 702 of the Code of Canon Law moreover ensuing.

Contrariis quibuslibet non obstantibus, ili.
Vatican City, 23 March, 1998.

O. D. Di Odoardo CP,	Jesus Torres CMF,
Principal of the Section	Undersecretary

Copy conformed to the original, Father Antonio Riccio.

43

24 MARCH, 1998

A Letter from Monsignor Ratko Perić to the Abbé René Laurentin, Protocol Number 265/98

ABBÉ RENÉ LAURENTIN,

I acknowledge receipt of your letter of 22 March and respond to it as follows:

1) One cannot speak privately on the "apparitions" of Medjugorje when they have become well known throughout the world these last fifteen years through your hundreds of thousands of copies of publications in various languages. It is therefore only right and just to publish, as we have done, the communiqué of our conversation in Mostar on 19 March, 1998, whilst dutifully notifying you beforehand.

2) Nothing was done except that which you already placed in your writings, as we demonstrated to you previously. Hence, you should be able to recognise yourself in your text. This chancery takes its responsibility for the Croatian and English texts. We now forward the communiqué with the exact references. We have not yet utilised your phrase which was written to the esteemed Benedictine Prior P. Touw, last August, that the Holy Father regrets my "action" regarding Medjugorje, which you denied writing when I asked you personally. Meanwhile your handwriting reveals the contrary. I would appreciate a response from you on this matter.

3) With your controversial books on the Medjugorje "apparitions" you have sown, not only in this country but also in the Catholic world, plenty of discord, ambiguity and explicit

untruths which will have to be eradicated with time. You are both competent and morally obliged to do this. We want to be at the service of the truth which can liberate us from many inauthenticities regarding Medjugorje, of which you have become a known herald.

4) With your stories on the "apparitions" of Medjugorje, which are truly regrettable, you have helped me come to the conviction and to the *constat de non supernaturalitate* of the so-called "apparitions" of Medjugorje. What motives you may have in the entire affair are for you to resolve before God.

5) From now on I cannot remain silent regarding any of your works containing the nonsenses of Medjugorje, which is destroying Catholic unity, ecclesial peace and the pastoral care of this local Church.

6) Besides making these deplorable things public, I also regularly inform the competent Dicasteries of the Holy See, which as *columna et firmamentum veritatis*, must be informed on the matters.

7) It would truly be regrettable if you were to wait till next year to cease writing on Medjugorje. On the other hand, it would be an honour to the Madonna if you were to stop immediately, except for writing the necessary *retractationes* if you wish to appear as a friend of the truth.

With regards,
✠ *Ratko Perić*, m.p.

44

26 MAY, 1998

Beautiful Gift or Pathetic Delusion?

On 26 May, 1998, a letter concerning Medjugorje was sent by the Congregation for the Doctrine of the Faith to the bishop of a French diocese in the Indian Ocean. The letter was flashed around the world on the Medjugorje Internet and is being represented as a change of attitude on the part of the congregation to the spurious "apparitions" in Herzegovina. The letter has been described in euphoric terms by spokesmen for the Medjugorje industry as a beautiful present to the Virgin from the Church on the 17th anniversary of her apparitions. The letter is, in fact, a clear reiteration of the totally negative attitude of the congregation to the Herzegovinian fraud.

THE BACKGROUND TO THE LETTER IS AS FOLLOWS: in September, 1997, Monsieur Thierry Boutet, secretary general of the association *Famille Chrétienne,* wrote to Monsignor Ratko Perić, Bishop of Mostar, asking him to explain, for the readers of his journal *Edifa*, his position apropos the alleged "apparitions" The full text of the bishop's reply, dated 2 October, 1997, reads as follows:

> Dear Monsieur Boutet,
> I am replying to your letter of 29 September received by fax at the nunciature in Sarajevo.
> As regards the curia of this diocese concerning the alleged apparitions or revelations at Medjugorje, in particular the formula *Non constat de supernaturalitate* or *Constat de non supernaturalitate,* this is what I can say:
> 1) The second diocesan commission, which worked from 1984 to 1986, voted explicitly on 2 May 1986 by an overwhelming majority for the *Non constat de supernaturalitate* (11 negative votes, 2 positive, 1 *in nucleo*, 1 abstention).

2) The declaration of the episcopal conference of 1991 stated: "On the basis of studies conducted so far it cannot be affirmed that supernatural apparitions and revelations are occurring."

3) The Congregation for the Doctrine of the Faith, citing in full the declaration of the bishops of the ex-Yugoslavia, in two identical letters sent to two French bishops, Monsignor Daloz, Archbishop of Besançon (4 July 1995) and Monsignor Tardivet, Bishop of Langres (23 March, 1996), stated: "From what has been said, it follows that official pilgrimages to Medjugorje, representing it as a place of authentic Marian apparitions, must not be organized either on a parish or diocesan level, because this would be a contradiction of what has been affirmed by the bishops of the ex-Yugoslavia in their previously cited declaration."

4) On the basis of a serious study by thirty of our researchers (including three commissions), of my experience as the bishop after five years in the diocese, of the scandalous disobedience which surrounds the phenomenon, of the lies that have been placed on occasions in the mouth of the "Blessed Virgin", of the uncharacteristic repetition of messages for 16 years, of the strange manner in which the "spiritual directors" of the self-styled "seers" accompany them throughout the world to disseminate their propaganda, on the principle that the "Blessed Virgin" appears at the *fiat* ("Let her appear") of the "seers":

My conviction and my position is not only *Non constat de supernaturalitate*, but also *Constat de non supernaturalitate* as regards the apparitions or revelations of Medjugorje.

5) Nevertheless, I am open to any study which the Holy See might undertake, with its supreme authority over the Catholic Church, to render a supreme and definitive judgement on this case, and that as quickly as possible for the good of souls, for the honour of the Church and that of the Blessed Virgin.

Monsignor Ratko Perić
Bishop of Mostar

Proprietors of the multi-million-dollar Medjugorje industry were outraged at the publication of Bishop Perić's letter, which could have affected their lucrative cash receipts. What particularly angered them was that Bishop Perić had not been content simply to reaffirm the 1991 Zadar statement by stating *Non constat de supernaturalitate* ("It cannot be affirmed that supernatural apparitions and revelations are occurring"), but that he expressed his personal conviction of *Constat de non supernaturalitate* ("It is confirmed that there is nothing supernatural"). The bishop makes it quite clear that this judgement is simply the expression of his personal opinion, and not the final definitive, official judgement. He mentions the possibility of the Holy See making its own study of the question, but at present it is not doing so, and has given no indication that it intends to do so. An interview with Bishop Perić by Yves Chiron, published in the French journal *Présent*, on 25 January, 1997, made clear that the episcopal conference of Bosnia-Herzegovina (which is composed of four bishops) had the authority to form a new commission of enquiry into the events at Medjugorje, but the four bishops were preoccupied with the consequences of the four years' war (1992-1995) and with the reconstruction of the life of the Church, and do not see the need to form a new commission of enquiry and to make a new declaration concerning Medjugorje. There is, therefore, no enquiry being made into the events at Medjugorje at present, and so the current official verdict remains: *Non constat de supernaturalitate*. There can not be the least doubt that the personal conviction of Bishop Perić, *Constat de non supernaturalitate,* will be endorsed by the other three bishops of Bosnia-Herzegovina should they eventually decide to establish a new commission of enquiry.

In a damage-control exercise circulated to the multi-national outlets of the Medjugorje industry it was stated that *Edifa* was not *l'Osservatore Romano* (no one had claimed that it was), that Cardinal Ratzinger had not ratified the *Constat de non supernaturalitate* of Bishop Perić (no one had claimed that he had), and that with his Polish background Pope John Paul II would be able to recognize that the tactics used by the bishop were those of the former Eastern bloc. This, it was explained, was said without any bitterness! The "Eastern bloc tactic" employed by Bishop Perić in his letter was simply to state a series of facts, which are indisputable, and to express his personal opinion. The damage-control response was written by one Father Daniel-Ange. As this priest is an uncritical disciple of Medjugorje he is, as a matter of course, described by proponents of the "apparitions" as an advocate of "the Light", and his response is "courageous".

The courageous response of this advocate of light contained, *inter alia*, the following points:

1) *The position expressed by Bishop Perić was not the official and definitive judgement of the Church.*

No one had claimed that it was.

2) Edifa *had no right to intervene in the question of Medjugorje or to carry out its own enquiry as the matter was very complex.*

Why should a Catholic journal not carry an article on Medjugorje? Dozens of Catholic journals have published favourable reports, to which Father Daniel-Ange has made no objection. What he is stating, therefore, is that Catholic journals are entitled to publish reports on Medjugorje only if they concur with his own opinion. Shades of the Eastern bloc!

3) *The* Edifa *enquiry was neither impartial, objective, or honest.*

This means that it contained facts that the Medjugorje industry did not want known.

As regards impartiality, the dossier included an interview with Father Daniel-Ange three times longer than the letter of Bishop Perić.

4) *The dossier did not include the declarations in favour of Medjugorje made (it is claimed) by numerous bishops.*

The only bishops with official authority to pronounce on the matter are the two bishops ruling the diocese during the course of the "apparitions", bishops Žanić and Perić, and members of the official episcopal commissions that had been established to examine the phenomenon. As no commission of enquiry into Medjugorje is established at present, Bishop Perić is the only bishop with the authority to make official pronouncements. But Father Daniel-Ange claims that pro-Medjugorje bishops from other countries have moral authority, and that this moral authority is recognized. Recognized by Father Daniel-Ange, presumably?

5) *Only negative aspects concerning Medjugorje are included in the dossier.*

This is a somewhat strange claim, as Father Daniel-Ange himself was given three pages to explain what he considered to be the positive aspects of the phenomenon, and testimonies from other Medjugorje disciples were included on pages 89–90, including one from the fanatically pro-Medjugorje bishop of Saint-Denis-de-la-Réunion, Gilbert Aubry. In reading the testimony of Bishop Aubry, bear in mind the claim of Father Daniel-Ange that no pro-Medjugorje bishop was permitted to exercise his "moral authority" and contribute to the *Edifa* dossier. Bishop Aubry comments:

> In the midst of winter, I went secretly to Medjugorje bearing the weight of my 20 years as a bishop. Pardon and thanks. While climbing Mount Krizevac I was sometimes on my knees with tears in my eyes. And in my breast was there not beating a sweet and humble heart that was not my own. Well then? My God! It is no longer I who live.... At the age of 53, I left with the strength of a new heart and a new spirit for the mission that inflames me and carries me to the faith. Joy and hope. Justice and peace. Together with Mary I give my testimony this day.

A BEAUTIFUL PRESENT?

In June, 1998 a euphoric Father Daniel-Ange announced to the world through the Medjugorje Internet that "the Church has offered a beautiful present to the Virgin" on the 17th anniversary of her apparitions. This "beautiful present" was a response from the Congregation for the Doctrine of the Faith to a bishop who had asked for clarification concerning Bishop Perić's affirmation of *Constat de non supernaturalitate*. The bishop in question was, surprise, surprise, Bishop Gilbert Aubry of Saint-Denis-de-la-Réunion! The full text of the Congregation's reply is as follows:

Congregation
Pro Doctrina Fidei.

Citta del Vaticano
Palazzo del S. Uffizio.
26 May, 1998

Pr. No 154/81-05922,

To His Excellency, Monsignor Gilbert Aubry,
Bishop of Saint-Denis-de-la-Réunion,

YOUR EXCELLENCY,

In your letter of 1 January, 1998, you submitted to this dicastery several questions about the position of the Holy See and of the bishop of Mostar in regard to the so-called apparitions of Medjugorje, private pilgrimages, and the pastoral care of the faithful who go there.

In regard to this matter, I think that it is impossible to reply to each question posed by Your Excellency. The main thing that I would like to point out is that the Holy See does not ordinarily take a position of its own regarding allegedly supernatural phenomena as a court of the first instance. As for the credibility of the "apparitions" in question, this dicastery holds to what was decided by the bishops of the former Yugoslavia in the Declaration of Zadar, 10 April, 1991: "On the basis of the investigations so far, it can not be affirmed that one is dealing with supernatural apparitions and revelations." Since the division of Yugoslavia into different independent nations it would now pertain to the members of the Episcopal Conference of Bosnia-Herzegovina to eventually reopen the examination of this case, and to make any new pronouncements that might be called for.

What Bishop Perić said in his letter to the Secretary General of *Famille Chrétienne*, declaring: "My conviction and my position is not only *Non constat de supernaturalitate*, but likewise *Constat de non supernaturalitate* of the 'apparitions' or revelations in Medjugorje", should be considered the expression of the personal conviction of the bishop of Mostar which he has the right to express as ordinary of the place, but which is and remains his personal opinion.

Finally, as regards pilgrimages to Medjugorje, which are conducted privately, this congregation points out that they are permitted on condition that they are not regarded as an authentification of events still taking place and which still call for an examination by the Church.

I hope that I have replied satisfactorily at least to the principal questions that you have presented to this dicastery, and I beg your Excellency to accept the expression of my devoted sentiments.

Archbishop Tarcisio Bertone
Secretary

PATHETIC DELUSION

Father Daniel-Ange provided a euphoric commentary on Archbishop Bertone's letter, proclaiming in large, bold letters:

WE CANNOT THANK GOD ENOUGH FOR THIS CLARIFICATION WHICH HAS BEEN WAITED FOR FOR SO LONG

Why unstinted thanks on behalf of the Medjugorje industry should be prompted by a letter that states nothing that was not already known is something that Father Daniel-Ange would find hard to explain, but he is fortunate in knowing that explanations are never required by the uncritical adepts of Medjugorje, provided that the statement in question coincides with their fantasies. Among the points made by Daniel-Ange are the following:

1) *The declarations of the bishop of Mostar reflect only his personal opinion. Consequently, they are not a definitive judgement of the Church. [Emphasis in original.]*

The first sentence contains a serious and manifest falsehood. Archbishop Bertone did not state that the declarations (plural) of Bishop Perić reflected his personal opinion, but only this particular statement which, the archbishop adds, "he has the right to express as ordinary of the place." The second sentence is completely unnecessary, since Bishop Perić's statement was made in his personal capacity, and not as "a definitive judgement of the Church". As very few of those who read

Beautiful Gift or Pathetic Delusion?

the Daniel-Ange commentary, which was transmitted on the Internet throughout the world, will have seen the text of Bishop Perić's letter, most will conclude that he had tried dishonestly to claim that his statement did indeed represent the "definitive judgement of the Church".

2) *One is directed to the judgement of Zadar, which leaves the door open for future investigations. In the meantime, pastoral pilgrimages with pastoral accompaniment for the faithful are permitted.*

Once again there is nothing new here. Daniel-Ange gives the impression that Bishop Perić had claimed that the door was not open to future investigations, whereas in his letter, as Daniel-Ange was fully aware, he made specific mention of such a possibility. Daniel-Ange also gives the impression that Bishop Perić had denied that private pilgrimages to Medjugorje were permitted. What Bishop Perić had included in his letter was the official response of Archbishop Bertone to two French bishops stating that: "From what has been said, it follows that official pilgrimages to Medjugorje, representing it as a place of authentic Marian apparitions, must not be organized either on a parish or diocesan level, because this would be a contradiction of what has been affirmed by the bishops of the ex-Yugoslavia in their previously cited declaration."

Archbishop Bertone makes precisely the same point in his letter to Bishop Aubry, explaining to him that even private pilgrimages are not permitted if they are "regarded as an authentification of events still taking place and which still call for an examination by the Church." As every pilgrimage organized by the Medjugorje industry is promoted as a pilgrimage to a place of authentic apparitions, it follows that every one of these pilgrimages is organized in defiance of the clearly expressed ruling of the Congregation for the Doctrine of the Faith. Many of the so-called Medjugorje centres throughout the world are in reality travel agencies that make a great deal of money by inducing naive Catholics to go to Medjugorje because they have been deluded into believing that Our Lady appears there several times a day.

3) *A new commission could eventually be named.*

This is not in dispute, and it is of great importance to note that Archbishop Bertone states that such a commission would be composed of the members of the Episcopal Conference of Bosnia-Herzegovina. This makes it clear, contrary to what some Medjugorje propagandists have been claiming, that the Holy See is *not* conducting its own investigation.

4) *In the meantime, all Catholics may go as pilgrims to Medjugorje.*

They may go, but not as members of an official pilgrimage, and not if they do so in the belief that Medjugorje is a place of authentic Marian apparitions.

To sum up, in describing Archbishop Bertone's letter to Bishop Aubry as "a beautiful present", Daniel-Ange and his fellow propagandists are deluding themselves and their dupes in the most pathetic manner possible. Nothing whatsoever has been changed in the attitude of the sacred congregation to Medjugorje. It should be noted that the sacred congregation always employs quotation marks when referring to the so-called apparitions. In view of the distorted interpretation of Archbishop Bertone's letter given in the pro-Medjugorje media, Bishop Perić felt it necessary to make a statement concerning this letter, which will now be quoted in full.

45

21 JULY, 1998

Private Visits to Unauthentic Apparitions
A Statement by Bishop Ratko Perić

THE LOCAL PRESS HAS ONCE AGAIN RETURNED to the phenomenon of Medjugorje. The reason is the letter of Archbishop Bertone, Secretary of the Congregation for the Doctrine of the Faith, dated 26 May, 1998, to Bishop Aubry of the French island of Réunion in the Indian Ocean. Motivated by the interpretation given to this letter in the media, we set out a brief chronology of expert opinion and the official position the Church, which to date remains unchanged, regarding the events of Medjugorje.

Unrecognized apparitions. The phenomenon of the "apparitions" in Medjugorje has been studied by three commissions. In the second commission, the local bishop of Mostar, Bishop Žanić, called in specialists from Church faculties and scientific institutions. On 2 May, 1986, the members of the commission voted *non constat de supernaturalitate*, that is, it does not follow that the "events" in Medjugorje involve supernatural apparitions. Having informed the congregation with the accord of the bishop of Mostar, the former bishops' conference established a new commission in 1987 that brought the results of its investigations to the bishops in the autumn of 1990. On the basis of the studies the bishops' conference, gathered in Zadar on 10 April, 1991, gave a negative declaration regarding Medjugorje: "On the basis of investigations made thus far, it is impossible to confirm that the events involve supernatural apparitions or revelations." These "apparitions" are to be considered "so-called" or "alleged". The Congregation for the Doctrine of the Faith also refers to them with quotation marks.

In the current circumstances, the question of further studying the alleged apparitions at Medjugorje has not been raised at the level of the Bishops' Conference of Bosnia and Herzegovina. These so-called apparitions and their "messages" have been aimed against the local bishop from the very beginning (1981) and are also closely tied to the "case of Herzegovina," which the Holy See very much takes to heart and would like to resolve as soon as possible. This refers to the disobedience of the Herzegovinian Franciscan province in its execution of a papal decree regarding certain parishes in the diocese of Mostar-Duvno.

"Private" Visits. Due to the lack of authenticity regarding "supernatural apparitions" in Medjugorje, the local bishop, Bishop Žanić, was against the organizing of visits to the place of the so-called apparitions. The former bishops' Conference declared that "organized official pilgrimages to Medjugorje, as if already taken to be accepted by the Church, are not allowed."

The Congregation for the Doctrine of the Faith wrote to the Italian Bishops' Conference in 1985, in order to study the suitability of suggesting to the Italian bishops "that they publicly dissuade the organization of pilgrimages to the aforementioned alleged place of 'apparitions', as well as all other methods of publicity, especially regarding the press, which could prejudice a calm examination of the 'events' on the part of the special commission which had been canonically established for this purpose."

The bishops' conference gathered in Zadar, in declaring that it is impossible to confirm the authenticity of the Medjugorje "apparitions" or "revelations", also mentioned that there exist "great gatherings of people from all parts of the world who come to Medjugorje for religious and other motives".

"Private" visits of this nature have never been a matter of controversy, since going to Medjugorje would then be similar to visiting any other Catholic parish. Yet it has always been clearly stated that this cannot be done officially, using the church and pulpit, in order to preach the authenticity of the alleged apparitions and proclaiming the place a "sanctuary" of unrecognized apparitions.

The Congregation for the Doctrine of the Faith wrote to the French Archbishop Daloz of Besançon in 1995, and to Bishop Taverdet of Langres in 1996, that "official pilgrimages to Medjugorje, perceived as a place of authentic Marian apparitions, cannot be organized at parish or diocesan levels, since they would contradict what the bishops of the former Yugoslavia stated earlier in their above-mentioned declaration."

Regarding "pilgrimages to Medjugorje of a private nature", the congregation maintains that they are allowed "under the condition that they are not considered an authentication of events still going on, which demand further investigation by the Church". Hence, nothing new here. Official or church pilgrimages are not allowed, nor are "private" visits allowed that have the intent of proving that the so-called apparitions and alleged "messages" are authentic. Therefore, the official position of the local bishop is the same as the official position of the bishops' conference of 1991. And both priests and the faithful as Catholics should adhere to this position.

Mostar, 21 July, 1998

✠ Ratko Perić
Bishop of Mostar

46

15 SEPTEMBER, 1998

An Unexpected Endorsement For Bishop Perić

A CONTRADICTION OF THE EUPHORIC JUDGEMENT of Father Daniel-Ange that Archbishop Bertone's letter constituted "a beautiful present" for devotees of Medjugorje came from a most unexpected source—none other than Father René Laurentin. His interpretation of the letter endorses the interpretation given to it by Bishop Perić. Writing in the 15 September, 1998, issue of *Chrétiens Magazine*, Father Laurentin insisted that the significance of the letter was negative for Medjugorje. The key section of his article reads:

> This clarification is valuable and will reassure consciences that have been troubled artificially, but the devotees of Medjugorje can not reassure themselves too quickly on the basis of the letter from Monsignor Bertone. This letter states specifically that from now on the decision has been returned to the episcopal conference of Bosnia. Now this conference consists of only four bishops who are in total solidarity with the diocesan bishop, with a more or less predominant concern to leave in his hands the liberty of judging events in his diocese. Monsignor Perić therefore is in a position of total control to impose his personal decision that the supernatural is excluded from Medjugorje. Our Lady is at his mercy, and he thinks that he has acquired the right to put an end to her pilgrimage to Medjugorje, after having published a book about her hostile to Medjugorje.
>
> Out of respect for the opinion of the Pope, which he does not ignore, he has stated prudently that he does not wish to precipitate hypotheses of a new

investigation. He has even suggested that Rome might take the judgement into its own hands. But here [in the letter of Archbishop Bertone] Rome has returned the ball into his court. The letter is, therefore, not the "good news", nor the "recognition" of Medjugorje that some have proclaimed.

47

16 NOVEMBER, 1998

Implementing Romanis Pontificibus

General Curia of the Friars Minor,
Via Santa Maria Mediatrice 25,
00165 Rome,
Italy

16 November, 1998

*To all Priests, Religious and Faithful
in the Diocese of Mostar-Duvno,*

ON THE EVE OF ADVENT, AS WE PREPARE TO CELebrate Christmas, wishing you abundant peace and prosperity, we announce the decision made in Rome on 10 November, 1998, at the Congregation for the Evangelization of the Peoples. Together with Cardinal Joseph Tomko, the prefect, and Archbishop Marcello Zago, the secretary of that congregation, we, the undersigned, the bishop of Mostar and Duvno and the general minister of the Order of Friars Minor were present, both charged with carrying into effect the decree *Romanis Pontificibus*, which was, as is well known, confirmed by Pope Paul VI in special form in 1975 and confirmed by the reigning Sovereign Pontiff, John Paul II. Also present were two members of the diocesan clergy from Mostar and four Franciscans representing the general curia and the Herzegovinian province. It was unanimously agreed that at the beginning of next Lent, that is to say, Sunday, 21 February, 1999, the OFM would place at the disposal of the bishop of the diocese the parishes mentioned in the papal decree.

We are conscious of the acknowledged historic contribution

Implementing Romanis Pontificibus 157

of the OFM to the life of the Church in Herzegovina. They have a part in the spiritual heritage of the diocese and its very Catholic identity. We therefore count on the Franciscans for the future too. More than a century ago, in the year 1881, Pope Leo XIII re-established the diocese of Mostar-Duvno, setting up a regular hierarchy. Since then vocations to the secular and religious clergy have enriched the local church ever more. Co-operation in a spirit of unity appears all the more important on that account, under the leadership of the ordinary (bishop) of the diocese, sharing pastoral work, and assisting with their respective gifts.

So with renewed strength we continue along the way of the Church, which we wish to be steeped in mutual respect and esteem, brotherly co-operation and unity between the religious and secular clergy.

Making known to you this agreement, we call upon you all, lay faithful, monks and nuns, secular and religious clergy, who are all the children of the same heavenly Father, that they should foster ever more the spirit of common good in the unity of the local Church which exists in Herzegovina. We particularly stress to every parish community and to each individual believer who belongs to it, that each and every one should advance that necessary brotherly unity, avoiding damaging divisions. Just as in the whole Church, so in the diocese of Mostar-Duvno, each and every community of Catholic believers must work in unity with the bishop.

Renewing our commitment for the good of the Church as a whole and locally, we have before our eyes and vigorously commend both the particular pastoral service of the secular clergy and the special gifts of the Franciscan religious.

There is a case in which, after repeated admonitions of the men in question by their lawful superiors, Holy Church has confirmed the dismissal from the Franciscan Order of two religious who used to belong to the Herzegovinian province, but who, sadly, declined to keep their vow of obedience. We pray to the Holy Ghost to enlighten them, so that they can find the way back to full unity with the Church.

Our heavenly Father, to whom the coming year of preparation for the great jubilee of the year 2000 is dedicated, urges us to ever more perfect unity with Himself and one another in the Church, which is a sign and instrument of that unity throughout the world. May Saint Joseph, the head of the Holy Family, and protector of the diocese of Mostar-Duvno, together with Mary, the most holy Mother of God, unite us before the Saviour's crib, which was particularly dear to Saint Francis, as it is to us all.

Rome, 16 November, 1998

Father Giacomo Bini ✠ *Ratko Perić*
General Minister, OFM Bishop of Mostar-Duvno

48

21 NOVEMBER, 1998

Dismissal of Three Franciscans From the Order of Friars Minor

General Curia of the Friars Minor,
Via Santa Maria Mediatrice 25,
00165 Rome,

Procurator General. Prot. No. 087753

YOUR EXCELLENCY,

It was agreed at the meeting held at the Congregation for the Evangelisation of the Peoples on 10 November that I was to inform you if decrees were made for the dismissal of Fra Boniface P. Barbarić and Fra Bože Radoš from the Order of Friars Minor. I now write to inform you how the matter has unfolded.

The general minister, Fra Hermann Schaluck, and the bishop of Mostar-Duvno, Monsignor Perić, had decided that, in order to bring into effect the decree *Romanis Pontificibus,* the parish of Čapljina, formerly entrusted to the Province of the Assumption of the Blessed Virgin Mary, would from 12 May, 1996, be handed over for the bishop to dispose of at his unfettered discretion. Accordingly, no Franciscan was authorized to reside within that parish and carry out pastoral duties within it. This was made known to all Franciscans in the province.

Fra Boniface P. Barbarić and Fra Bože Radoš declined to be transferred, and remained in Čapljina, despite repeated and authoritative requests and orders to the contrary.

Since they have persisted in disobedience, the procedure for their dismissal from the order was set in train. On 28 February, 1998, a general consistory of the Order voted unanimously in a secret ballot to expel Fra Boniface P. Barbarić and Fra Bože Radoš of the province of the Assumption of the Blessed Virgin Mary in Bosnia and Herzegovina from the Order of Friars Minor, in accordance with the provisions of section 1 of canon 699.

The Congregation for the Religious confirmed the decrees for the dismissal of the above-mentioned Brothers on 23 March, 1998.

Since there is no record of their having lodged any appeal in the time fixed for so doing, the decrees take effect according to the canon, with the result that Fra Boniface P. Barbarić and Fra Bože Radoš no longer belong to the order of Friars Minor.

Your respectful servant in the Lord,
Father Antonio Riccio, OFM
Procurator General

Monsignor Ratko Perić
The Episcopal Residence,
88000 Mostar, Bosnia and Herzegovina

49

14 DECEMBER, 1998

Further Implementation of the Decree Romanis Pontificibus—*Communiqué*

ON 13 AND 14 DECEMBER, 1998, THE GENERAL minister of the Order of Friars Minor, Fra Giacomo Bini, and Monsignor Ratko Perić, Bishop of Mostar-Duvno, as the persons charged with carrying the decree *Romanis Pontificibus* into effect, met in Mostar in the presence of a representative of the Holy See, Archbishop Marcello Zago, Secretary of the Congregation for the Evangelization of the Peoples, and of the Provincial of the Franciscan Province of Herzegovina, Fra Tomislav Pervan.

Joint meetings with a section of the diocesan clergy and of the Franciscans took place in a brotherly atmosphere of unity both at local level and with the whole Church.

In the course of the above-mentioned meetings the question of the transfer of the parishes mentioned in the decree to the administration of the diocesan clergy was dealt with energetically. Both sides undertook their transfer in accordance with canon law, the decisions of the general minister and his council and the provincial.

The Holy See and the order are well aware of the steps that are being taken. Disobedient Franciscans should know that they are liable to be punished according to canon law and the rules of their order. It is desired that the decree should at long last be implemented for the good of the Church, the diocese, the Franciscan province, and, above all, the faithful.

We remind Christian believers that sacraments which they receive from the punished Franciscans are invalid.[1]

It is important that all, both clerics and the faithful, should see the local bishop, who is working with the secular and religious clergy, as the centre and point of reference of diocesan ecclesiastical life.

A special appeal is made to all members of the (Franciscan) community in this diocese, which has always been faithful to the Catholic Church, to follow the precepts of the Holy Father, the Holy See and the authorities which they have appointed, in a spirit of brotherly unity with one another, for the sake of spiritual and temporal progress in this diocese which the Pope loves, and whose affairs he is closely following.

Mostar, 14th December, 1998

✠ *Marcello Zago, OMI.*

✠ *Ratko Perić*
Fra. Giacomo Bini, OFM

---

[1] This statement would not, of course, refer to Baptism and the Eucharist, which would be valid if celebrated even by an excommunicated priest who intended to do what the Church does in these sacraments.

50

JANUARY, 1999

With Truth Against Lies Concerning the Parish of Čapljina

The article that follows appeared in the January, 1999, edition of Crkva na Kamenu *(The Church on the Rock), the pastoral bulletin of the dioceses of Herzegovina.*

AT THE END OF NOVEMBER 1998, OFFICIAL DOCuments appeared in the Croatian press regarding the dismissal from the Order of Friars Minor of Brothers Boniface Barbarić and Bože Radoš, who were illicitly officiating in the parish of Čapljina. The reactions of the two former Franciscans appeared in various newspapers, such as *Slobodna Bosna I Herzegovina, Vecernji List, Jutarnji List, Globus* and *Nacional,* and on radio and television. Even certain Muslim and Serbian media carried the story. Out of regard for the truth about the Church and the Faith, and for the sake of relationships within the Church, we have asked the bishop of Mostar-Duvno, Monsignor Ratko Perić, to deal with these articles as we read them.

Crkva na Kamenu: Is it true that the dismissed Franciscans were not permitted to put forward any defence and that their order expelled them without affording them any opportunity to put forward a defence (as is suggested in *Slobodna*)?

Bishop Perić: They need not have been expelled, had they been willing to obey their order and the Holy See. Following the lawful decision [at first instance] they might have defended themselves within the permitted time limits; that is to say, they could have lodged an appeal to the Holy See (more particularly, to the Congregation for Religious) questioning the decision of their order, had they wished to do so. So serious a step as dismissal from a religious order can not validly be taken, according to canon law, unless the wrongdoer has been admonished at least once to desist from his stubborn disobedience, and has been allowed a reasonable time to come to his senses. Admonitions reached Čapljina within the prescribed time limits from the lawful superiors and from the provincial and from the general curia of the Franciscan Order. It is quite another question whether the expelled Franciscans were willing to accept the admonitions; if such letters and such emissaries are not received, the fault does not lie with the superiors. But if the expelled were perhaps under the impression that it was sufficient that they should be defended by an unauthorized assembly of the faithful, they unfortunately took yet another false step in the preparation of their defence.

Crkva na Kamenu: The expelled Franciscans believe that the Pope "does not know the whole truth about them" *(Globus, Jutarnji List, Nacional)*. What do you say to that?

Bishop Perić: They may believe that and say it till the cows come home, yet all persons in authority were and are fully apprised of these grave matters, beginning with the Vatican dicasteries and the Holy Father himself. This matter was not dealt with overnight; rather, it proceeded strictly according to canon law, with due regard to all eleven canons concerning the dismissal of religious (canons 694 to 704). Indeed, eight months passed from their dismissal from their order until notice thereof appeared in the newspapers, from 23 March to 23 November, 1998. Accordingly, nothing was done contrary to canon law, or without the knowledge of the two former Franciscans.

Crkva na Kamenu: They claim (see *Globus* and *Nacional*) that three bishops of Mostar, namely Bishop Cule, Bishop Žanić and you yourself have deceived the Holy See and that the Pope does not know about the papal decree concerning the allocation of parishes. Is that possible?

Bishop Perić: That is neither possible nor the case. Pope Paul VI knew of the Holy See's decree concerning the allocation of parishes dated 6 June, 1975. He personally confirmed it on 5 June, 1975, *in forma specifica*. Moreover, Pope Paul VI sent a letter on 25 June, 1975 to all the members of the Franciscan province of Herzegovina, saying "Know for certain, beloved sons, that the decree prepared by the Sacred Congregation for the Evangelization of the Peoples, which we confirm and commend to you in every particular, was recently delivered to the bishops of Mostar and Duvno and the general minister of our beloved Order of Friars Minor." Probably there were even then some who denied that the Pope knew of all this, so the Supreme Pontiff decided to write a letter to the whole province.

Crkva na Kamenu: What was the principal reason for the dismissals from the order in this case?

Bishop Perić: According to the published official documents the principal ground which the General of the Franciscan Order submitted to the congregation for Religious, and which the Congregation submitted to the Holy Father, was that the two Franciscans were absent without leave from the house of their order. Their superiors summoned them to come to the house, in, for example, Široki Brijeg or Mostar or Duvno, but they refused to obey. They remained outside the house of their order, in this case in Čapljina, for months, indeed for years.

Crkva na Kamenu: One of those expelled says that "the Franciscans are the opposition to the Church establishment, as the religious orders ever were, but as time went by, they fell asleep".

Bishop Perić: I have never heard that said before, nor do I believe it now. I have always believed that religious are called to bear witness to the Church's second defining characteristic "one, *holy*...." Religious of both sexes are called by their lawful keeping of their vows and obedience to their superiors, and in the last analysis to the pope and the bishops, to follow Christ particularly closely. The structures of the episcopate and the religious orders are not the same. Christ willed and established the Apostles and their successors, the bishops, whereas the religious orders were established as the centuries went by. The Church by her distinguished members, the founders of the particular orders and congregations, desires and regulates their conduct within the Church. The bishops are the structure of the Church, whereas the religious are a structure within the Church. The bishops go back to the first century, whereas the Franciscans and the Dominicans go back to the thirteenth century, the Jesuits to the sixteenth, the Salesians to the nineteenth, and Mother Teresa's Missionaries of Love to 1948. It is not right that either bishops or religious should sleep, but if there is unhealthy opposition, then they must be expelled, even though it were the case of an archbishop, such as Marcel Lefebvre, who was once excommunicated.

Crkva na Kamenu: One of those expelled says that you said: "Even if I should drive all the faithful to take Islam and lose their Christian faith, I would do anything to make all the Franciscans fall at my feet" *(Nacional)*.

Bishop Perić: No sane man could say such things. The journalist must have known that it was fantasy, yet he repeated the allegation.

Crkva na Kamenu: Might I ask you to comment upon a phrase that is heard often enough from certain Franciscans in Herzegovina, and which the expelled Franciscans formulate thus: "Even before he went to Rome to study, Perić held spiritual exercises for nuns in Virovitica. Even then he coarsely said: 'I will break the necks of the Herzegovinian Franciscans. I will break their backs'."

Bishop Perić: Bishop Petar Cule sent me to study theology in Rome in 1965, after two years studying philosophy in Zagreb. I was ordained in 1969, and finished my studies on taking my doctorate in 1971. It is quite impossible that nuns would have summoned a mere theology student to conduct spiritual exercises for them. While I have conducted spiritual exercises on ninety occasions in the course of seventeen years as a priest, beginning in 1975, and six years as a bishop, I have never conducted spiritual exercises in Virovitica. I have never uttered such words, for it would be not only coarse, but senseless. Since I was consecrated a bishop, I have always asked the Franciscan Fathers who are entrusted with the care of souls in my diocese to carry the Pope's decree concerning the parishes into effect in accordance with canon law and in a spirit of obedience. Only their superiors admit them into their order, and expel them from it; the Congregation for the Religious has the final word in the Pope's name.

Crkva na Kamenu: One of those expelled says that "Bishop Perić's interference (or that of any other bishop) is an act of violence against his faith and conscience." He appeals to the example of Blessed Cardinal Stepinac, who was "a victim of his conscience". What do you say to that?

Bishop Perić: Religious of both sexes make three vows to God, exclusively through the instrumentality of the Church, which confirms and accepts their vows of poverty, chastity and obedience. Private vows of private persons made in private are quite another matter. They are not in issue in this case. Accordingly, whosoever confirmed the vows of members of religious orders and bound them in conscience, can release them from those vows and send the professed into the world, if they do not keep their vows. Every monk and nun knows that simple rule. The ordinary neither administers vows to Franciscans, nor releases them from their vows. Their superior does so, and our Holy Father the Pope.

Secondly, it is quite incredible to draw a comparison between this case and that of Blessed Cardinal Stepinac, who never sought to set his conscience above the Church, but subordinated his conscience to the Holy Church, the Holy Father and the Holy See, and was "ready to die not only for the Church generally, but if God in His providence should so require it, for every paragraph of the Code of Canon Law" (letter of 12 April, 1952).

He was a martyr precisely because he remained faithful to Christ's Church, to the See of St. Peter and so to his own conscience. In this painful case, everything is the other way around. The canon law of the Church has been broken, and these men were in truth expelled from their order in accordance with the Church's canons. A man may appeal to his own conscience in defiance of the Holy See, and his Franciscan

Order, but then he separates himself from the Church, which was unfortunately the case (as I have mentioned) with Archbishop Lefebvre.

Crkva na Kamenu: They say that they will not "separate themselves from the Vatican, and form a 'Croatian Catholic Church'" *(Nacional)*.

Bishop Perić: The Holy Church relies on obedient and not disobedient sons. They will persuade us when they show by their deeds and by obedience that they are not separating themselves from the Holy See.

Crkva na Kamenu: One of those expelled reproaches you with having forbidden a religious work that he has written, so that it can not be obtained in parish churches. When did you forbid it?

Bishop Perić: I did not do so at all; that is one of one-thousand-and-one lies. On the contrary, that expellee recently sent me a copy of his book *The Sacred Heart of Fra Barika Dermic*, and on the fly sheet he wrote a dedication: "To the most enlightened bishop in the world, regardless of all the others, my bishop, Ratko Perić, Čapljina, 21 November, 1998, Fra Bože Radoš, defender of the truth and the very Truth."

By coincidence on the same day, 21 November, a faxed letter arrived from Rome, declaring that he had been expelled from his order. I neither recommended nor forbade his book, nor did I even know that he had published it, until I read the dedication.

Crkva na Kamenu: Incidentally, the same journalist recounts how Fra Barika Dermic did not obey the then provincial of the Franciscans, Fra Rufina Sialic. Yet was not Fra Barika Dermic a holy Franciscan?

Bishop Perić: How was he to obey him, when Fra Barika died in 1932, but Fra Rufina Sialic became provincial in 1967? In this fashion the journalist corrupts his readers with his lies.

Crkva na Kamenu: Journalists maintain that the majority of the Franciscans see the fault for the present difficult situation in Herzegovina as lying at your door, in that you showed no understanding at all for the Church in Herzegovina, and failed to realize that the Franciscans would vigorously oppose you. A great number of Franciscans in Herzegovina (it is alleged) refuse to accept the bishop's decisions, but no one wants to confirm officially that it is so, and the bishop himself is striving to conceal the widespread disobedience throughout the Franciscan province. How much truth is there in that?

Bishop Perić: That is quite untrue, so far as I am concerned; these are just tales that journalists dream up as part of their trade. When I was appointed bishop in 1992, I took the motto: "Through many tribulations we must enter the Kingdom of God" (Acts 14:21). One of them is this unhappy affair. I therefore had at least some inkling of what awaited me. Secondly, no sensible person can expect a bishop to show understanding for disobedience. The Herzegovinian Franciscans are no fools, and so could not have expected that of me. Thirdly, neither is it true that I concealed the disobedience with regard to the parishes. Whenever it was necessary to speak of it officially or in writing, it was said officially or put in writing, and when it was necessary to say so publicly in the pulpit or on television, it was said publicly without flinching, and all the evidence, in Mostar and in Duvno. I did not shrink from speaking of it even at the bishops' synod concerning the Religious in the Vatican in the presence of the Holy Father and of two hundred and fifty cardinals and bishops, saying that in the past the Holy See had showered our religious with privileges, whereas today it strikes them with sanctions. That was published in *L'Osservatore Romano*. So much at least is public knowledge.

***Crkva na Kamenu*:** What do you say to the headline attributed to one of those expelled: "I would, if necessary, prefer to go to hell with my Croatian flock than to the bishop's heaven without my people!"

Bishop Perić: Matters do not stand thus, and there is no such dilemma, but rather they stand as the Pope said in Sarajevo in 1997 and in Solin in 1998. When he was in Solin, the Holy Father quoted St. Ignatius of Antioch word for word: "Be with the bishop, so that God should be with you." Father Barbarić knows that, and is bound to abide by those words, if he wishes to remain in God's Church, assuming that his bishop is in communion with the Pope.[1]

Crkva na Kamenu: What is their present status? They are not Franciscans, yet they wear Franciscan habits, saying that they can do no other.

Bishop Perić: They are no longer Franciscan religious, but they remain secular clergy. If they wish to re-enter the Franciscan Order, they would have to go back as novices.

Crkva na Kamenu: If, therefore, they are secular priests, under whose authority do they come?

Bishop Perić: I am not aware that they are under anyone's authority, yet they are bound to belong to some canonically constituted structure within the Church, that is to say, to a diocese. Canon 701 prescribes: "Vows, rights and obligations, derived from (a religious) profession cease *ipso facto* by legitimate dismissal. However, if the member is a cleric, he cannot exercise sacred orders until he finds a bishop who receives him after a suitable probationary period in the diocese according to canon 693 or at least allows him to exercise sacred orders."

Crkva na Kamenu: In the joint communique of 14 December, 1998, it is said that sacraments received at the hands of the expelled Franciscans are not valid.

Bishop Perić: The Church's law (canon 701) provides that a religious who has been ordained a priest and is expelled from his order may not perform his priestly duties until the question of his status has been resolved. The message of the communiqué is that the expelled Franciscans are illicitly present in the parish of Čapljina and all that they do as priests under no one's authority is illicit and against the Church. Regarding the sacraments, and speaking as a theologian, a priest cannot bestow the sacrament of orders in any event. If he illicitly administers confirmation or confession, or officiates at a wedding, it is invalid. A priest in good standing regularly administers baptisms, says Mass, and administers

---

[1] As he is no longer a Franciscan he has no right to the title Frater (Fra.), i.e. "Fra".

extreme unction, but these men are illicitly in possession of the presbytery and the parish, and they are aware that they sin not only against the Church's laws and the sacraments but also against conscience. The faithful are called upon to turn to their legitimate parish priest for the sacraments and other functions of the Church.

Crkva na Kamenu: Might they contact that bishop who affirmed that he had been to Medjugorje on many occasions and, in October 1997, confirmed children in Čapljina (*Slobodna*, 6 October, 1997) so that they should be his priests?

Bishop Perić: Were they to do that we might then know a little more about that scandal too, and that illicit confirmation and that "far away land".

Crkva na Kamenu: Were they to contact you, would you receive them?

Bishop Perić: As yet they have not contacted me, but were they to do so, I would invite them for discussions.

Crkva na Kamenu: What is the status of the parish of Čapljina: is it a Franciscan parish or a diocesan parish?

Bishop Perić: Since the Provincial has handed over the parish to the ordinary by a notarized deed, this parish is no longer in any sense a Franciscan parish, as the expression is. *De jure* it is a diocesan parish, but *de facto* it is occupied contrary to law. So far as the priests are concerned, they are no longer Franciscans, but Čapljina is a diocesan parish with secular priests. One must be patient towards men, as gentle as a dove, and filled with the wisdom of the gospels, and all will fall into place with God's help.

Crkva na Kamenu: During the war [with the Bosnian Serbs], when parishes [i.e., staffed by secular priests] were set up in Mostar, it was commonly asked why the bishop felt the need to start a second war?

Bishop Perić: Well, now peace of a kind prevails, yet still there is no obedience, nor any valid excuses for disobedience, any more than in the time of war. God's people know where the true Church is, and the false!

51

20 FEBRUARY, 1999

The Franciscan Rebellion in Herzegovina: Rome Acts

Congregation for the Religious
Communiqué

FOLLOWING THE JOINT LETTER THAT THE GENeral minister of the OFM, Fra Giacomo Bini, and the bishop of Mostar-Duvno, Monsignor Ratko Perić, both signed on 16 November, 1998, and following the communiqué of 14 December, 1998, issued by Archbishop Marcello Zago, Secretary of the Congregation for the Evangelization of the Peoples, and the above-mentioned general minister and diocesan bishop, the representative of the general minister, Fra Stephan Ottenbreit, the vicar general of the order, and the diocesan bishop met in Mostar from 17 to 20 February, 1999, so as to bring into effect at long last the Holy See's decree *Romanis Pontificibus*. Monsignor Mario R. Cassari, *ad interim chargé d'affaires* of the apostolic nunciature in Bosnia and Herzegovina, was present in the name of the Holy See.

The two persons charged with carrying the decree into effect decided the following:

1. The general curia of the OFM, together with the Herzegovinian Franciscan province, in unity with the diocesan bishop, announce that in complete accord and unity of intention it wishes to carry into effect the Holy See's decree and the decision of the general chapter of the Franciscan Order.

2. Alas, the date of 21 February, 1999, previously agreed upon with a view to the transfer of the parishes mentioned in the decree from the administration of the Franciscans to the secular clergy could not be kept, despite the good will of

The Franciscan Rebellion in Herzegovina: Rome Acts 173

those charged with carrying it into effect, for the following reasons. Physical resistance has been organized. Grave threats have been made both verbally and in writing, parish churches and presbyteries have been occupied, parish registers and seals have been seized.

3. With effect from 22 February of this year the present parish priests and persons pastorally responsible for the parishes mentioned in the decree are relieved of their pastoral responsibilities. They are:

> Fra Petar Vlašić in Blagaj on the Buna;
> Fra Leonard Hrkać in Crnac;
> Fra Marko Dragicević and Fra Miro Sego in Grude;
> Fra Alojzije Bosnjak in Jablanica;
> Fra Tihomir Kutle in Mostarski Gradac;
> Fra Oton Bilic in Nevesinje; and
> Fra Drago Skrobo in Ploce-Tepčići.

These Franciscans, to whom the provincial and his council have allocated houses in the province, will carry out pastoral duties in the diocese in accordance with the decisions which the provincial administration takes in agreement with the diocesan bishop.

4. While expecting the situation to return to normal in very early course, that is to say, that the selected priests can take over the mentioned parishes in accordance with canon law, the diocesan bishop undertakes, as he is duty bound to do, to ensure pastoral care for the faithful.

Accordingly, the parishioners of Blagaj on the Buna and Nevesinje are asked to attend the parishes of St. John the Evangelist or the cathedral in Mostar; the parishioners of Crnac and Mostarski Gradac the parishes of Polog and Jare; the parishioners of Grude the parishes of Ledinac and Raskrizje; the parishioners of Jablanica the parishes of St. Matthew the Evangelist or the cathedral in Mostar.

The bishop and the priests working in the diocesan curia are at the disposal of each and every one of the faithful for their pastoral needs.

5. So far as the present situation in Čapljina is concerned, the persons charged with carrying the decree into effect wish to make it particularly clear to the faithful that the priests Boniface Petar Barbarić and Bože Radoš were expelled from the OFM on 28 February, 1998, which expulsion the Holy See confirmed on 23 March, 1998. Accordingly, they are no longer entitled to wear the Franciscan habit. They were suspended *a divinis* by the Holy See on 17 December, 1998, and are forbidden to celebrate any of the sacraments. Proceedings are pending for the expulsion from his order of the third disobedient priest resident in Čapljina, Fra Mile Vlašić.

The sacrament of penance which the three above-mentioned persons administer and the sacrament of Christian matrimony at which they assist are invalid.

6. Similar sanctions under canon law will be taken against those Franciscans who do not abide by the directions of the Holy See and the general minister and his council. Canon law authorizes the local ordinary to forbid the use of unlawfully occupied churches as a last resort.

7. The general administration of the order, together with the administration of the Franciscan province of Herzegovina, wishes publicly to restate that it distances itself from the "Association of Catholic faithful *Peace and Good*". Since the Catholic Church has not recognized that association, it has no legitimacy in its eyes.

8. In this moment of suffering, the Catholic believers of the diocese of Mostar and Duvno, true to their past, are urged to redouble their sense of unity and fidelity to the Apostolic See and the Holy Father.

9. The local ordinary, with his clergy and faithful, would like to express his deep gratitude to the OFM and the Franciscan province of Herzegovina for their uninterrupted work for the growth and unity of the Church in the region, and once again express their need for the order's future witness and pastoral co-operation.

By the intercession of the Blessed Virgin Mary, Mother of the Church, may this time of Lent, so apt for repentance, and the whole year consecrated to our heavenly Father bring us spiritual succour, so that we may go through the Cross to the Resurrection.

Mostar, 20 February, 1999

Fra Stephan Ottenbreit
Vicar General of the Order of Friars Minor

✠ *Monsignor Ratko Perić*
Bishop of Mostar-Duvno

7 JANUARY, 2000

The Position of the French Episcopal Conference Regarding Medjugorje

During the 2001 assembly of the bishops of France, a question put by a member of the conference was the subject of a written response by Monsignor H. Brincard, Bishop of Puy-en-Velay, responsible for overseeing the Association of Marian Organisations. This response was made at the request of the permanent council. Regarding some facts having a certain reverberation, Bishop Brincard wanted solely to bring an ecclesial light, which we may hope will contribute to strengthening the unity of the People of God. Is not the Virgin Mary, Mother of the Church, in a very particular way, the servant of this unity? The text is taken from the official bulletin of the French Episcopal Conference (SNOP), No. 1064, printed in La Documentation Catholique of 7 January, 2000. Translated by Jim Gallagher for the May 2002 issue of Christian Order.

REGARDING MEDJUGORJE:

Question put.

Is there an authorised and official position of the Church concerning the events which motivate pilgrimages to Medjugorje?

We know that a true devotion towards the Virgin Mary is based not on alleged apparitions, nor on those that the Church recognises as authentic, nor on private revelations. We know also that these extraordinary interventions can be signs that we should not neglect once the Church, having operated the necessary discernments, has authenticated them.

Today the events of Medjugorje, in Bosnia-Herzegovina,

attract our attention, not only because of their reverberation, but also by reason of the pastoral solicitude necessitated by the numerous faithful of our dioceses who go on pilgrimage to this place.

If we want to have an informed opinion on the subject of what has happened at Medjugorje and what is still unfolding there, it is essential to ask ourselves the question: "Who has authority to speak about this in the name of the Church?"

THE COMPETENT ECCLESIASTICAL AUTHORITIES:
The Local Ordinary

The norms relative to the discernment of private revelations, published on 24 February, 1978, by the Congregation for the Doctrine of the Faith, signed by its Prefect, Cardinal Francis Seper, specify: "It belongs in the first and foremost to the local ordinary to investigate and to intervene."

There was in fact an investigation, from 1982 to 1986, overseen by Monsignor Pavao Žanić, bishop of Mostar. Let us recall briefly the stages of this investigation:

On 11 January, 1982, a commission of investigation is constituted composed of four members (two Franciscan priests and two secular priests),

In January, 1984, this investigating commission is enlarged by the nomination of a dozen ecclesiastics "chosen from experts in theological matters from different theological faculties in Croatia and Slovenia",[1] and medical doctors.

The Yugoslav Episcopal Conference is informed of the work of this commission of investigation. In a declaration of 12 October, 1984, this same conference makes it known that the bishops are asking "not to organise official pilgrimages to Medjugorje [...], not to prejudge the verdict."

On 30 October, 1984, with the prospect of an imminent completion of the works of the commission of investigation, Bishop Žanić publishes a report entitled *"Posizione attuale, non uffiziale, della Curia vescovile di Mostar nel confronti degli eventi di Medjugorje"*. ("Current non-official position of the episcopal

---

[1] *Posizione* of Bishop Zanic, 30 October, 1984.

curia of Mostar on the subject of events in Medjugorje".)

People reproached Bishop Žanić for publishing this document. Nevertheless, it is normal that before the publication of an official judgement itself, the ordinaries of the places concerned by the said events publish notes of information in order to orient pastors and faithful and to thus prepare them to receive the judgement of the Church.

The Episcopal Conference

The norms previously cited add:

> But the regional or national episcopal conference can become involved:
> —if the local ordinary, after having fulfilled the obligations pertaining to him, has recourse to it to study the whole phenomenon;
> —if the phenomenon equally concerns the region or the nation, by way of the prior consent of the ordinary of the place.

Bishop Žanić did not have recourse to the episcopal conference. However, on the suggestion of the Congregation for the Doctrine of the Faith, he accepted that the study of the dossier be confided to the Yugoslav Episcopal Conference, as the reverberation of the "event" extended well beyond the limits of his diocese.

The Congregation for the Doctrine of the Faith

"The Apostolic See may intervene, either at the request of the ordinary himself, or at the request of a qualified group of faithful, this by reason of the immediate right of universal jurisdiction of the Sovereign Pontiff" (Norms of 1978).

The sole Roman dicastery capacitated to intervene in the name of the Pope is the Congregation for the Doctrine of the Faith. The Holy Father never intervenes directly in affairs of this kind.

The norms of 1978 specify:

> The intervention of the sacred congregation may be sought either by the ordinary, after he has fulfilled

the obligations incumbent upon him, or by a qualified group of faithful. In the latter case, vigilance will be exercised that the recourse to the sacred congregation not be motivated by suspect reasons (for example, wanting to lead, by one faction or another, the ordinary to modify his legitimate decisions, or to have the sectarian position of a group ratified, etc).

It belongs to the sacred congregation to intervene of its own accord in serious cases, notably when the phenomenon affects a large part of the Church; but the ordinary will always be consulted, as well as the episcopal conference, if the situation requires it.

Bishop Žanić did not solicit the intervention of the Congregation for the Doctrine of the Faith. However, he well fulfilled the obligations incumbent on him, as this same congregation affirmed that it "appreciated the work accomplished by the diocesan commission, under the responsibility of Bishop Žanić."

Moreover, let us recall that on 2 June, 1982, Bishop Žanić submits a first report to the Congregation for the Doctrine of the Faith and, on 26 April, 1986, he delivers to Cardinal Ratzinger, prefect of the congregation, a plan of negative judgement, as the conclusions of the commission of investigation appear to be going in this sense. The cardinal therefore asks him to hold back the publication of a definitive judgement.

On 2 May, 1986, the commission of investigation votes, in a secret ballot, by eleven votes to four, against the recognition of the supernatural character of the events: *non constat de supernaturalitate*. At the same time, having concluded its work, it accepts its own dissolution, the affair being from then on in the hands of Rome.[2] On 15 May, 1986, Bishop Žanić transmits to the congregation the negative finding of the commission. It is therefore not correct to state that Bishop Žanić was relieved of the dossier. Furthermore, while the phenomenon "affects a large portion of the Church", the congregation did not intervene of its own accord.

---

2 Homily of Bishop Zanic of 25 July, 1987, in I. SIVRIC, "La face cachée du Medjugorje".

It is Bishop Franic, Archbishop of Split, who, on 17 April, 1985, during the plenary assembly of the Yugoslav episcopate, addresses to the bishop of Mostar the following request: "I ask His Excellency the bishop of Mostar to ascertain the facts about Medjugorje, while also accepting the help of the Holy See and of competent persons abroad so as to act in conformity with the maxim *'cum Petro et sub Petro'*."

The congregation thus applies that which is foreseen by the Norms of 1978: "It belongs to the sacred congregation to discern and to approve the action of the ordinary or, if such proves necessary, to proceed to a new examination of the events distinct from that which the ordinary has effected; this new examination of the events will be accomplished either by the sacred congregation itself, or by a commission especially established to this end."

The Roman dicastery charges the Episcopal Conference of Yugoslavia to take up the dossier, with the help of a new commission established to this end.[3] The work of this commission results in the Zadar Declaration of 10 April, 1991.

THE JUDGMENT OF THE COMPETENT ECCLESIASTICAL AUTHORITIES

Up to this day, only the bishops of Mostar—Bishop Žanić, then Bishop Perić—and the Yugoslav Episcopal Conference (dissolved *de facto* by the partition of the country after the war) have expressed a judgement on the events of Medjugorje. The Congregation for the Doctrine of the Faith, on the other hand, has never issued an official judgement. It has only given directives of a pastoral order.

The Personal Judgements of the Successive Bishops of Mostar-Duvno

The judgements of the bishops of Mostar are "personal" judgements rendered public within the limits of their diocese. They are negative judgements. They are exposed in the

---

3 Declaration of Cardinal Kuharic and Bishop Zanic, 9 January, 1987, published in *l'Osservatore Romano* of 14 February, 1987.

Posizione of Bishop Žanić (30 October, 1984), then in a notification in twenty-eight points dated March, 1990. Bishop Perić adopted the negative judgment of his predecessor in a work entitled "Seat of Wisdom" (1995). A chapter of that work is devoted to the question of Medjugorje. Here is the conclusion:

> It is therefore forbidden to claim or to declare in churches and religious communities that Our Lady has appeared or will yet appear in Medjugorje."

These episcopal interventions occurred after long and laborious official investigations, several elements of which are not known to us. It is to be noted that the Congregation for the Doctrine of the Faith never expressed the least reservation regarding these judgements when they were published. Bearing in mind the authority which this congregation recognises pertaining "first and foremost" to the local ordinary, in matters of discernment and of intervention, it would not be wise to take lightly that which the successive bishops of the diocese of Mostar-Duvno have said.

The Zadar Declaration (1991)

The judgement of the Yugoslav Episcopal Conference, in the declaration known as the "Zadar Declaration", dated 10 April, 1991, was a provisional reserved judgement, formulated thus: "Based on the investigations carried out thus far, it has not been possible to establish that it involves apparitions or supernatural revelations."

That is what is called a *"non constat de supernaturalitate"*. The disappearance of the Yugoslav Episcopal Conference has not permitted this same to pursue its investigations. But the fact that in 1991, ten years after the beginning of the events, not one single decisive element in favour of a possible supernatural origin of the apparitions could be put forward, underlines not only the complexity of the dossier, but leads also to suppose that there were also at the time important questions left unanswered.

Since February 1999, the Episcopal Conference of Bosnia-Herzegovina has received from the Congregation for the

Doctrine of the Faith the task of pronouncing definitively, after a new and final investigation. At the present moment, that conference has not pronounced.

The history of the Church teaches us that Rome always remits *in fine* to the authority and the competence of the local ordinary. That is true for the apparition of La Salette—where the bishop of Grenoble, Bishop de Bruillard, was able to pronounce, despite the opposition of his metropolitan, Cardinal de Bonald, Archbishop of Lyon. It goes also for the events of Beauraing (1932-33) and of Banneux (1933) in Belgium. The bishops of Namur and of Liege, dispossessed for a time of the power to pronounce—in favour of Van Roey, Archbishop of Malines and Primate of Belgium, to whom was confided the totality of the dossier on the "Belgian apparitions" of 1932-34—in the end obtained the faculty to bring a positive judgement on the events arising in their dioceses, despite the remaining very negative opinion of Cardinal Van Roey and of the commission which he established. It is once again confirmed in Japan for the events of Akita (1974-1981) where Bishop Ito, bishop of Niigata and local ordinary, was able, on 22 April, 1984, to pronounce favourably in their regard despite the opposition of the Japanese Episcopal Conference.

INTERVENTION OF THE CONGREGATION FOR THE DOCTRINE OF THE FAITH:
The question of pilgrimages

Regarding Medjugorje, the Congregation for the Doctrine of the Faith has intervened only on the pastoral level. In this matter official acts are very rare:

—On 23 May, 1985, a warning. Monsignor Bovone, Secretary of the Congregation for the Doctrine of the Faith, wrote to Monsignor Caporello, Secretary of the Italian Episcopal Conference.

Here is the content of his letter:

> From several sides—and particularly the competent ordinary (the bishop of Mostar)—we note and deplore a real propaganda for the "events" linked to the alleged

apparitions of Medjugorje. A special organisation for pilgrimages has been set up and other initiatives have been taken which contribute to sowing confusion among the faithful and to hindering the work of delicate examination which the special commission for the study of the "events" in question is currently carrying out. In order to avoid the spread of the above-mentioned propaganda and the speculation which it provokes in Italy, despite the advice and recommendations of the Yugoslav Episcopal Conference, may the presidency (of the Italian Episcopal Conference) consider well the opportunity of advising the Italian episcopate to discourage publicly the organisation of pilgrimages to the above-mentioned centre of "apparitions", as well as every other form of publicity, particularly editorial, judged prejudicial to a serene study of the "events" in question by the special canonically constituted commission to this end.

— On 23 March, 1996, then in June, 1996, Monsignor Bertone, Secretary of the Congregation for the Doctrine of the Faith, replies to questions which have been addressed to the congregation by Bishop Taverdet, bishop of Langres, and by Bishop Daloz, archbishop of Besançon. Referring to the Zadar Declaration, Monsignor Bertone reminds them above all that the cult is not authorised.

— On 26 May, 1998, Monsignor Bertone replies, this time to Bishop Aubry, bishop of Saint-Denis-de-la-Réunion. After having recalled the Zadar Declaration, he adds:

> I point out first of all that it is not the habit of the Holy See to assume, in the first instance, its own position vis-à-vis supposed supernatural phenomena.

Addressing the question of pilgrimages, the secretary of the congregation points out:

> Finally, concerning pilgrimages to Medjugorje which take place in a private manner, this congregation holds that they are permitted on condition that they are not considered as an authentication of events in course which still necessitate an examination by the Church.

Let us recognise that it is not easy to apply faithfully this recommendation. How, in fact, to organise a private pilgrimage without it being motivated by the conviction that the events of Medjugorje are of a supernatural origin? Since this conviction is at the origin of the pilgrimage, does not this latter not become *de facto* "an authentication of events in course which still necessitate an examination by the Church"?

It is just this difficulty which Cardinal Kuharic and Bishop Žanić foresaw in their joint declaration of 9 January, 1987.

The Criterion of Fruits

On this subject, let us make an introductory remark. It emerges from the document published in 1978 by the Congregation for the Doctrine of the Faith that one must "in the first place" judge the event according to positive and negative criteria and "then, if this examination results favourably, allow certain public manifestations of cult and devotion, all the while pursuing into the events an investigation of an extreme prudence (which amounts to the saying: for the moment, there is nothing against it)."

The examination of the events must, consequently, precede the examination of the fruits. When this order is not respected errors of judgment can arise.[4]

If we examine the events of Medjugorje in the light of the fruits, what do we observe? It is first of all undeniable that at Medjugorje there are returns to God and "spiritual" healings. It is no less evident that the sacramental life there is regular and the prayer fervent. One could not deny these good fruits *in situ*. We should even rejoice in them. But can we say that they continue in our parishes? Difficult question, for we must note unfortunately that the susceptibility, even aggressiveness, of some partisans of Medjugorje towards those who do not share their enthusiasm is such that in some places it provokes serious tensions that attack the unity of the People of God.

---

4 The story of the Mariavites in Poland at the beginning of the century provides sad confirmation.

The Position of the French Episcopal Conference

From where do these good fruits, observed in an indisputable manner at Medjugorje, come? A declaration of Bishop Perić, our confrère of Mostar, may on this point usefully enrich our meditations: "The fruits, so often mentioned, do not prove that they flow from apparitions or supernatural revelations of Our Lady. But in the measure that they are authentically Christian, they may be interpreted as a product of the normal work of divine grace, by faith in God, by the intercession of the Virgin Mary, Mother of Christ, and by the sacraments of the Catholic Church. And this to say nothing of the negative fruits."

Finally, it is opportune to ask ourselves if the events of Medjugorje have produced good fruits in the visionaries who, at least during the duration of the "apparitions", must by their lives be the first witnesses of the grace from which they say they benefit. From there it follows that we ask ourselves the following questions: "Have they obeyed the bishop of Mostar? Have they respected him?..." Such questions and still others yet, are habitually part of a serious investigation into an event of apparitions. In order for the investigation to arrive at a solid conclusion, it is necessary that these fundamental questions receive a clear and objective response.

We would like to say nothing about the doubtful or even bad fruits. But the truth obliges us to say that they exist. Let us quote, as examples, the calling into question, even to the point of defamation, of the local ordinary as well as the disobedience with regard to his legitimate authority; the exacerbation of the Herzegovina "question" following the words attributed to "the *Gospa*", words in favour of the Franciscans and against the bishop. In conclusion, allow me to make the following reflection:

I have no authority to pronounce any ecclesial judgement whatsoever on the events of Medjugorje. I am therefore the first to have to give an example of obedience, notably in respecting the pastoral decisions of my confrère of Mostar and in complying with joy to his wishes. "I do not see how I can go to Medjugorje without giving my support, by the very fact of my arriving there, to the events whose discernment and assessment rests henceforth with the Episcopal Conference of Bosnia-Herzegovina. Such support would fly in the face of a traditional teaching of the Church, recalled in *Lumen Gentium* and applicable to all the successors of the Apostles: 'Individual bishops, in so far as they are set over particular Churches, exercise their pastoral office over the portion of the People of God assigned to them, not over other Churches nor the Church universal'."

My wish, which I share with you, is to be able to further in my diocese a real renewal of Marian piety, in having frequent recourse to the habitual means which the Church puts at our disposal and which the Holy Father does not cease to recommend to us.

✠ *Henri Brincard*
Bishop of Puy-en-Velay,
Accompanying Bishop of the
Association of Marian Organisations

53
11 JANUARY, 2000
Death of Bishop Pavao Žanić

BISHOP PAVAO ŽANIĆ DIED ON 11 JANUARY, 2000, in a hospital in Split, Croatia at the age of 81. His Requiem was celebrated on 13 January at Kastel Novi, his birthplace, where he had been living since his retirement in 1993. He was buried in the local cemetery.

54

24 JANUARY, 2000

Newsweek *Report:* "Visions of the Virgin"

Thousands of believers throng to hear the Mother of Jesus speak through a man who lives in Boston

By Kevin Peraino
Newsweek International, January 24, 2000

IVAN DRAGICEVIĆ IS GETTING MOBBED. AT THE Sacred Heart Roman Catholic Church in a suburb of Boston, people are lunging, straining to get their hands on him. "I'm a friend of Ivan's," claims a white-haired man jockeying to get closer; Dragicević doesn't know him. Another man railroads his way through the congregation and pleads for a picture; Dragicević demurs. Dragicević's wife, a former Miss Massachusetts, is poised nearby as flashbulbs flicker. Ivan looks overwhelmed. An aide whisks him away from the crowd and out the back door. "They expect me to be a saint," he says after catching his breath. "I'm a man like everyone else. I'm fighting to be humble."

Navigating crowds is part of life when you're one of the Medjugorje visionaries—the six Croatian children who reported in 1981 that they began receiving daily visits from the Virgin Mary in what was then Yugoslavia. Since they were first reported, the visions have sparked a worldwide phenomenon, drawing more than twenty million tourists to Medjugorje. And at the busy intersection of sanctity and celebrity in America, Dragicević is a man in demand. Never mind that the apparitions have never been authenticated by the Catholic Church. These days Dragicević draws crowds of thousands at stops around the United States—four thousand in Dallas in

November, three thousand a few days later in San Antonio. Other stops are planned for later this month, and in February he'll be the keynote speaker at a weekend conference near Oakland, California. Devotees come to watch him commune with Mary, then translate her messages to the crowd.

Now thirty-four and living in Boston, he jets from Hong Kong to Honolulu, shepherded by an entourage. Dragicević isn't getting rich from it—he lives modestly off rental income from a bed-and-breakfast-style house in Medjugorje, plus occasional stipends from appearances. So why does he do it? "I have a duty," he says. "People are hungry for God." In the United States there are more than one hundred and fifty Marian groups—well-organized Catholics, many of whom have made the pilgrimage to Apparition Hill, site of the original visions at Medjugorje. The visions have spawned a cottage industry in the United States of pilgrimage guides and merchandisers. There is, of course, a web site, and *Medjugorje* magazine accepts advertising from for-profit book retailers and travel agencies. Boasts the magazine's ad-rate card: "Readers of *Medjugorje* magazine are active buyers and stimulated by advertising."

But many rank-and-file Catholics remain unconvinced. In 1987 the bishops of Yugoslavia declared that "one cannot affirm that supernatural apparitions are involved." Even the Vatican says only that the Holy See continues to investigate the matter. But the Madonna remains a popular figure. "She's a role model in a microwave age," says Rosemarie Marando, a Medjugorje pilgrim from New York. And the messages rarely conflict with Catholic teachings. A recent example: "Only through prayer will you become my apostles of peace in this world without peace."

Dragicević says his first encounter with the Virgin Mary occurred on a hot day 18 years ago when he was out for a walk with a friend during halftime of a Croatian basketball game. Some girls he knew called him over, and that's when he says he saw her for the first time, floating on a cloud. He says she appears to him largely the same as on that day:

black hair, blue eyes, rosy cheeks, a white veil and a crown of stars. It usually happens at 6:40 p.m. What makes him so sure it's really the Virgin Mary? Says Dragicević: "Hey, I'm certain because I see her as I see you." After his talk at Sacred Heart, Dragicević opens the floor to questions. "How old does she look?" asks a child with black hair and glasses. Around twenty-six, Dragicević says. Someone asks whether Dragicević has seen heaven, and what it looks like. "Yes," he says. "Hang on, you'll see." The hands show no sign of stopping. Finally, he says, "If you pray more, you'll have no more questions to ask me." Dragicević is tired, his ulcers are acting up and he's ready to get out of here. And anyway, he has to get up early tomorrow. He has a plane to catch.

55

7 FEBRUARY, 2000

A Letter From Bishop Ratko Perić Concerning Father Zovko

Mostar, 7 February, 2000 Prot.: 131/2000

DEAR FATHER FRANKEN:

I answer to your letter of 6 February, 2000. Thank you for your book *Een Reis naar Medjugorje*, Van Spijk Venlo, Antwerpen, 1999. I hope to have an English version soon.

Regarding Father Fra Jozo Zovko, OFM, member of the Franciscan province of Herzegovina (several times mentioned in your book, especially p. 102), I am obliged to inform you that he was revoked of "every faculty and canonical mission in the diocese of Mostar-Duvno and Trebinje-Mrkan" by my predecessor Monsignor Pavao Žanić, who died on the last 11 January, in a letter of his diocesan chancery office, Nr. 622/89, of 23 August, 1989.

As the present diocesan bishop of these two dioceses of Herzegovina, I uphold this decision, and action. Furthermore, since he has heard confessions without the necessary faculty, he has also fallen into the penalties prescribed in canon 1378 § 2, 1º. I notified him of this in my letter, Nr. 423/94, of 14 June, 1994.

The Congregation for the Evangelization of the Peoples requested in 1990 that he go away from Medjugorje, into a "convento lontano", but he is still very involved in the Medjugorje affair, residing in Široki Brijeg and visiting Medjugorje. Father Jozo Zovko is a disobedient Franciscan.

Father Zovko is constructing a convent of great proportions in Široki Brijeg in this diocese without the permission of the ecclesiastical authority. According to the project, of 1997, it will cost about 8 million DEM. From where, I do not know.

Availing myself of this opportunity, I wish to express to you my regards and greetings,

Monsignor Ratko Perić
Bishop of Mostar-Duvno and
Administrator of Trebinje-Mrkan.

Reverend Father Rudo Franken
Markt 7, 6088 BP Roggel
The Netherlands

1 JULY, 2000

Confirmation Homily by Bishop Ratko Perić

The Immaculate Heart of Mary, Medjugorje

DEAR CANDIDATES FOR CONFIRMATION AND GOD-loving faithful:

Yesterday we celebrated the Solemnity of the Sacred Heart of Jesus in various places in our two dioceses. Today the Church celebrates the liturgical memory of the Immaculate Heart of Mary. This celebration used to fall on the 22nd of August (I recall with gratitude to God that I chose to celebrate my first Mass on that day in 1969). For many years now this memory is celebrated the day after the Solemnity of the Sacred Heart, one after the other, and rightfully so. Today's memory moves us to say a few words on the Blessed Virgin Mary, who was filled with the Holy Spirit and to especially refer to her motherly heart.

Holy Scripture twice mentions Mary's motherly heart:

> After the events regarding Jesus' birth, St. Luke writes: "Mary kept all these things, pondering them in her heart" (Lk 2:19).

After the encounter in the temple, when Jesus was twelve years old, St. Luke writes once again: "His mother kept all these things in her heart" (Lk 2:51).

This is truly a simple, motherly and humane reaction! She kept all these events with gratitude inside her and reflected upon them with love in her motherly heart. In both, the first and second occasions, not only words are mentioned which Mary heard, since the Greek original *rhemata* means words, news, teaching, events, memories. The Madonna pondered these events in her heart, just as one ponders upon the glorious mysteries of the Rosary, keeps them as a great treasure, thanks God and prays to Him that she may thoughtfully unite them in her mind and heart. Mary surely spoke of these events to Jesus when He grew up. She also could have heard directly from Him and experienced during His and her lifetime the full meaning of these memories and events.

The gospels contain a few moments where Mary speaks up, asks questions and says a prayer. For instance, the gospels of St. Matthew and St. Mark do not contain any of Mary's direct words. In the gospels of St. Luke and St. John, there are a few, five or six of her direct interventions.

In Nazareth she asked the archangel Gabriel: "How can this be, since I have no husband?" (Lk 1:34). And when the angel explained in his own way how this will come about, then she accepted and said: "Let it be to me according to your word" (Lk 1:38). This word of the Madonna, we Catholics say at least once if not three times a day, when we pray the Angelus.

The Magnificat is her prayer of praise and thanksgiving, which follows the Old Testament way of Samuel's mother Anne, arranged in ten lines: "My soul magnifies the Lord, and my spirit rejoices in God my Saviour... and his mercy is on those who fear him from generation to generation..." (Lk 1:46-56). This prayer of praise we priests, religious and sisters pray or sing each evening during the liturgy of the hours.

Then come two words that Mary puts to Jesus:

> When He was twelve years old, while at the temple, when they found Him, she said: "Son, why have you treated us so? Behold, your father and I have been looking for you anxiously" (Lk 2:48), which we heard in today's gospel reading, and at the beginning of Jesus' public ministry, at Cana of Galilee, during a wedding banquet: "They have no wine" (Jn 2:3). Right after this she said to the servants: "Do whatever He tells you" (Jn 2:5). There could be other similar occasions in the future.

Regarding these few lines where Mary directly asks, speaks or prays something, and other moments when she listens to

Confirmation Homily by Bishop Ratko Perić

others and in which she is described as Virgin and Mother, countless theological books have been written, numerous Marian conferences have been held and many masters' and doctoral theses on Mariology have been defended. These biblical words are the foundation of our faith and relationship to Mary as Mother of Jesus and exemplary believer in God. She is an example and guide in this faith. We especially appreciate Mary's words that God's mercy is on those who fear Him, on those who have a sense of fear of God and His commandments. Dear candidates for Confirmation, remember to pray today and always for the gift of fear of God which comes from the Holy Spirit!

When one keeps this in mind, and arrives at a biblical knowledge of Mary as the humble and silent virgin, as a worried and prudent mother, who ponders all these events in her heart and speaks very little of them, then a true believer can only remain amazed at the talk that here in Medjugorje, for almost twenty years now, day by day, Mary has been presumably "appearing" for five, ten or fifteen minutes to so-called "seers"; that she is presumably handing something over, in the form of so-called "messages", or "ten secrets"; it's not sure if there are exactly ten, if each person has received the same number, or if there are six times more, meaning that each person received a different amount.

Does this mean that this "apparition" up until this time has appeared 6,940 times (19 years multiplied by 365/6 days)? And that constantly, every day, she is speaking, and that only once in a month she leaves a "message", and thanks the so-called "seers" for responding to her call? And this has been going on for almost twenty years now, and could keep on going another ten, twenty or even more years?

The official statements of the Church, starting from the local bishop up to the bishops' conference has not in this case recognized a single "apparition" as authentic. The Church has clearly declared that it is impossible to affirm that these events involve supernatural apparitions. For this reason I wrote decisively and clearly on 14 February, 1998, to the local pastor:

"Therefore, let no official Church premises belonging to the parish be used for these so-called, presumed and imagined apparitions which have never been recognized or accepted by the Catholic Church". The parish priest willingly obeyed. Therefore, I hereby declare with no doubt in my mind, as the local ordinary and bishop, that not a single so-called "apparition" or so-called "message" convinces me that these events involve supernatural appearances. Messages on peace and grace, regarding fasting and prayer, on love and the need for penance are already known at the most official levels of the Bible's teachings and those of the Church.

And what are we to do with the acclaimed "spiritual fruits"? Dear believers, in whichever church you enter in order to pray to God with faith, sincerely confess and repent of your sins, and piously receive Holy Communion, you may receive spiritual fruits. Candidates for Confirmation receive the sevenfold gift of the Holy Spirit, not because they are in Medjugorje, or Mostar or Rome, but because it is conferred upon them by an authorized minister of the Church. No one in his right mind who believes in God would ever say that in those parishes around the world where the sacraments are celebrated and received legitimately, there will be no spiritual fruits. Wherever the Holy Spirit is found there will be spiritual fruits as well!

The Catholic Church, in her mission of teaching and upholding the truth of salvation, is not influenced by large or small numbers of peoples or nations present. She holds instead to that which God has revealed about Himself, on mankind, and on Mary, of whom we believe and hold:

- that she was immaculately conceived;
- that she is the Mother of God; according to the Father's plan in time, by conceiving through the Holy Spirit, she gave birth to our Saviour Jesus Christ, the Son of God, the Second Person of the Holy Trinity;
- that she remained a virgin always;
- that she was taken up body and soul into the glory of heaven.

The Church upholds and believes that the Blessed Virgin Mary can appear, and that she has appeared at different times in history and also that up to this day there is no proof or convincing arguments that she ever appeared in a supernatural way in Medjugorje.

All of us, you candidates for Confirmation and the rest of us, should pray to the Blessed Virgin Mary, the Mother of Jesus and our spiritual mother, that through the love of her Immaculate Heart she intercede for us before the Father, that through her motherly care, she watch over us, over this parish, our diocese and the entire world.

✠ *Ratko Perić*
diocesan bishop

57

3 DECEMBER, 2000

A Medjugorje Canonisation

THE 3 DECEMBER, 2000, ISSUE OF THE *CATHOLIC Times* reported the death of Father Slavko Barbaric, and the astonishing news that the seers claimed that Our Lady had appeared to them and assured them that their mentor had been "borne into heaven" and was "interceding for them"—in other words, he had been canonised. Amanda Toon, a national leader of Youth 2000, the spiritual initiative which holds retreats for young people in Britain and Ireland, told the *Catholic Times*: "Our Lady has never ever specified anything about anyone before. Father Slavko is a saint in heaven without a shadow of a doubt."

In February, 2000, Bishop Perić had withdrawn the faculties to hear confession from Father Barbaric, who was living and ministering in Medjugorje contrary to the express prohibition of the bishop. Father Barbaric had appealed to Rome, but no decision had been reached before his death. Bishop Perić came in person to celebrate the requiem of the priest who had caused him so many difficulties, a gesture that is typical of the charity of the bishop who, like his predecessor, is a true shepherd.

58

28 MAY, 2001

Communiqué from Monsignor Luka Pavlović, Vicar General of Mostar-Duvno

A communiqué regarding an imposter bishop and the illicit confirmations

FROM THE CHANCERY OFFICE OF THE DIOCESE OF MOSTAR-DUVNO

This chancery office has already issued communiqués on May 16, 19 and 21 of this year that "Bishop Srecko Franjo Novak," upon the invitation of the Franciscan priests who have occupied the parish of Grude: S. Pavlović, A. Soljic, B. Maric and A. Saravanja—13 May; then upon the invitation of the dismissed Franciscans who have usurped the parish of Čapljina: Boniface Barbaric, B. Radoš and M. Vlašić—20 May; and finally upon the invitation of Fra Martin Planinic, who has seized the parish of Tepčići 27 May, 2001, conducted the rite of "confirmation".

According to his Certificate of Baptism, Novak is the son of parents who were not married in the Church and only legitimate p.f.c. (= *pro foro civili*). Yet he was baptised in the Catholic Church (enclosure N. 1-photocopy of the Certificate of Baptism of 1968 and 2001).

Having been expelled from the Catholic seminary, he joined the Old Catholics. The Sacrament of Holy Orders has three levels: diaconate, presbyterate and episcopate. To this day, Novak has not provided any documented proof of his ordination to the priesthood or episcopacy. He has stated: "I possess all the documents regarding my high school diploma, my scientific title and proof of completion of theological studies as well as my episcopal ordination in Switzerland in 1989" (*Slobodna Dalmacija*, 23 May, 2001, 9). He is hence obliged to prove: who ordained him a priest and bishop? When and where? Who can testify to these events? Where are the originals or the diploma of ordination (*testimonium ordinis*)? Where can this be verified? The people have a right to know the origins of public figures.

The position of the chancery office of the diocese of Mostar regarding the documents received of Srecko Franjo Novak is as follows:

1) A deacon who was denied priestly ordination and never consecrated bishop! Novak was ordained a deacon of the Old Catholic Church. He was denied ordination to the priesthood and never became a bishop in that community. This is what the Old Catholic bishop Hans Gerny from Switzerland wrote on 23 May, 2001: "Novak studied theology at the Old Catholic theological faculty in Berne. He was ordained deacon by Bishop Leon Gauthier. Ordination to the priesthood was denied to him. From that time onward, he has had nothing to do with the Christian-Catholic Church nor with any other Old Catholic Church of the Union of Utrecht. He never received episcopal consecration according to the rite of the Old Catholic Church" (enclosure N. 2: photocopy of Gerny's letter; enclosure N. 3: photocopy of the Old Catholic Dr. Ivo Hrsak's letter from Zagreb, 23 May, 2001).

2) Self-proclaimed bishop and even archbishop! We have managed to obtain a copy of the "List of succession" which Novak refers to in speaking to journalists (*Slobodna Dalmacija*, 23 May, 2001, 9). In fact, it is the "List of successors of the International Christian Community" (*Christengemeinde International-die Successorenliste*). This "List of succession" has not been presented to the public by Novak because being a false document it does not give him honour. This document begins by listing the names of ten successors of the Canadian community, the current bishop being "Serge Thériault, from Hull, Canada".

A new title then follows: A list of succession of the International Christian Community, and one can see the first name as Leon, 2 May, 1983, and then a double cross (indicating an archbishop) with the signature: ✠ Leon Felix (Srecko) Novak. Under his name there are listed six more German and Croatian names of "archbishops" and "bishops" with their signatures, which Leon Felix Srecko Franjo Novak, the self-proclaimed "archbishop", "ordained" himself or together with those he "ordained" earlier (enclosure N. 4: copy of the "List of succession" of "arch/bishop" Novak).

This "List" only proves Novak's religious megalomania. During his seminary days he was known to dress up in a priest's cassock and march through the streets of Zagreb! Many of his superiors and colleagues who are priests today can testify to this.

3) Questions to Thériault and his responses. Having obtained the "List of succession", for the love of Truth and with all ecumenical respect, we sent forth 10 questions via e-mail on 24 May to Serge Thériault regarding S. F. Novak. Amongst the inquiries: Was Novak ever regularly ordained by someone with "apostolic succession"? Who ordained him as bishop? Someone has said that you personally ordained him bishop? If this is true, when and where did this take place? (enclosure N. 5: copy of e-mail with Croatian translation).

Serge Thériault wrote back the same day he received the letter, 24 May, 2001, and responded: "I did not ordain him a deacon, priest or bishop..." (enclosure N. 6: copy of Thériault's letter with a Croatian translation of Questions and Answers). From the response one can understand that up until May of 1983 Novak was not even a deacon, yet on the "List of succession" 2 May, 1983, his signature appears as "archbishop" Leon!

4) Thériault's solemn declaration. The next day, 25 May, 2001, we sent Serge Thériault a copy of the "List of succession", according to which he "ordained" Novak a "bishop". Thériault was so upset that he immediately called a meeting of the Synod Council and the same day, 25 May, issued a resolute "Statement regarding Srecko Novak...."

As the "4th Bishop Ordinary of the Christian Catholic Rite of Community Churches" he declares "that Srecko Novak, Harald Scheffler, Franz Budweiser and others are not, and never have been, canonical clergymen in our jurisdiction, and that no ordination to the diaconate, the priesthood or the episcopate in the historical apostolic succession has been conferred on them by me or by my predecessor, Monsignor O'Neill M. Coté, 1939–1986... and in consequence, it is false that an episcopal lineage in Apostolic Succession is claimed from and through us, as stated in the attached document titled 'Die Successorenliste of the Christengemeinde International'" (enclosure N. 7: copy of the declaration in English with a Croatian translation).

5) "Professor and doctor of Theology"? Srecko Novak, together with Dragan Hazler, from the "Croatian Academy of Sciences and Arts in Diaspora" in Basel, issued an *honoris causa* doctorate diploma with his signature as secretarius with a little cross (indicating that he is a bishop) with the following: "Prof. Dr. th. ✠ Srecko Novak", thus suggesting that he is a doctor of theology. This is how he signed the diploma given to Hans Joachim Dombrowsky on 7 March, 1994, (enclosure N. 8: photocopy of the diploma).

If it is true that he is a "professor and doctor of theology" as his signature indicates, then he should at least provide his diploma or any other authentic document of a theological faculty indicating where, when and from whom he received his doctorate in theology. If this is not true, then one knows what this is called in academic circles. What is known, though, is that he was expelled from the seminary of Zagreb as well as from the Old Catholic theological school before he completed the first level of studies towards a diploma in theology.

Such are the facts of the matter regarding Novak as a pseudo-professor, deceptive doctor of theology, phoney priest, bogus bishop and spurious "successor of the apostles"—all this documented with his signature. From his signatures and the documents which others have received from him, we are convinced that we are dealing with not only a dismissed Catholic seminarian, an expelled Old Catholic deacon, but also with a scientific and ecclesiastical falsifier, whom the above-mentioned dismissed, and disobedient Franciscans of the province of Herzegovina have promoted to be their "bishop"! These sad events probably best describe how deep the disease of disobedience can go in the Church and concretely in the entire "Herzegovinian affair"!

According to the documents which we have obtained and Novak's statements, we hereby declare that all Novak's Masses are invalid and sacrilegious since he has no proof that he was validly ordained a priest, and that all his confirmations are also invalid and sacrilegious since he has no proof that he was validly ordained a bishop!

Conclusion. All of this can be summarised in a single word: TRAGEDY! This is a religious, moral, liturgical, sacramental, dogmatic, Catholic, "ecumenical" and especially a Franciscan tragedy! We appreciate the Communiqué given by the provincialate of the Franciscan province of Herzegovina of 23 May, in which the province firmly distances itself "from the actions of certain Franciscans who are already under sanctions by the generalate of the Franciscan Order and by the local ordinary. Neither the Franciscans of Herzegovina nor the Franciscan Province of Herzegovina, which is truly Catholic, stand by these actions..." (enclosure N. 9: copy of the Statement).

It is scandalous how some disobedient Franciscans have strayed from the principles, hierarchy and order of the Catholic Church, deceiving hundreds of candidates for confirmation, thousands of sponsors and parents and giving way to offence and sacrilege against the Holy Spirit. It is evident here that the use of reason has failed and moral idiocy has taken over. "If Gypsies can have their own bishop... then why can't a Franciscan be consecrated bishop?" Fra Bernard Maric asks (*Jutarnji list*, 19 May, 2001, 3). Is this the way to resolve the "Herzegovinian affair"? Is this, then, an attempt to separate from the Catholic Church through a validly ordained bishop who would not recognise the Holy See? Would such a disobedient or dismissed Franciscan be ordained a "bishop" by the dismissed Old Catholic deacon Srecko Novak, so that "the last fraud will be worse than the first" (Mt 27:64)?

We humbly pray that the Holy Trinity may keep us, guide us and consecrate us in our holy faith and our faithfulness to the Catholic Church.

Mostar, 28 May, 2001
Monsignor Luka Pavlović
Vicar General

59

29 MAY, 2001

Communiqué of the Bishops' Conference of Bosnia-Herzegovina

WE THE BISHOPS OF BOSNIA-HERZEGOVINA, MOTIvated by our responsibility to maintain unity in the Church and by our pastoral care for the good of souls, having gathered together for a special session in Mostar, wish to communicate to the Catholic faithful and the general public the following:

The appearance of a member of a non-Catholic community who recently held the rite of confirmation in three parishes of the diocese of Mostar-Duvno is an overt attempt to disintegrate the unity of the Roman Catholic Church in this country and to break its centuries-old bond of communion with the Apostolic See of St. Peter.

The priests dismissed from the Franciscan Order, as well as those who in disobedience to their religious and Church superiors invited a non-Catholic to preside at a Catholic rite, are directly acting against the holiness of the sacraments and the unity of the Church.

Those candidates who for whatever reason agreed to participate in these scandalous acts, through which Catholic Church unity is not strengthened but destroyed, did not receive the sacrament of Confirmation of the Catholic Church.

It seems that the aim and the method in which the abovementioned rite was conducted serve only to increase the difficulties which the Croatian people and the Catholic Church in Bosnia and Herzegovina have been exposed to recently.

Therefore, we wholeheartedly implore the Catholics of B-H, the priests, religious and all the faithful, especially those in the diocese of Mostar-Duvno, to not allow anyone to deceive or confuse them in the solid faith of their fathers, in their faithfulness to the Holy Father and the Holy See, as well as their unity with the local bishops. We invite everyone to pray to our heavenly Father and to Christ the Good Shepherd, so that all the faithful of the holy Church may receive the gift of the Holy Spirit, who is the only guarantee of the Church's unity of faith and her communion of love and peace.

Through the intercession of the Blessed Virgin Mary, Mother of the Church, we pray that all may receive an abundance of blessings and peace of the Holy Trinity!

Mostar, 29 May, 2001
✠ *Vinko Cardinal Puljic*, Archbishop of Vrhbosna (Sarajevo).
✠ *Franjo Komarica*, Bishop of Banja Luka.
✠ *Ratko Perić*, Bishop of Mostar-Duvno.
✠ *Pero Sudar*, Auxiliary Bishop of Vrhbosna (Sarajevo).

60

14 JUNE, 2001

Homily by Bishop Perić

Given in Medjugorje, in Which He Speaks of the Disobedience of the Local Franciscans Involving Invalid Confirmations and Attempted Invalid Priestly Ordinations

CHRIST, BE OUR JOY!
HOLY SPIRIT, GIVE US YOUR WISDOM!
Medjugorje, Solemnity of the Body and Blood of Christ, 14 June, 2001

TODAY THE CHURCH CELEBRATES THE SOLEMNITY of the Body and Blood of Christ. We sing in a Croatian Eucharistic song to Jesus: Christ, be our joy! Christ, be our happiness! Christ, be our life! Amongst these three great words: joy, happiness and life, we shall reflect on only one: happiness and its opposite.

Happiness. Christ, be our happiness! We don't ask Christ to be our lucky break, our chance opportunity, something totally unexpected. In Latin there are two meanings for happiness: *felicitas*—this is happiness which is earned, merited, for which one has worked towards and prayed hard for, and fortune—this is sheer luck, winning a lottery, finding a thousand deutschmarks on the street. Someone might be crying over that loss while you are rejoicing over your newly discovered fortune, which you should instead report to the police.

In our faith we are not talking about the fortune of chance events. Instead, we refer to the happiness which comes from an encounter (in Croatian sreca—*felicitas* comes from sresti—encounter) with a person, parents, brothers, sisters, with people you respect, love and to whom you owe a debt of gratitude. A true encounter is happiness. An encounter with God is the ultimate happiness and God has prepared that encounter for us. We owe Him our encounters and our happiness.

We also pray to Christ that He be our happiness and that we may encounter Him. Today we celebrate Him in his Sacred Body as our encounter and our happiness. We encounter Him every day in the Eucharist, in prayer and adoration. Let us pray for vocations in our local Church, so that He may choose new labourers according to the Father's plan. The harvest is great, yet the labourers are far too few (Lk 10:2).

In the Church there has always existed the practical rule that: "If you wish to be happy and if you want to make others happy, then don't personally ask for anything and don't refuse anything". Don't push your own candidacy forward and don't bury your talents! Others know about you.

Don't seek to become the Father Provincial! But if you are legitimately elected, then don't run away, but try your best to lead the province to happiness, not to adversity. Don't seek to become a bishop! Yet if you are legitimately nominated, stay faithful to the end in truth and justice and govern the diocese in unity of faith and love with the Holy Father the Pope.

If anyone is cheerful, let him sing praise (James 5:13). If anyone is happy, may he make others happy as well.

Misfortune. Maybe happiness can be better understood when one mentions misfortune: misfortunes at work, during travels, in marriage, in the sky, during the night, misfortunes as tragedies, an automobile accident or train crash, injury, loss, failure, death. There are various types of misfortunes, willed and accidental, all the way up to great Church misfortunes.

Many local and foreign journalists have asked me by phone or fax these last days: "What do you think of the so-called apparitions, which haven't stopped being a mass-media craze these last twenty years?" My response is that I think what I have always thought, and as the local ordinary of this diocese still hold to what I said from this holy place last year. I think and state that which the Catholic Church on the basis of competent and responsible investigations officially claims: taking into account all the events of the last twenty years, there hasn't been recognized any authentic and accepted supernatural apparition, nor has any supernatural message been recognised, nor has any supernatural revelation been acknowledged.

This is what I believe and what I publicly and clearly proclaim, so that there may be absolutely no doubt regarding the so-called apparitions. At the same time, I express my deep faith in the Blessed Virgin Mary, the humble and obedient servant of the Lord and her role in Christ's work of salvation according to the teachings of the Church.

Yet amongst all these curious questions, very few enquire about the local Church situation which is making many faithful unhappy in this diocese. The situation I'm speaking of is the inhuman, unchristian, irreligious and unpriestly disobedience that continues against the decisions of the highest Church authorities.

Had they asked me, I would have responded with a sorrowful heart that according to revealed facts that have not been repudiated by anyone so far with sound arguments, the disobedience that has been nurtured for years against the Holy See, the Franciscan OFM order and the local Church, has recently produced the bitter fruits of invalid and sacrilegious confessions, invalid confirmations and sacrilegious Masses.

Those Franciscan priests who in previous years took it upon themselves to confirm invalidly or invited others to celebrate "confirmation", have descended this year into such a depth of misfortune that they avoided the local ordinary and invited someone who not only is not a bishop nor priest, but who isn't even a Catholic to "confirm". This person stated: "Our aim is to make the Pope revoke the *Romanis Pontificibus* decree through these confirmations... the Franciscans and I believe in Mary's apparitions in Medjugorje".

Regarding celibacy he said: "When it is abolished, priests will be able to marry. This is what we want". Being a non-Catholic, he also said: "The impeccability of the Pope cannot regard dogmas" (statement, 23 May, 2001). He was probably referring to the Pope's infallibility in faith and morals. These are the beliefs of the person who was invited to three parishes of this diocese: Grude, Čapljina and Tepčići, to "confirm" 779 candidates illegitimately. What is at hand here are not only invalid confirmations and a sacrilege against the Holy Spirit but also invalid Masses, which this non-priest acted out before the faithful who were led astray by a hireling, like sheep without a pastor (Jn 10).

I would have responded with a sorrowful heart to questions on the local situation with first-hand testimony that last year some Franciscans approached an Old Catholic bishop in Switzerland and asked him to ordain a "secret bishop" (*Geheimbischof*) so that through the sacrament of holy orders they could ordain new priests and celebrate the sacrament of confirmation. The Old Catholic bishop obviously refused their request and ended the discussion (our question: 25 May, 2001, and his response 28 May, 2001). I have no reason not to believe the Old Catholic bishop from Switzerland, who acted in the current ecumenical spirit of non-proselytising. I have also informed the responsible authorities of the Church on this matter.

I would have responded with a sorrowful heart that I was recently officially informed that the Franciscan Order has dismissed another three members of the province of Herzegovina from the order due to their continuous disobedience, and that three others were suspended of their priestly faculties. I would also have mentioned that forty members of the province refused to sign the statement regarding obedience, which was agreed upon by the general of the Franciscan Order, the local bishop and authorised by the Holy See.

Yet with gratitude I also mention that two-thirds of the Franciscan Fathers signed the statement and thereby expressed their desire to maintain a true spirit of ecclesiastical obedience. I will be counting on them and their participation in the pastoral work within the diocese. I further stress that the Franciscans currently assigned to this parish of Medjugorje have been presented by the provincialate and legitimately nominated by the chancery office of Mostar.

The latter pleases us greatly, whereas the former, the attempt to break Catholic unity on the part of some in the areas of faith, cult and discipline, hurts to the bottom of the heart. I am bringing this out in the context of this celebration of the sacrament of confirmation with my appeal to all in the diocese, in the country and the world, accompanied by a heartfelt prayer that the Holy Trinity save us from similar misfortunes and unfortunate Church tragedies.

Therefore, I pray for you today, dear candidates for confirmation, and I invite you after having validly received the sacrament of confirmation, to be true witnesses of Catholic unity and faith, authentic witnesses of the Holy Spirit and His seven gifts, from wisdom to holy fear of God, witnesses for Jesus Christ who has revealed the Father to us.

Christ, be our joy! Holy Spirit, send forth your gifts: "love, joy, peace, patience, kindness, goodness, faithfulness, gentleness, self-control" (Gal 5:22–23).

✠ *Ratko Perić*
Bishop of Mostar-Duvno

10 OCTOBER, 2001

Bosnia-Herzegovina Cardinal Critical of Medjugorje Franciscans

Catholic World News Service, Reference 16570

IN AN EXTREMELY IMPORTANT DEVELOPMENT the highest-ranking Church official in Bosnia-Herzegovina, Cardinal Vinko Puljic (Archbishop of Vrhbosna, Sarajevo), has commented on aspects of the Medjugorje phenomenon in the presence of the Holy Father, at the current Synod of Bishops in Rome. This is what he said:

> As pertains to the Church in Bosnia-Herzegovina, its shepherds commit themselves, together with their priests, consecrated persons and faithful laity, to make their witness become the leaven of society and to make it possible to transmit the light of the Gospel into the economic, social and political realities of their nation.
>
> While most of the consecrated persons operating on the territory of the local ecclesial districts remain faithful to the charism of their institutes and commit themselves without reservation to the promotion of apostolic works, for the good of the Church and civic society; unfortunately, certain members of the Franciscan Order of Friars Minor and those expelled try to impose their own points of view in the individual dioceses, substituting the authentic charisms of their institute with pseudo-charisms, a serious threat for the Church and for her organizational and doctrinal unity.
>
> Suffice it to recall the sad events last summer when the protagonists of the aforementioned order and a

self-declared bishop: an old-style Catholic deacon expelled from his community, or a systematic disobedience to the same religious persons who for years have been in the diocese of Mostar-Duvno.

62

MOSTAR, 2001

Final Chapter of the Book Ogledalo Pravde ("Mirror of Justice"), by Bishop Perić

PP. 313-314

CONCLUSION: THE CHURCH'S POSITION

According to an official communiqué dated 10 April, 1991, composed on the basis of the thorough and comprehensive work of the commissions of experts, the bishops[1] did not find a single indication or sign that might have led them to say that the phenomena in Medjugorje are of supernatural origin.

Nor has anything of significance since happened with regard to the "apparitions" and "messages" so as to lead to a reconsideration. It follows that those who preach in our churches from the very altars about these phenomena, as if they were recognized and authentic apparitions and messages, are not acting in accordance with the Church's position.

An interpretation of the "pilgrimage"

The Secretary of the Congregation for the Propagation of the Faith twice (in 1996 and 1997) cited the episcopal pronouncement of 1991 and concluded:

> From what has very rightly been said about the matter, it follows that official pilgrimages to Medjugorje, taken to be a place of authentic Marian apparitions, may not be organised whether at parish or diocesan level, for to do so would be in conflict with the solemn pronouncement of the bishops of the former Yugoslavia in their previously mentioned communiqué.

---

1 *Sc.* of the former Yugoslavia

Final Chapter of the Book Ogledalo Pravde ("Mirror of Justice")   215

On 26 June, 1998, the selfsame secretary of the congregation expressed an opinion to the like effect, saying that "unofficial pilgrimages" to Medjugorje were permitted only on condition that they were not to be deemed to amount to recognition of the authenticity of the "apparitions," from which it follows that even "unofficial pilgrimages" are not permitted if they involve the recognition of the authenticity of the "apparitions".

Accordingly, those who come to Medjugorje with the intention of recognizing the so-called apparitions and "messages" are not working in harmony with the Church's position. There is no apparent need for the faithful to come to Medjugorje from the four corners of the earth to say the Rosary, make their confessions or receive communion, when they may do all these things religiously in their own parishes, where Our Lord Jesus Christ is present in the sacrament of the altar, and Our Lady is always ready to offer a mother's care.

From disobedience to schism

For many years the diocese of Mostar and Duvno has been afflicted by the incomprehensible disobedience of a small number of members of the Franciscan province of Herzegovina with regard to handing over a number of parishes "to the free disposition of the [diocesan] bishop", in accordance with a papal decree of 1975.

In 1997 the general administration of the OFM took the most serious measures as a result of such disobedience, including the expulsion of disobedient members from the order. Eight members have been expelled from the Franciscan Order in this way. The Holy See has confirmed their expulsions. Some of them have occupied a number of parishes, in which, even though they have been punished by suspension *a divinis*, they illicitly and sacrilegiously act as clerics, hearing invalid confessions, officiating at invalid weddings, and administering invalid confirmations.

Bishops and priests who come to Medjugorje from all over the world and at the request of parishioners or other moving spirits make pronouncements about the "apparitions" and "messages" of Medjugorje as though they were authentic, do not help order, peace and the necessary unity of this diocese and the Church by their presence or by their pronouncements.

A serious sin against the unity of the Church was committed on 5 October, 1997, when some purported bishop, telling neither his name nor whence he came, but passing through Medjugorje at the request of the disobedient Franciscans, confirmed more than four hundred children in the neighbouring parish of Čapljina, against the express provisions of canon law. According to information received later, the officiating cleric was a Herzegovinian Franciscan who had blasphemously represented himself as a bishop. In 2001 he was expelled from the Franciscan Order.

An even worse scandal occurred last year in June 2001, when some disobedient elements invited an Old Catholic deacon, who falsely represented himself to be a bishop, announcing that he accepted the "apparitions" of Medjugorje, and who officiated at the invalid confirmations of hundreds of candidates for confirmation in three parishes.

Commendation

We humbly commend the ecclesiastical unity of this diocese to the Immaculate Virgin who conceived by the power of the Holy Ghost and gave birth to the Light of the World, Jesus Christ, the Lord of Righteousness (1 John 2:1). We accordingly turn to her, calling upon her as we do in her litany: "Mirror of truth, pray for us!"

✠ *Ratko Perić*, Bishop

63

5 JULY, 2002

Catholic Herald *Report*

This report by Simon Caldwell is of considerable significance, being the first article critical of the Medjugorje phenomenon to appear in a mainstream Catholic weekly newspaper in Britain. It has been slightly abbreviated.

ON TUESDAY LAST WEEK, THE MADONNA OF MEDjugorje came of age. The 21st anniversary of the first reported apparition on a hillside in Herzegovina was marked in this country by a statement to the Catholic press from the Medjugorje Apostolate of England and Wales (formerly the Medjugorje Network). In the statement, the organisation boasted that worldwide interest in the "apparitions" has been mounting every year and that now "millions of people from all five continents make their private pilgrimages to this shrine, including many cardinals, bishops, priests and nuns".

Indeed, it is true that many positive spiritual "fruits" have been linked to the claims of apparitions; almost every Catholic knows someone who claims their lives have been changed by a visit to the shrine. Some pilgrims come back with stories about spinning suns, and rosaries turning to gold; others undergo conversions that are sincere and lasting, and some become vigorous promoters of Our Lady Queen of Peace, known to devotees as the *"Gospa"*, and her mission to bring about world peace through reconciliation and prayer. So, it is ironic that Medjugorje has become one of the biggest threats to the unity of the Catholic Church today.

What many devout pilgrims to Medjugorje may not realise is that the Church does not want them to go there at all. The Congregation for the Doctrine of the Faith (CDF) has forbidden all public pilgrimages to the shrine since 1995. Bishop Ratko

Perić of Mostar, who, as local ordinary, is the only man alive to whom the Church has given authority to determine the veracity of the "apparitions", is convinced they are fraudulent; so was his predecessor, the late Bishop Pavao Žanić, so is the ex-Yugoslavian bishops' conference, so are the members of three official commissions, each of which ruled negatively, and so are all the Mostar diocesan clergy and most of the Franciscans there.

There will be one final investigation, conducted by Rome, and it will conclude only when either the reports of the "apparitions" end or the last of the seers dies, since Church norms warn that errors might arise if the study of the "fruits" are not preceded by the study of the "events".[1] But a definitive ruling is unlikely to come in the near future because three of the original six visionaries are saying the *Gospa* promised them apparitions for life, and a second generation of seers has also emerged.

This is convenient for the visionaries since they derive income from their status as seers. They have courted and won celebrity status and some have since toured the world with the *Gospa*, whom they can summon on demand anywhere. She has an apparent flexibility that has surprised even some of her most ardent devotees. On one trip to England, the seer Ivan Dragicević was said to have postponed a scheduled apparition so he could watch a soccer match instead, promising that Our Lady would appear after the final whistle. Ivan, who is married to former Miss Massachusetts beauty queen Laureen Murphy, was once touted by U. S. tour operator Peter Miller as able to offer a personal introduction to the Madonna for just $500.

He owns a BMW and a Mercedes as well as a German-style mansion on the local millionaires' row. It stands opposite that which belongs to fellow seer Mirjana Dragicević, who has converted part of her home into a guesthouse for pilgrims, including "apparitions" as part of the deal. All of the seers are

---

[1] This is not correct since the entire question of Medjugorje is in the hands of the four bishops of Herzegovina, not one of whom accepts the authenticity of the alleged apparitions. Rome is not involved in the matter in any way.

married and all but one of them own hotels in Medjugorje, in stark contrast to, say, Lucia Dos Santos and Saint Bernadette Soubirous, who went on to lead less worldly lives after they received apparitions at Fatima and Lourdes.

It was the belief of the late Bishop Žanić that the whole thing began as a joke, and at first that's how it appears. The children would laugh hysterically during the *Gospa*'s early appearances, not least when Jakov Colo asked if his football team, Dynamo Zagreb, would win the championship. After an initial week of visions, the children said the *Gospa* would appear for "just three more days", that the visions would end by 4 July 1981. But, since then, she has spoken on an additional thirty thousand occasions, has promised the seers ten secrets each, promised great signs from heaven that never materialised and, contrary to the teachings of the Church over two millennia, has declared "all religions are equal before God". She became the number one apologist for a group of disobedient Herzegovinian Franciscans only when Father Jozo Zovko, the parish priest at St James Church, Medjugorje, where the "apparitions" were said to be appearing, established himself as the children's "spiritual adviser". But, even then, she would continue to drop the occasional gaffe, describing, for instance, *The Poem of the Man God*, a book by Maria Valtorta, as "good reading" (Cardinal Joseph Ratzinger, the Prefect of the CDF, had said it was a "heap of pseudo-religiosity").

What really swayed the local bishops against the *Gospa*, however, was her partisan approach to "the Herzegovina question". This is the Vatican's term for a *de facto* schism involving a large minority of Herzegovinian Franciscan friars who not only refuse to obey their bishop but also defy the Father General of their order and Rome itself.

In the 1980s two such friars, Father Ivica Vego and Ivan Prusina, were expelled from their order for disobedience by a Vatican tribunal, acting on the advice of Bishop Žanić and the Franciscan Father General in Rome, but they continued to celebrate the sacraments. Thirteen times the *Gospa* told the seer, Vicka Ivanković, that the bishop was wrong and her "saints" were innocent, even threatening him with God's "justice" unless he reversed their expulsion (Father Vego, for the record, soon showed just how saintly he was by impregnating a Franciscan nun).

When Bishop Žanić later investigated the "apparitions", he should have had the co-operation of the Franciscans. Instead, they publicly slandered him, calling him a "wolf", "Satan" and a "hypocrite". It was hardly a surprise, then, that Bishop Žanić soon concluded that the six children were lying, and publicly accused Father Zovko and his collaborator, Father Tomislav Vlašić, of putting words into the mouth of Our Lady. Indeed, he was not only concerned about the spiritual well-being of his people but also about their corporal welfare. In 1985 he wrote to Father René Laurentin, a chief promoter of the visions, complaining that "a fierce frenzy has taken hold of many of the faithful who were good until now; they have become excessive and peculiar penitents... one can look forward to a religious war here...."

Pope Pius XII first moved against the friars by appointing a secular rather than a local Franciscan bishop to the See of Mostar in 1942. The rebellion that ensued came to a head in 1975 when Pope Paul VI issued the decree *Romanus Pontificibus*, which gave the friars a deadline of a year to hand over contested parishes. Predictably, they refused.

Promoters of Medjugorje insist that the Herzegovina question and the "apparitions" are not connected. The diocese of Mostar insists they are intimately linked. Bishop Žanić said the *Gospa* was used to justify the disobedience of the friars, while Don Ante Luburic, chancellor of the diocese, in 1997 went as far as to describe Medjugorje as a place of "religious disorder, disobedience and anti-ecclesiastical activity".

Sadly, this situation has been exacerbated by the trusting support for the friars of "millions of people from all five continents", for the Church has made little progress on the Herzegovina question since 1941. During the Bosnian War... an estimated £10 million was raised in the West for war orphans under the banner of the Queen of Peace. But all there has ever been to show for the money is a 40-place crèche in Medjugorje for the children of working mothers. Few, not least the bishop of Mostar, have a clue where the rest of the money went, but some sources suggest that about seventy per cent ended up in the hands of warlords and organised criminals. This is not fanciful: in the mid-1990s, the Charity Commission froze the assets of Britain's Medjugorje Appeal when it was found to be buying handcuffs for the HVO Croatian militia.

The Yugoslavian bishops, unanimous in their rejection of the *Gospa*, raised the Herzegovina question in the presence of the Pope at last year's Synod of Bishops in Rome when Cardinal Vinko Puljic of Sarajevo warned of the serious threat posed to the unity of the entire Catholic Church as a result of the disobedient monks "serving in Medjugorje who impose their own points of view with the aid of pseudo-charisms".

The Pope, for his part, has been silent on Medjugorje, leaving the matter to the discretion of the local bishops. Indeed, with some three hundred reported cases of private revelations going on in the world at any one time, he would have little time to do anything else if he were to investigate and rule on each one personally.

Nevertheless, Medjugorje promoters continuously insist the Pope has privately signalled his approval of the "apparitions" and list a number of comments he has supposedly made in their favour, perhaps most famously, "Let the people go to Medjugorje if they convert, pray, confess, do penance". An American Catholic once asked Archbishop Pio Laghi, then papal nuncio to the United States, if there was any truth in the remarks, and he received a reply that read: "Although there have been made observations about Medjugorje attributed to the Holy Father or other officials of the Holy See, none of these have been acknowledged as authentic."

Perhaps the most telling indication of all was the Pope's visit to Bosnia in April 1997, when he not only declined to visit Medjugorje (he visited the Muslim community of Mostar just fifteen miles away) but also failed to mention the disputed shrine even once.

In short, all the arguments are stacked against the possibility that the Medjugorje "apparitions" could be authentic. The most compelling argument in their favour remains the so-called "fruits"—the converted lives, the increase in piety and devotion, the recovery of lost faith, and so on.

On this subject, Bishop Perić, not surprisingly, has an opinion. "The fruits, so often mentioned, do not prove that they flow from apparitions or supernatural revelations of Our Lady," he said. "But in the measure that they are authentically Christian, they may be interpreted as a product of the normal work of divine grace, by faith in God, by the intercession of the Virgin Mary, Mother of Christ, and by the Sacraments of the Catholic Church. And this is to say nothing of the negative fruits."

According to Church teaching, fruits of authentic supernatural interventions are first born in those who receive them, yet the two men closest to the children from the outset do not appear to have been converted in the proper sense.

Father Vlašić, who fathered a child by a nun in a mixed-sex convent in Zagreb in the 1970s, now lives in Italy, where, funnily enough, he's trying for the second time to set up a mixed religious community. Father Zovko, on the other hand, is one of sixteen Herzegovinian friars either suspended by Bishop Perić, or expelled from the Franciscan order by the Father General, Giacomo Bini, a man who for the last eight years has also threatened to suspend the entire Herzegovina province. Like his rebellious confreres, Zovko ignores the penalties of the bishop, not only continuing to celebrate Mass and hear confessions, though he has no faculties to do so, but building, without the bishop's permission, a huge convent in Široki Brijeg, near Mostar, the source of funding of which remains a mystery. Last year, Bishop Perić wrote to each of the one hundred and twenty friars to ask for their obedience, and about a third refused to give it. Earlier in the year, the rebels used a bogus archbishop, Srecko Franjo Novak, an expelled seminarian, to confirm seven hundred children in three churches. The confirmations, of course, were invalid and caused a great deal of anxiety to loyal clergy and to the bishop.

To many, Medjugorje is not so much about apparitions of the Blessed Virgin Mary but of disobedience to the legitimate authority of the Church: about friars who defy their superiors, and Catholics from overseas who ignore the directions of the Church not to go on pilgrimage there. Most seriously of all, it is a manifestation of the disobedience of the cardinals and bishops who go there too: by wilfully ignoring the wishes of the local ordinary these men are offending against the principle of collegiality, as defined in section 23 of *Lumen Gentium*.

They are also helping to perpetuate what could be one of the most subversive hoaxes in the history of the Catholic Church.

12 JULY, 2002

Catholic Herald:
A Defence of Medjugorje

Simon Caldwell's article, in a journal that is sold in most Catholic parishes in England and Wales, provoked outrage among devotees of Medjugorje. The letter that follows was written by Monsignor George Tutto, a longstanding believer in the authenticity of the alleged apparitions.

SIR:

The devotees of Our Lady of Medjugorje are used to the rather un-Christian attacks by a vociferous group of antagonists of Medjugorje, but the feature article by Simon Caldwell (July 5) surpasses them all, unworthy of your well-respected paper.

The article is full of untruths and distortions and I cannot go into all. I mention only two facts, which are enough to render the article a malicious attempt to hurt and confuse many believers. The first untruth in the article is this: "What many devout pilgrims to Medjugorje may not realise is that the Church does not want them to go there at all. The Congregation for the Doctrine of the Faith has forbidden all public pilgrimages to the shrine since 1995."

Against this nonsense I quote a few passages from the letter of the Secretary of the above Congregation (CDF), Archbishop Tarcisio Bertone, to Bishop Gilbert Aubry of Saint Denis de la Réunion on 26th May, 1998:

"The main thing I would like to point out is that the Holy See does not ordinarily take a position on its own regarding supposed supernatural phenomena as a court of first instance. As for the credibility of the 'apparitions' in question, this dicastery respects what was decided by the bishops of the former Yugoslavia, in the Declaration of Zadar, 10 April, 1991:

"On this basis of the investigations so far, it cannot be affirmed that one is dealing with supernatural apparitions and revelations. Since the division of Yugoslavia into different independent nations it would now pertain to the members of the Episcopal Conference of Bosnia-Herzegovina to eventually reopen the examination of this case, and to make any new pronouncements that might be called for.

"What Bishop Perić said in his letter to the Secretary General of *Famille Chrétienne*, declaring: 'My conviction and my position is not only *Non constat de supernaturalitate*, but likewise, *constat de non-supernaturalitate* of the apparitions or revelations in Medjugorje', should be considered as the expression of the personal conviction of the Bishop of Mostar, which he has the right to express as ordinary of the place, but which is and remains his personal opinion.

"Finally, as regards pilgrimages to Medjugorje, which are conducted privately, this congregation points out that they are permitted on condition that they are not regarded as an authentification of events still taking place and which still call for an examination by the Church."

The second untruth concerns the two suspended friars by Bishop Žanić: "In the 1980s two such friars, Fathers Ivica Vego and Ivan Prusina, were expelled from their order for disobedience by a Vatican tribunal, acting on the advice of Bishop Žanić...." Just the opposite is the truth.

Bishop Žanić demanded on the 17 January, 1983, that the friars should be reduced to laity status. Father Vego, I gather, got married later on, but the case of Father Prusina was taken up by the supreme tribunal of the Holy See, the *Signatura Apostolica*. After many years of investigation, the tribunal arrived at its decision on 27 March, 1993. In document 17907/86 CA, it is stated that Father Ivan Prusina's expulsion from the order and Bishop Žanić's demand to declare Prusina *ad statem laicalem* was both wrong and illegal. The Catholic Press failed to take note of this. But I blame partly also the Roman authorities. When I wrote a letter to the Secretary of the tribunal, Bishop Zenon Grocholewski, on 1 June, 1995, asking for a copy of the tribunal's sentence, the Bishop expressed his regret for being unable to accede to my request, but I was forbidden to publish the contents of his letter. I received information regarding Father Prusina from other sources.[1]

In view of the above facts, it is beyond my comprehension that Mr. Caldwell could write such critical words against cardinals and bishops who went to Medjugorje to pray there.

"Most seriously of all, it is a manifestation of the disobedience of the cardinals and bishops who go to Medjugorje too: by wilfully ignoring the wishes of the local ordinary these men are offending against the principle of collegiality, as defined in section 23 of *Lumen Gentium*".

I hope and pray that the readers of your paper will ignore this article with contempt.

Yours faithfully,
GEORGE TUTTO,
Hungarian Roman Catholic Chaplaincy of Our Lady,
London, W.3.

* * * * *

A SCANDALOUS ALLEGATION

A letter from Mr. Bernard Ellis published in the same issue of the *Catholic Herald* contained the following scandalous allegation.

> Simon Caldwell's article about Medjugorje is full of inaccuracies but does contain one crucial truth, namely that "almost every Catholic knows someone who claims their lives have been changed by a visit to the shrine" and "others undergo conversions that are sincere and lasting". As Bishop Perić told Father John Chisholm, a theologian well respected by the Vatican, that he personally did not believe in the apparitions

---

1 As explained in note 39 the expulsion was overturned on a technicality. The facts that prompted it have not been disputed. In the case of Vego the annulment is irrelevant as he has married his mistress and is hence no longer a Franciscan. (See Bishop Ratko Perić, *Ogledalo Pravde*, 64.) Prusina now lives in Germany and is not permitted to exercise his priesthood in Herzegovina.

at Lourdes and Fatima, it is hardly surprising that he refuses to attribute these fruits to a supernatural visitation in Medjugorje.

I contacted Bishop Perić immediately upon reading this letter and he assured me that the allegation was false. The claim that Father Chisholm is "a theologian well respected by the Vatican" is simply a gratuitous claim by Mr. Ellis. I obtained the address of this priest, a private home and not an ecclesiastical establishment, and wrote to him on 15 July, 2002, to ask whether he had made the statement that Mr. Ellis had attributed to him. My letter included the following:

> You may be aware of the fact that you were quoted in the *Catholic Herald* of 12 July as stating that Bishop Perić had told you that he did not believe in the apparitions at Lourdes and Fatima. I immediately telephoned Bishop Perić, with whom I am in regular contact, and he denied emphatically that he had ever made any such statement to anyone. He confirmed this by fax and tells me that although you spent some time with his secretary, he does not recollect granting you an interview.

Father Chisholm did not reply.

19 JULY, 2002

Catholic Herald: *My Reply to Monsignor Tutto*

SIR:

Having read the excellent article on Medjugorje by Simon Caldwell, I was not surprised at the negative and emotional response that it evoked among some of your readers. Medjugorje is a topic upon which I can write with some authority, for since 1987, with the help of my Croatian wife, I have worked closely with the two bishops of Mostar who have occupied that see since the alleged apparitions began in 1981. My wife has translated many of the episcopal statements and other official documents that I have published in a book, which has been through five updated editions, and will appear in a considerably updated sixth edition in the spring of 2003.[1] In a letter concerning my book the present bishop of Mostar, Monsignor Perić, was kind enough to remark: "You write with Catholic conviction and Christian frankness.... In your book you base yourself upon the official documents and teaching of the Church. There are far too many inaccurate versions of events spread throughout the world, above all through the efforts and the agency of those in the service of the so-called apparitions at Medjugorje."

The reaction of Monsignor George Tutto is typical of those who have been deluded into accepting what may be the greatest confidence trick since World War II. Those who point out the facts are always unchristian, vociferous, malicious, guilty of untruths and distortions. In stating that public pilgrimages

---

[1] I was, alas, unable to have the new edition ready for publication until the summer of 2004. [Note: Mr. Davies died on 25th September, 2004 just as he had finished his final draft]

to Medjugorje are forbidden Mr. Caldwell is not lying, and he is not guilty of "a malicious attempt to hurt and confuse many believers", nor is he talking "nonsense" when he states that "the Congregation for the Doctrine of the Faith has forbidden all public pilgrimages to the shrine since 1995." On 23 May, 1985, Monsignor Bovone, then Secretary of the Congregation for the Doctrine of the Faith, wrote to Monsignor Caporello, Secretary of the Italian Episcopal Conference, stating that it should "discourage publicly the organisation of pilgrimages to Medjugorje". On 23 March, 1996, and then in June, 1996, Monsignor Bertone, Secretary of the Congregation for the Doctrine of the Faith, informed two French bishops that the cult of Medjugorje "is not authorised". Monsignor Tutto is correct in stating that Monsignor Bertone informed Bishop Aubry, Bishop of Saint-Denis-de-la-Réunion, that private pilgrimages were permitted on condition that they were "not considered as an authentication of events in course which still necessitate an examination by the Church." Could Monsignor Tutto deny that the pilgrimages to Medjugorje advertised in the Catholic press are organised on the presumption that the events that have taken place there "are of a supernatural origin", and are therefore forbidden?

In a statement made on behalf of the entire French episcopal conference, a somewhat more authoritative source than the opinion of Monsignor Tutto, printed in *La Documentation Catholique* of 7 January, 2000, Monsignor Henri Brincard concludes by stating: "I do not see how I can go to Medjugorje without giving my support, by the very fact of having come there, to events the discernment and assessment of which rest henceforth with the Episcopal Conference of Bosnia-Herzegovina. Such support would fly in the face of the traditional teaching of the Church, recalled in *Lumen Gentium*, and applicable to all the successors of the Apostles."

This is a complete justification of the position taken by Simon Caldwell.

As regards the alleged "second untruth" by Mr. Caldwell, the fact that Father Prusina's expulsion from the Franciscan Order had been revoked, does not alter the fact that the expulsion of Father Ivica Vego, who made a nun pregnant, was not. The self-styled seers informed Bishop Žanić on thirteen occasions that the Blessed Virgin had told them that Father Vego was innocent. Let me quote from the diary of Vicka, a diary which on frequent occasions she insisted did not exist, but of which I have a photocopy:

> **Saturday, 3 January, 1982.** "All we seers together asked the Madonna about Father Ivica Vego. The Madonna replied: 'Ivica is not to blame. If he is expelled from the Franciscan Order, let him remain steadfast. Every day I say: 'Peace, peace', but there is ever more strife. Let him remain; Ivica is not at fault. She (i.e., the Madonna) repeated this three times. We all heard it, and we told him (Father Vego). 'The bishop is not maintaining order and that is why he is to blame. He will not be bishop for ever. I will show justice in the (heavenly) kingdom.'"

I urge readers of the *Catholic Herald* to take careful note of this. Our Lady is alleged to have stated thirteen times that this scandalously immoral Franciscan was in no way to blame, and that the guilty party was Bishop Žanić, who remarked correctly that this fact alone should convince anyone "well instructed in the faith to come to the conclusion that the 'apparitions' are not of the supernatural."

What explanation would Monsignor Tutto give for the rejection of the authenticity of the alleged apparitions at Medjugorje not simply by Bishop Žanić and Bishop Perić but also by every current member of the hierarchy of the former Yugoslavia? Are they inspired by malice? Is this a conspiracy? Are they possessed by Satan?

If Monsignor Tutto wishes to challenge me I would have no problem in providing him with more examples of blatant untruths uttered by the self-styled seers. I cannot recollect a single instance of lying on the part of St. Bernadette or the children of Fatima.

I was so shocked at the claim by Mr. Bernard Ellis that Bishop Perić had stated "that he personally did not believe in the apparitions at Lourdes and Fatima" that I telephoned him at once, and he denied with indignation that he had ever made such a statement. He confirmed this in a fax dated 12 July in which he stated, "Never in my life did I say to anybody that I do not believe in Lourdes or Fatima." It appears that there are no lengths to which devotees of Medjugorje will not go to denigrate this erudite and profoundly Marian successor of the Apostles. In his fax, Bishop Perić stressed that: "The three canonical commissions which were engaged in examining the Medjugorje phenomena came to the conclusion that there has been no sign, no message, and no miracle, by which it could be concluded that this was a case of supernatural apparitions and messages. That is why pilgrimages to Medjugorje are not permitted if they attribute a supernatural character to the events that have taken place there. This remains true to this day."

Perhaps Monsignor Tutto and Mr. Ellis could explain why we should accept their personal opinions rather than the carefully evaluated statements of the three commissions. The investigation into the authenticity of the alleged apparitions has been placed by the Congregation for the Doctrine of the Faith in the hands of the bishops of Herzegovina, who all agree with Bishop Žanić and Bishop Perić that nothing supernatural has occurred or is occurring at Medjugorje. To the best of my knowledge, no alleged apparition has ever been deemed worthy of credence by the Church without first obtaining the approval of the diocesan bishop. No such approval will ever be forthcoming in the case of Medjugorje. What is taking place there is a calculated and cynical financial fraud.

Yours faithfully,
Michael Davies

66

26 JULY, 2002

Catholic Herald *Editorial: The Mixed Fruits of Medjugorje*

The following editorial is of even greater significance than the report by Simon Caldwell, as it commits this newspaper to the position that there is no supernatural basis to the events in Medjugorje.

IT WAS NEVER GOING TO BE EASY FOR THIS NEWSpaper to come to an editorial conclusion on the subject of Medjugorje. We have received an almost unprecedented response both to Simon Caldwell's original article (which concluded that the Medjugorje phenomenon is fraudulent and encourages disobedience to legitimate ecclesial authority) and to Paul Burnell's wholehearted defence of the shrine and its effect on the lives of many who have gone there on pilgrimage.

It is these "fruits" of the Medjugorje experience which to its defenders are the ultimate sign of its authenticity; this has emerged from letter after letter, often in very moving personal testimonies. We have no doubt that the journey to Medjugorje, often in the company of good holy priests, in search of Our Lady, has often been the occasion of a deepening of the spiritual life of those involved. That is absolutely clear, and has to be respected.

The question is whether or not these "fruits" constitute evidence for the truthfulness of the visionaries of Medjugorje. For, it has to be said, firstly, that good fruits often occur even in the midst of evil, for God is never closer to those who love Him than where there is spiritual danger. We have to ask, too, the painful question of whether there are bad fruits as well as good. The French bishops concluded that this is indeed the case: "The truth", they declared in January, 2000, "obliges us to say that [evil fruits] exist... the calling into question, even to the point of defamation, of the local ordinary as well as the disobedience with regard to his legitimate authority; the exacerbation of the 'Herzegovina question' following the words attributed to the *Gospa*, words in favour of the Franciscans and against the bishop".[1]

The French bishops' statement was a response to the question, "Is there an authorised and official position of the Church concerning the events in Medjugorje?" They quote the Congregation for the Doctrine of the Faith on the norms relative to the discernment of private revelations: "It belongs in the first place (pre-eminently) to the local ordinary to investigate and to intervene".

In the case of Medjugorje the only official ruling to date has been that of successive bishops of Mostar and it reads as follows: "It is... forbidden to claim or to declare in churches and religious communities that Our Lady appeared or will yet appear in Medjugorje." The late Bishop Pavao Žanić had studied the "events" and had concluded that the visionaries were lying and that they were being manipulated by Franciscan friars who were disobedient to legitimate authority. The ex-Yugoslavian Bishops' Conference in 1990 made a provisional reserved judgement in support of him, and the CDF expressed solidarity through pastoral directives which forbade even private pilgrimages to the shrine *if they were motivated by a conviction that the events there were of supernatural origin*. (Though one might ask why one would go there if one were not so convinced.)

Bishop Žanić himself said that "if all the ugly things could be made public, then surely the answer would be clearly negative to everyone". There is the case of Father Ivica Vego, a friar suspended by Rome but who, according to the bishop, "continued to celebrate Mass, distribute the sacraments and pass time with his mistress", a nun who later became pregnant.

---

[1] Bishop Žanić, *Posizione*, 3–4, 9–10, and *passim*.

There are the *Gospa*'s theologically untenable statements, such as "all religions are equal before God", reported by Mirjana Dragicević on 1 October, 1981, in a tape-recorded interview with Bishop Žanić.

The authenticity of this particular statement is beyond question. Nevertheless, defenders of Medjugorje consistently deny that it was ever uttered, or give significantly different more defensible versions of it. One apologist indicated to the *Catholic Herald* last week that the words Mirjana actually attributed to Our Lady were "all religions are not equal before God but all men are". But that is not what Mirjana said to Bishop Žanić.

Such rewriting or adjustments of the record are by no means unique. In most cases, perhaps, they are the result of innocent wishful thinking rather than conscious dishonesty. But the record, nevertheless, is habitually misrepresented. One writer last week said that "Cardinal Vinko Puljic [Archbishop of Sarajevo] made no mention of Medjugorje at the Synod of Bishops in Rome 2001", the implication being that he was silent on the issue. But he was not. This is what he said: "Certain members of the Order of Franciscan Friars Minor and those expelled try to impose their own points of view in the individual dioceses by substituting the authentic charisms of their institute with pseudo-charisms which pose a serious threat for the Church and for her organisational and doctrinal unity." Cardinal Puljic was alluding to the Herzegovina question and to the *Gospa*, which the local bishops see as having become inseparably linked. An attempt in a letter published (to our regret) in our previous week's issue, which claimed that the current Bishop of Mostar does not even believe that Our Lady appeared in either Lourdes or Fatima, was indignantly scotched by the bishop himself. Many other denials or assertions have been made — often these are claims of the support of prominent Churchmen — which tend to evaporate in the light of day; the most obvious example is the frequently made claim that the Pope himself is a secret supporter, but according to Cardinal Pio Laghi no such claim has been authenticated.

What we do know about the Pope is that he believes that "within the Church community the multiplication of supposed apparitions or visions is sowing confusion", and it is this precisely, this confusion which is one of the most dangerous fruits of Medjugorje. In an age in which the disobedience of Catholics to the authority of the Church in matters of faith and morals is proving so demonically destructive, the example of the visionaries themselves is purely disastrous. As the French bishops put it, "It is opportune to ask ourselves if the events of Medjugorje have produced good fruits if the visionaries who, at least during the duration of the 'apparitions' must by their lives be the first witnesses of the grace from which they say they benefit. From there it follows that we ask ourselves the following questions: 'Have they obeyed the bishop of Mostar? Have they respected him?'"

We, too, must ask questions which flow from these. Is not obedience the first mark which distinguishes—has always distinguished—the lives of those who have been touched by the Mother of God? And is it conceivable that Our Lady would appear in order to encourage disobedience among the faithful to their bishop? *Has she ever done so?* They are surely questions to which defenders of the visionaries of Medjugorje need to give grave and prayerful attention.

67

24 AUGUST, 2002

A Bogus Papal Blessing

THE LENGTHS TO WHICH PROPONENTS OF MEDjugorje will go to deceive faithful Catholics into believing that Pope John Paul II believes in the authenticity was made clear on 24 August, 2002, in a report in the Zagreb daily newspaper, *Vercernji List*. It was reproduced in the Medjugorje propaganda journal *Glas Mira Medjugorje—The Medjugorje Voice of Peace*, a copy of which Bishop Perić sent to me. The report was immediately circulated throughout the world via Medjugorje websites. A typical example is that of Denis and Cathy Nolan of the Children of Medjugorje, South Bend, Indiana.[1] Their report was as follows:

> SOUTH BEND, IN—An unexpected event for Father Jozo Zovko broke out in the Croatian media! We want to share with you what was reported last Saturday evening, 24 August, 2002, in the Zagreb daily newspaper, *The Vercernji List*. (note the attached scan of the newspaper article). The headline states, "A surprising gesture from the Vatican. The Pope thanks Father Jozo for Medjugorje!"
>
> Father Jozo Zovko is a member of the Hercegovinian Franciscan Province. As a witness to the Medjugorje apparitions, he has become one of the best-known priests in the world. Many tribes have made him their chief and he is connected with many miraculous healings. According to a poll conducted by *The Daily Catholic*, Father Jozo has been elected among the 29 Catholics of the century." (J. P.)

---

1 P. O. Box 1110, Notre Dame, IN 46556 (USA). Email: dnolan@childrenofmedjugorje.com

A Bogus Papal Blessing

The original text in Italian of the Pope's letter (a scan of the original is also attached) reads:

"Imparto di cuore una particolare Benedizione Apostolica a Padre Jozo Zovko, O. F. M., ed invoco nuova effusione di grazie e favori celesti e la continua protezione della Beata Vergine Maria".—Joannes Paulus II

English translation:

"I grant from the heart a particular blessing to Father Jozo Zovko, O. F. M., and I invoke a new outpouring of graces and heavenly favors, and the continuous protection of the Blessed Virgin Mary".

Then, his handwritten signature: Joannes Paulus II.

End of the Children of Medjugorje Report.

While the Nolans no doubt published this report in good faith the information on which it is based can best be described as mendacious nonsense. What other word but nonsense can be used to describe the claim that Father Jozo Zovko, who is unknown outside the Medjugorje movement, "is one of the best-known priests in the world"? And as for his being made the chief of many tribes (how many tribes and where are they located?), and being connected with "many miraculous healings" (how many, who was cured, and cured of what?), and being "elected among the twenty-nine Catholics of the century" (elected when, and elected by whom?), the only possible reply must be that given by the Duke of Wellington to the man who greeted him with the words: "Mr. Smith, I believe". "If you believe that," replied the duke, "you'll believe anything."

The fact is that anyone who is prepared to believe that Our Lady has appeared on even one occasion at Medjugorje is certainly prepared to believe anything. Devotees of Medjugorje will, in fact, believe anything: believe that the *Gospa* has appeared more than 31,000 times, standing on a cloud; believe that she writes secrets in an unknown language on parchment made from an unknown material; believe that rosaries turn to gold; and that credence can be given to calculating liars who have grown rich on the income they derive from naive Catholics from what could well be described as the greatest fraud in the history of the Church. Bishop Perić, the representative of Our Lord in the diocese of Mostar-Duvno, has rightly denounced "the contradictions, falsehoods and banalities, which cannot be attributed at all to our heavenly Mother *Sedes Sapientiae* — Seat of Wisdom."[2]

What credibility can be given to the claim that Pope John Paul II personally sent "a letter" conveying his blessing to Father Zovko. In order to make this clear it is first necessary to provide some background information for those who are not fully informed concerning this "world-renowned Franciscan." Where the dupes of Medjugorje are concerned, he is beyond criticism. Father Richard Beyer writes:

> Father Jozo Zovko was the pastor at Medjugorje when the apparitions began. Because of his defence of the visionaries and courageous preaching, he was imprisoned by the Communist government for a year and one-half on a charge of "fostering sedition". He now resides in a parish about 25 minutes from Medjugorje, but continues to minister to the many pilgrims who come from all over the world. His spiritual gifts and holiness are now legendary, and he has been gifted with visions of the Madonna, although he rarely discusses the fact.[3]

A report in *The Catholic Herald* of 29 November, 2002, reported that Father Zovko had been forbidden to celebrate Mass in the national shrine of the Immaculate Conception in Washington after the rector, Monsignor Michael J. Bransfield, had written to Bishop Perić asking him to clarify the Franciscan's juridical status. In his reply, dated 18 November, 2002, the bishop explained that Father Zovko is a disobedient Franciscan whose faculties and canonical mission in the dioceses of Mostar-Duvno and Trebinje-Mrkan were revoked by Monsignor Pavao Žanić on 23 August, 1989. Bishop Perić upholds the decision of his predecessor, and adds that, as Father Zovko

---

2 See Appendix I.   3 Beyer, *op. cit.*

has heard confessions without the necessary faculties, he has incurred the penalties prescribed in canon 1378 of the Code of Canon Law, i.e. an automatic (*latae sententiae*) suspension. In 1990, the Congregation for the Evangelization of Peoples required him to leave Medjugorje and take up residence in a distant convent (*convento lontano*), but he has refused to do so and is still actively involved in Medjugorje.

As regards the cover photograph showing the Pope allegedly welcoming Father Jozo in 1992, it depicts not a private audience to welcome the Franciscan, but a general audience for a large number of people. The Holy Father is simply moving along the front row and does not appear to be looking at Father Zovko. A photographer is always present at these audiences and takes numerous photographs that can be seen and ordered from the Vatican Press Office the next day. The Pope would not have known who Father Zovko was, and it is no more than a gratuitous assertion to claim that he said: "I am with you, protect Medjugorje! Protect Our Lady's messages!"

As regards the so-called "thank you note...personally signed by the shaky hand of...John Paul II", it is simply the standard blessing that can be purchased at any bookstall or souvenir shop in Vatican City. One simply selects a card or more expensive parchment blessing, gives the name of the person for whom the blessing is required, pays the price, and a week or so later it will arrive at the designated address. The one purchased for Father Zovko is of the cheaper variety and is not even dated. In order to prove how easy it is to obtain these blessings I asked a priest resident in Rome to obtain another one for Father Zovko. He went for a "top of the range" parchment blessing with identical wording to the one received by Father Zovko, but written out in beautiful calligraphy with floral decorations and dated 14 November, 2002. It cost me thirty-five euros. I sent it to Bishop Perić.

According to one report, a "visibly shaken" Father Zovko told a Catholic paper: "So far, I have received hundreds of gifts and thank you notes but none can compare with this one. I am most pleasantly surprised."

If Father Zovko was indeed "visibly shaken" when presented with the pre-printed standard blessing (not a thank-you note), and made the effusive remarks attributed to him, it denotes rank dishonesty, since he must certainly be aware that these "particular apostolic blessings" are on sale in Rome for anyone willing to pay the fee. Photocopies of the blessing are now on sale in Medjugorje as proof that the Pope believes in the authenticity of the alleged apparitions, and of course those naive enough to spend their money to make the trip will certainly not question its authenticity.

68

OCTOBER, 2002

Unexpected Support for the False Apparitions
The Catholic Truth Society of England and Wales

ONE OF THE MOST ASTONISHING AND DEPRESSING episodes in the entire squalid history of the Medjugore phenomenon occurred in England in October, 2002. The Catholic Truth Society (CTS) of England took it upon itself to publish a booklet calculated to induce Catholics to ignore the clearly expressed will of the Bishop of Mostar-Duvno and take part in pilgrimages to Medjugorje, which is within his diocese.

The CTS informs us that it works to develop and disseminate as widely as possible completely reliable publications about the faith, teaching, and life of the Catholic Church. It does so thanks to the generosity of Catholics throughout the world. Before examining the reliability of the booklet with the snappy title *Medjugorje* one must examine it within the entire context of CTS publications since the foundation of the Society in 1868. The Congregation for the Doctrine of the Faith (CDF) warns that there has appeared a veritable explosion of all kinds of "apparitions" which are being reported not only to the local bishop but also to the Holy See. In just the last ninety years (1905-1995) out of two hundred and ninety-five reported "apparitions" the Church has given its approval to eleven only, and said "no" to two hundred and eighty-four. In many cases false seers have been unmasked and pecuniary transactions have been discovered, and whenever they "announced" a sign from heaven it turned out to be human trickery. This is precisely what is taking place at Medjugorje.

Since its foundation the CTS has maintained an inflexible policy of giving no publicity to any alleged apparition until it has received Church approval. Mr. Fergal Martin, the General Secretary of the CTS, who is quite taken (or better still, taken in) by Medjugorje, decided to change this policy on the basis of his predilection for the Herzegovinian phenomenon. One might have hoped that Mr. Martin would have considered it his duty to serve the best interests of the Society rather than use the Society to promote his personal predilections.

Mr. Martin's booklet claims "to provide a popular, accurate and balanced account... of what is happening in Medjugorje, using authentic sources." Just how accurate and balanced the account is can be demonstrated by its many examples of *suppressio veri*. The technique it uses is not that of stating outright falsehoods but of suppressing the truth. It does, however, contain some serious falsehoods that were probably included due to ignorance rather than dishonesty. On page 66, for example, it is claimed that the Pope sent Father Jozo Zovko his Apostolic Blessing with the words: "I grant from the heart a particular Apostolic Blessing to Father Jozo Zovko, OFM, and I invoke a new outpouring of graces and heavenly favours, and the continuous protection of the Blessed Virgin Mary." Pictures of the blessing appeared on Medjugorje websites throughout the world, and it could immediately be recognized as the certificate that is sold in Rome in the shops and on the stalls in the area of St. Peter's Basilica. The certificates include a picture of the Pope and the wording just cited. They come in various qualities from cheap cardboard to parchment, but the text is always identical. I purchased an identical blessing for Father Jozo to prove how meaningless they are. Unfortunately, most readers of Mr. Martin's booklet will imagine that the Holy Father really did send his blessing to Father Jozo, and that this proves his support for the "apparitions". Any publisher of integrity would withdraw the publication from sale to prevent its readers from being deceived in this way.

The booklet is correct in stating that Bishop Žanić, the Bishop of Mostar-Duvno, was open to the veracity of the

Unexpected Support for the False Apparitions

"apparitions" in the beginning, but changed his mind in response to "reported messages via the 'visionaries' from Our Lady disagreeing with the bishop's stance, and lending strong support to the Franciscans."

Just how accurate and balanced this account is can be made clear by explaining the precise content of the messages allegedly from Our Lady transmitted to Bishop Žanić by the self-styled seers. He changed his mind when it became apparent that the seers were lying when they told him on thirteen occasions that Our Lady had supported two disobedient Franciscan priests in their opposition to him. One of these priests, Father Ivica Vego, was dispensed from his vows and expelled from the Franciscan Order after seducing a nun, Sister Leopolda, and when she became pregnant they both left the religious life and began to live together near Medjugorje, where their child was born. They now have two children. But prior to this, Father Vego refused to accept his expulsion and continued to celebrate Mass, administer the sacraments, and pass the time with his mistress.

Why mention such a distasteful affair? The reason is that the seers claimed that Our Lady appeared to them on thirteen occasions, stating that Father Vego was innocent, that he was as entitled to celebrate Mass as any other priest, and that the bishop was harsh! Any reader with a *sensus catholicus* will need to read no further to realise the full extent of the mendacity of the seers, a mendacity that cannot be excused simply on the grounds that they have been manipulated by their Franciscan mentors. What credibility can be given to those who claim that the Mother of God told them repeatedly that an immoral priest, expelled from his order is innocent, and that the bishop, who had taken the only course open to him, was the guilty party!

The answer is that Mr. Martin is bound to give credibility to the lies of Vicka; otherwise, he could not in good conscience, use the CTS to promote Medjugorje. But how can he explain the fact that Mr. Vego is now married to the nun he seduced? Any answer he could give would be very interesting.

One must also presume that he finds the bloody handkerchief story convincing (May, 1990, Part 6).

Many more examples of blatant deceit by the self-styled seers are included in this book. Some of them appear to be pathological liars. Two more examples will suffice. Vicka has a friend whose father wished to build an hotel. Vicka was asked to tell a group of Medjugorje adepts in Holland that Our Lady had asked for the construction of a 100-bedroom hotel for which they were requested to supply a large sum of deutschmarks. Some members of the Dutch groups became suspicious and asked for more details; Vicka eventually admitted that she had been lying, but did not think it important. So, lying is "not all that important," even when the lies are put into the mouth of the Blessed Virgin. It is a point of view, not a very Catholic point of view, but one must presume that it is one with which Mr. Martin agrees; otherwise, he would not be distributing a book in which Vicka is described as an "extrovert, quick-witted, and forthright". Quick-witted perhaps, but forthright? (See November, 1997, *Medjugorje Incredibilities*.)

Bishop Žanić makes clear (May, 1990, Part 15), that Marija Pavlović has decisively proven that no confidence can be placed in her veracity—"Marija has consciously spoken falsehoods." In 1987, Father Tomislav Vlašić, the principal manipulator of the alleged seers, established a bizarre community in Parma, Italy, with an enigmatic German lady named Agnes Heupel who claimed to have been cured of an illness at Medjugorje. In this community, guided by Vlašić and Heupel, young men and women lived together—which, Bishop Žanić comments, is something unheard of in the history of the Church. The founding of the Vlašić/Heupel community caused such scandal that Vlašić decided to silence his critics by claiming that the community had been established in obedience to a command from Our Lady. Marija Pavlović was a member of the community, and in response to a request by Vlašić duly "revealed" that the community had been established at Our Lady's express command. In July, 1988, great consternation was caused among the Medjugorists when Pavlović swore

Unexpected Support for the False Apparitions

before the Blessed Sacrament that her previous statement had been false and that the Vlašić/Heupel community had in no way been endorsed by Our Lady. I suspect that even Mr. Martin would find it hard to cover up the fact that Pavlović must have been lying on at least one occasion (see 11 July, 1988: *Marija Pavlović Contradicts Herself*).

Approval by the diocesan bishop is the first step in the acceptance of an apparition as authentic, and no apparition has been recognised by the Church without such approval. The two bishops of Mostar-Duvno during the period of alleged apparitions are both absolutely adamant that Our Lady has not appeared at Medjugorje on a single occasion. In a letter to Father Hugh Thwaites, SJ, dated 17 August, 1987, Bishop Žanić wrote: "I am sure that Our Lady does not appear. No miracles. The 'Messages' cannot be of our Virgin. They are the fruit of a fabrication, fraud and disobedience to the Church. It is about big money and personal interest too."

This judgement is shared by the successor of Bishop Žanić, Bishop Ratko Perić, who warns:

> In some of the statements made by the so-called seers of Medjugorje published in the last fourteen years, there are such contradictions, falsehoods and banalities, which cannot be attributed at all to our heavenly Mother *Sedes Sapientiae* — Seat of Wisdom, since there does not exist even a minimal guarantee of credibility. On the basis of such statements and the events tied to the statements, it cannot be affirmed that these matters concern "supernatural apparitions or revelations", of the Madonna or others. The talk of a "great sign", of "ten secrets", which Our Lady conveyed to the children, resembles the scare tactics which are typical of non-Catholic communities and not the sound teachings of the Catholic Church.

The squalid reality of what is taking place in Medjugorje is not so much as hinted at in Mr. Martin's "accurate and balanced account... of what is happening in Medjugorje, using authentic sources." The source of the CTS propaganda tracts is one David Baldwin, whose uncritical effusions make clear that he has been completely duped by the duplicitous "seers".

Mr. Martin's booklet is not only contrary to the entire tradition of the CTS in its promotion of unapproved apparitions (and what is more, apparitions that have been condemned as false by legitimate authority). His booklet also constitutes gross and calculated interference in the diocese of exemplary Catholic bishops in communion with the Holy See. Bishop Žanić expressed the situation perfectly:

> By divine law I am the pastor in this diocese, the teacher of the Faith, and the judge in questions concerning the Faith. Since the events in Medjugorje have caused strife and division in the Church—some people believing, others not believing—because there are those who have refused to submit themselves to the authority of the Church. Because the recommendations and decisions of the above-mentioned authorities, commissions, congregations of the bishops' conference had no effect, I, the bishop of Mostar, answerable before God for the discipline in this diocese, repeat and confirm earlier decisions of ecclesiastical bodies, and I forbid pilgrimages to come here and attribute a supernatural character to these events before the Commission of the Bishops' Conference completes its work.

Mr. Martin would, I hope, accept that this is true, but it in no way dissuaded him from using the CTS to interfere in the internal affairs of Mostar-Duvno and incite English Catholics to go there on pilgrimage. Let us make the position of legitimate Church authority concerning pilgrimages to Medjugorje absolutely clear. The Secretary of the Congregation for the Doctrine of the Faith twice (in 1996 and 1997) cited the episcopal pronouncement of 1991 and concluded:

> From what has very rightly been said about the matter, it follows that official pilgrimages to Medjugorje, taken to be a place of authentic Marian apparitions, may not be organised whether at parish or diocesan level, for to do so would be in conflict with the solemn

Unexpected Support for the False Apparitions 247

pronouncement of the bishops of the former Yugoslavia in their previously mentioned communiqué.

Bishop Perić comments:

> On 26 June, 1998, the selfsame secretary of the congregation expressed an opinion to the like effect, saying that "unofficial pilgrimages" to Medjugorje are permitted only on condition that they are not to be deemed to amount to recognition of the authenticity of the "apparitions," from which it follows that even "unofficial pilgrimages" are not permitted if they involve the recognition of the authenticity of the "apparitions".

Mr. Martin's booklet accepts that this is the position of legitimate authority (pp. 70-71) but observes: "There is therefore no bar whatsoever to the laity organising themselves as individuals or into pilgrim groups to make the journey to Medjugorje, accompanied by their parish priest, or any other priest, to tend to their pastoral needs."

Such pilgrimages are permitted only on the basis that those taking part do not accept the authenticity of the alleged apparitions. But what possible reason exists for anyone to go there who does not accept their authenticity? As Bishop Perić wrote:

> Accordingly, those who come to Medjugorje with the intention of recognizing the so-called apparitions and "messages" are not working in harmony with the Church's position. There is no apparent need for the faithful to come to Medjugorje from the four corners of the earth to say the Rosary, make their confessions or receive communion, when they may do all these things religiously in their own parishes, where Our Lord Jesus Christ is present in the sacrament of the altar, and Our Lady is always ready to offer a mother's care.

For any group to make a pilgrimage to Medjugorje and claim that it is not motivated by a belief that that place is the site of supernatural visions constitutes sheer hypocrisy. On 17 January, 2001, a considered judgement on behalf of the

French hierarchy was published by Monsignor Henri Brincard, Bishop of Puy-en-Velay. With all respect due to Mr. Martin I hold the considered judgement of the French hierarchy to be somewhat more authoritative than his personal opinion. Bishop Brincard writes:

> It is opportune to ask ourselves if the events of Medjugorje have produced good fruits in the visionaries who, at least during the duration of the "apparitions", must by their lives be the first witnesses of the grace from which they say they benefit. From there it follows that we ask ourselves the following questions: "Have they obeyed the bishop of Mostar? Have they respected him?..." Such questions and still others yet are habitually part of a serious investigation into an event of apparitions. In order for the investigation to arrive at a solid conclusion, it is necessary that these fundamental questions receive a clear and objective response.
>
> We would like to say nothing about the doubtful or even bad fruits. But the truth obliges us to say that they exist. Let us quote, as examples, the calling into question, even to the point of defamation, of the local ordinary as well as the disobedience with regard to his legitimate authority; the exacerbation of the Herzegovina "question" following the words attributed to "the *Gospa*", words in favour of the Franciscans and against the bishop. In conclusion, allow me to make the following reflection:
>
> I have no authority to pronounce any ecclesial judgement whatsoever on the events of Medjugorje. I am therefore the first to have to give an example of obedience, notably in respecting the pastoral decisions of my confrère of Mostar and in complying with joy to his wishes. "I do not see how I can go to Medjugorje without giving my support, by the very fact of my arriving there, to the events whose discernment and assessment rests henceforth with the Episcopal Conference of Bosnia-Herzegovina. Such support would fly in the face of a traditional teaching of the Church, recalled in *Lumen Gentium* and applicable to all the

successors of the Apostles: 'Individual bishops, in so far as they are set over particular Churches, exercise their pastoral office over the portion of the People of God assigned to them, not over other Churches nor the Church universal'."

In conclusion, by endorsing alleged apparitions that are not only not approved but have been declared by legitimate authority as lacking any basis in fact, and by undermining the authority of the legitimate bishops of the diocese, Mr. Fergal Martin has brought disgrace upon the CTS. He insisted in a letter to me dated 25 March, 2004 that he considers "the book to be a sufficiently balanced and informative presentation of the matter and the issues surrounding it." Of the one hundred diocesan priests in the dioceses of Herzegovina, not one believes in the apparitions. Of the forty-two bishops of Yugoslavia (ordinaries, auxiliaries and retired), only one has been outspoken in declaring his belief and has defended the events. Of the fifteen members of the first commission, which was formed by the bishop of Mostar with the help of the bishops and provincials from Yugoslavia, eleven of the members said that there was nothing supernatural in the events of Medjugorje, two (Franciscans) claimed that the apparitions were authentic, one member said that there was something *in nucleo* (in the beginning) and one abstained. The fact that these clergy of every rank either live in Herzegovina or elsewhere in the former Yugoslavia, and are ideally placed to make an informed and balanced judgement, does not trouble Mr. Martin at all. He is convinced that in his office at 40-46 Harleyford Road, London, SE11 5AY he is far better placed to make a balanced judgement.

A somewhat contrasting view from the standpoint of legitimate authority in the Church was published by Bishop Perić on 17 February, 2004:

> The Church, from the local to supreme level, from the beginning to this very day, has clearly and constantly repeated: *Non constat de supernaturalitate*!

No to pilgrimages that would ascribe a supernatural nature to the apparitions, no shrine of the Madonna, no authentic messages or revelations, no true visions! This is the state of things today. How will things be tomorrow? We'll leave them in God's hands and under Our Lady's protection!

8 NOVEMBER, 2002

Crkva Na Kamenu: A Pronouncement by the Congregation for the Doctrine of the Faith on the Current Spate of Apparitions

The following article appeared in the November, 2002, issue of Crkva na Kamenu ("The Church on the Rock"), the newspaper of the diocese of Mostar-Duvno.

IN THE YEAR BOOK *ATTIVITÀ DELLA SANTA SEDE* for 2001, which came out a few days ago, we read on page 707 the following text from the Congregation for the Doctrine of the Faith (CDF):

> It has been noticed during the course of this year that the CDF has received an increased number of reports of *extraordinary events*: of so-called Marian apparitions, messages, stigmata, and weeping statues of Our Lady or of Our Lord, and all sorts of Eucharistic "miracles", and so on.
>
> The Holy See is receiving news from various parts of the Catholic world of strong pressure being put by groups of the faithful upon the local diocesan bishop to force him to recognise the veracity of Marian apparitions, sometimes even those which took place a good time ago. Sometimes there is long and worrying tension between the faithful who believe in the "apparitions" and the local bishop who is unwilling to give official recognition to them. This enduring tension

is a danger to the unity of the local Church. The CDF is aware that in this sensitive matter it must give an exemplary pastoral response to these continuous demands which are arriving from all over the Catholic world, as well as to give God's people and His pastors further and more up-to-date criteria for guidance in the hope of clarifying the meaning of apparitions, messages, and extraordinary events in general, in keeping with the teaching of the faith, and the consequent practical criteria which could bring about a resolution.

The CDF makes the following points:

1. There has appeared a veritable explosion of all kinds of "apparitions" which are being reported not only to the local bishop but also to the Holy See. In just the last ninety years (1905-1995) out of two hundred and ninety-five reported "apparitions" the Church has given its approval to eleven only, and said "no" to two hundred and eighty-four. In many cases false seers have been unmasked and pecuniary transactions have been discovered, and whenever they "announced" a sign from heaven it turned out be human trickery.

Within the diocese of Mostar-Duvno, in the parish of St. James in Medjugorje, "apparitions" that have been lasting from 1981 have reached a total that is beyond calculation. These are not remarkable for anything new in their content, but only for their huge number. It is being maintained that a female "seer" even had up to ten "apparitions" a day! The bishops' conference declared on 10 April, 1991: "On the basis of investigations to date, it is impossible to confirm that we are dealing with apparitions and supernatural revelations."

2. Those who promote "apparitions", be they "seers" or their mentors or followers, are putting enormous pressure on the bishops and on the Holy See to recognise as true these extraordinary events, and so there exist lasting tensions between the faithful who believe in the "apparitions" and the bishops who do not recognise them.

In the parish of Medjugorje in the eighties some "seers" put pressure upon Bishop Žanić, both verbally and in writing, to recognise the "apparitions" threatening him with heavenly judgement. If he failed to recognize them Our Lady's judgement and that of her Son would be waiting for him. The more often he received these false threats from the "seers" the more convinced the bishop became that it was a question of false apparitions. (See Bishop Perić's book *Ogledalo Pravde*, Mostar, 2001, 88–91.)

3. The CDF points out that such pressure can become a real threat to the unity of the local Church. Threats to the unity of the local Church are particularly pronounced in Medjugorje, where the "apparitions" have from the very beginning been bound up with the solution to the "case of Herzegovina", which is characterised by disobedience to the Pope and the decisions of the Holy See. In 1994 the local bishop, speaking at the Synod of Bishops in Rome, at which the Pope himself was present, stressed that the so-called apparitions at Medjugorje "are creating no small measure of trouble and division, and not only in the local Church. We accordingly expect that the Holy See will use its own methods to create complete and unshakable unity in this particular Church" (*L'Osservatore Romano*, 13 October, 1994, 7).

Since numerous requests that the "apparitions" should be recognised as authentic arrive in Rome from all over the Catholic world, the CDF has decided to lay down guidelines for the entire Church explaining the meaning of such events and laying down practical criteria for distinguishing true from false apparitions.

Such directions from the Holy See can only help us to avoid exposing our faith and the faith of others to danger, and to build up the unity of our Church on the firm foundation which is Christ the Lord, Head of the Church, which is His Body, Ephesians 1: 22-23.

Mostar, 8 November, 2002,
Monsignor Luka Pavlović
Vicar-General

70

29 DECEMBER, 2002

The Sunday Times

The following report from a secular newspaper indicates the extent to which the Medjugorje phenomenon can best be described as an industry.

VILLAGE GROWS RICH ON VIRGIN VISIONS
Tom Walker, Medjugorje, Bosnia

They call it Apparition Hill. Past the pizzerias, boarding houses, shops and gift stalls, high on a slope of broken rock and scrub, stands a statue of the Virgin Mary.

On a bitingly cold winter's day last week snow shrouded the peaks in the distance, but a handful of devout worshippers stared intently at the statue. One woman wept openly; others nervously fingered their rosary beads.

This is the Bosnian village of Medjugorje, where in 1981 six local children aged between ten and sixteen swore they had seen an apparition. Since then, their powers have supposedly allowed them to remain in touch with the Virgin Mary on a regular basis. What was once a hamlet of a few dozen houses has expanded tenfold and Medjugorje, which is said to have attracted up to twenty-two million pilgrims, now has the air of an established tourist resort.

Mere hundreds arrived for Christmas, but from Easter onwards the town will be packed until the autumn.

To local businessmen this is manna from heaven, but to the Vatican it is distinctly dubious. The Catholic bishop of Mostar, Ratko Perić, has denounced the money-spinning and the Pope, who has refused invitations to visit, has ordered an inquiry into the phenomenon.[1]

---

1 This is not correct.

Medjugorje lies in Herzegovina, one of the most fiercely nationalist Croatian areas of Bosnia, where strangers have traditionally been viewed with suspicion. A wall of silence meets most queries from non-pilgrims.

Three of the six "seers", as they are known, have stayed in the town and their prosperity has risen to reflect the Madonna gold rush. Two of them, Jakov Colo, 31, and Mirjana Dragicević-Soldo, 37, live in smart executive houses with immaculate gardens, double garages and security gates. On the other side of town, the residence of Ivanka Ivanković-Elez, 36, is even more sumptuous, with a brand-new tennis court.

All three refused to discuss their experiences and the huge wealth it has generated. Local Franciscan monks who gave credence to the visions preferred to say nothing, demanding that any questions be sent by fax.

Perić, however, does not mince his words. In a booklet handed out by his office he complains of the "incomprehensible disobedience" of the Franciscans and says he told the Pope that "no competent authority has recognised any apparition in Medjugorje".

Compiled by a Dutch priest, Rudo Franken, the booklet asks fundamental questions including why the Virgin appears to the visionaries — while remaining invisible to everybody else — daily at 6:40 p.m. in the summer when the tourist trade is at its peak, then limits her appearances to once a month in the winter. He also picks out inconsistencies in the seers' accounts.

The international authority in Bosnia, the Office of the High Representative, is also looking at Medjugorje, where Madonna profits are suspected to have swollen the coffers of the Croatian nationalist parties that are hoping to break Bosnia apart.

The Vatican has been alarmed since the apparitions began. The Catholic Church in Italy was thrown into disarray in 1995 by a Madonna brought back from Medjugorje that was said to have wept tears of blood. Soon dozens of weeping statues were reported all over the country; almost all were later unmasked as cases of people splashing red paint or water over the figures and then proclaiming a miracle.

Before he travelled to Croatia in 1998 the Pope refused to cross the border to Medjugorje, instead visiting the lesser-known shrine of Marija Bistrica near Zagreb.

The Vatican is drawing up new guidelines with "updated criteria" for establishing the authenticity of apparitions. A ruling on Medjugorje is expected early next year and is likely to rule that there is no evidence of supernatural visions there.

Since 1905 only twelve visions of the Madonna have been approved by Catholic bishops and two hundred and eighty-four have been rejected. But Monsignor Arthur Calkins, an American expert working in the Vatican, said that if Medjugorje were to close down, pilgrims would soon be attracted elsewhere.

One of the Franciscans who has always defended the reclusive seers of Medjugorje, Father Jozo Zovko, says he was imprisoned by the "communists" of the former Yugoslavia for his views and is prepared to be jailed again to protect the good name of the village.

The bishop of Mostar was entitled to his opinion, he said in his faxed reply to questions, "but I believe in Our Lady's apparitions. She told the parish that she has chosen it. The reason for this choice remains a mystery to us."

FINAL NOTE

MICHAEL DAVIES DID NOT ADD ANY FURTHER pages to this manuscript before his death. Its abrupt ending reminds us that he primarily saw himself as a compiler of documents and information otherwise unavailable to those in the Anglosphere who were curious about Medjugorje. It is likely that, had he lived longer, he would have developed the present work into a more complete treatment. Fortunately, that has been done recently by another Mariologist who expressly notes his indebtedness to Michael Davies, namely, Donal Anthony Foley in his *Medjugorje Complete: The Definitive Account of the Visions and Visionaries* (Brooklyn: Angelico Press, 2021). Readers who are interested in picking up the thread of the story down to the present are strongly advised to continue with Foley.

APPENDICES

APPENDIX I

17 FEBRUARY, 2004

A Definitive Statement by Bishop Perić
Medjugorje: Secrets, Messages, Vocations, Prayers, Confessions, Commissions

Although this book is intended to document the Medjugorje phenomenon up to 2002 I decided to include this statement by Bishop Perić summarizing the situation at the beginning of 2004. Although much of what the bishop states is already included in the book it is appended here in full.

Maynooth/Dublin, 17 February, 2004.

MEDJUGORJE IS A PARISH IN THE DIOCESE OF Mostar-Duvno in Bosnia-Herzegovina, with a population of about 4,000 persons, which has been entrusted to the pastoral care of the Franciscan friars, OFM. From 24 June, 1981, onwards, some events have been occurring that many people, some Franciscans included, have attributed to so-called apparitions of the Blessed Virgin Mary, who has seemingly presented herself as the "Queen of Peace".

I. HOW MANY SO-CALLED VISIONARIES AND VISIONS ARE THERE?

1. Vicka Ivanković, born on 3 September, 1964, in the parish of Medjugorje, has been receiving "apparitions" from 24 June, 1981. Every day. There have been pauses, but there have also been days with up to ten "visions". Vicka married Mario Mijatovic in 2002 and now has one child and lives in Krehin Gradac, near Medjugorje.

How many "visions" has she had till now? According to a simple calculation of the days, it would be 8,270 including yesterday's. These "apparitions" were with the other "seers" during the first years, yet for many years now she has been having them alone, separately, in the evening, regardless of her location. As if they were programmed.

2. Marija Pavlović, born on 1 April, 1965, in the parish of Medjugorje, has been a "seer" from the second day of the "apparitions", 25 June, 1981, every day up till now. In 1993 she married an Italian, Paolo Lunetti. She has three children and is now living in Monza, near Milano, Italy.

How many "visions" has she had till now? Around 8,270 including yesterday's, together with the other "privileged" few or separately. The "apparitions" are not tied so much to the locality of Medjugorje as to persons: wherever these persons travel in the world, the "apparitions" travel with them.

3. Ivan Dragicević, born in Mostar on 25 May, 1965, has had daily "apparitions" from 24 June, 1981, to this day. He married the former Miss Massachusetts, Laureen Murphy, in 1994 and has four children. He lives with his family part of the time in Boston and the rest of the time in Medjugorje.

How many "visions" has Ivan had till now? About 8,270 with last night's, together with the other "seers" or separately.

4. Mirjana Dragicević, born in Sarajevo on 18 March, 1965, has had "visions" from 24 June, 1981. Her last regular encounter was on Christmas Day 1982. From that day onward, she has received an "apparition" once a year—on her birthday—18 March. Along with this, from 2 August, 1987, on each second day of the month, she hears the Madonna's voice and sometimes sees her. That would make it 17 years times 12 months, she either hears or sees the Madonna. Mirjana married Marko Soldo in 1989 and has two children. She is now living in Medjugorje.

How many "visions" has Mirjana had till now? All totalled: about 770.

5. Ivanka Ivanković was born in Bijakovici in the parish of Medjugorje on 21 June, 1966. The phenomenon appeared

A Definitive Statement by Bishop Perić   263

to her from 25 June, 1981, to 7 May, 1985. She now has a "vision" once a year, on 25 June, on the anniversary of the "apparitions". She married Rajko Elez and has three children. She is currently living in Medjugorje.

How many "visions" has Ivanka had till now? About 1,450 altogether.

6. Jakov Colo was born on 6 March, 1971, in Bijakovici in the parish of Medjugorje. From 25 June, 1981, he received daily "apparitions" until 12 September, 1998. From this date onward, he has only had one a year—on Christmas Day. In 1993 he married Anna-Lisa Barozzi from Italy. They have three children and now live in Medjugorje.

How many "visions" has he had till now? Together with the others and separately, around 6,290.

The Madonna has been presumably "appearing" on a regular basis and at one and the same time, even if one of the "seers" is in America, another "visionary" in Herzegovina, a third in Italy or a fourth in Maynooth. Adding all this up together makes for 33,320 "apparitions" up till now. Please don't ask me about the accuracy of these statistics, because a thousand "apparitions" more or less have no role to play here! The hierarchical Church at various levels-diocesan, national and Holy See-hasn't accepted a single apparition as authentic.

Let us now compare Medjugorje to two recognized Marian shrines:

At Lourdes in 1858, the Madonna appeared as the "Immaculate Conception", eighteen times to Bernadette. The Church accepted these apparitions and four years afterwards declared them authentic, in 1862.

At Fatima in 1917, the Madonna appeared as "Our Lady of the Rosary" six times to the ten-year-old shepherd children Lucia, Francisco and Jacinta. Thirteen years later the Church accepted these apparitions as authentic.

Three of the Medjugorje "seers", who say they have daily "apparitions", live most of the time outside of Medjugorje, while the remaining three who live in Medjugorje supposedly have only one "apparition" a year.

II. HOW MANY SECRETS HAS THE ALLEGED MADONNA GIVEN TO THE SO-CALLED SEERS?

Those who have daily "visions" have received nine secrets, while those who have "apparitions" once a year have ten secrets. It is not clear if nine or ten secrets have been given and are known to each of the "seers", or if each of the "seers" has his/her own number of secrets that differ from the rest.

If we compare this to the authentic apparitions, then one can see that at Lourdes there were no secrets for the world, while at Fatima one secret was divided into three parts. Yet at Medjugorje till now there have been nine or ten, or even fifty-seven possible secrets, which have been divided by three "seers" who have received ten and another three who have received nine. To this day not a single secret has been revealed.

In the first years there was apocalyptic talk about a "great sign" to happen, yet to this day this "great sign" has not occurred, and the expectation of a sign has diminished.

III. HOW MANY PRESUMED MESSAGES HAVE THERE BEEN?

All the "messages" of Medjugorje can be summed up into five basic ones, as is usually the case, yet these "five" are actually the following "fourteen": peace, conversion, prayer, fasting, vigilance, penance, adoration, witnessing, faith, call to holiness, Eucharist, Word of God, monthly confession, Rosary.

Many authors greatly differ which five should be taken from these fourteen. Italian, French and Croat authors, all have their own interpretations. It's important to mention here that besides the daily "messages", there are also special monthly "messages" on the twenty-fifth of each month that are given to Marija in Italy, which she then sends to the parish rectory of Medjugorje for verification and are then sent out into the world.

All these "messages" of the various interpreters of Medjugorje are heard every Sunday in churches. For us, the novelty of Medjugorje would be that the "Queen of Peace" on the twenty-fifth of each month sends out a special communication with the message: "Thank you, children, for responding to my invitation". The Madonna thanks the "seers" for having the time, for wanting to, and deigning to meet and talk with her. According to these words the "Madonna" is amazed and grateful to the "seers" who have responded to her invitation! This is somewhat like parents thanking their children for being born, or physicians thanking the infirm for seeking their health back! (*Ogledalo Pravde [Mirror of Justice]*, Mostar, 2001, 249-250). [Bishop Perić's book *Ogledalo Pravde* is referred to in subsequent references as OP.]

IV. HOW MANY VOCATIONS HAVE RESULTED FROM THE "APPARITIONS"?

Of the six "seers" of Medjugorje, none of them has achieved a religious vocation. Three of them mentioned that they were going to enter and two even went on to follow this inexplicable voice, yet with time everything vanished.

Ivan Dragicević became a candidate for the Franciscan Province of Herzegovina. In 1981 he went to the minor seminary of Visoko, where he continued with the "apparitions". Due to his failure to pass his repeat examination, it was decided that he could possibly do better if he went to the minor seminary in Dubrovnik. While in Dubrovnik, he managed to pass his repeat examination and enter into the second year, but he didn't show an equal aptitude for school as he did for the "apparitions", and hence he returned home in January, 1983.

Having said farewell to the seminary, Ivan continued not only with daily "apparitions" to this day, but at a certain point began imposing the harsh demands of this phenomenon of his upon the local bishop, Pavao Žanić, that he accept the "messages" of Medjugorje. In 1994 he married an American woman in Boston and thereby irrevocably transformed his religious vocation into a marriage (OP, 34).

Vicka Ivanković from the outset demonstrated enthusiasm for the religious life. In September, 1981, she confided this to an Italian weekly: *I would like to enter a convent and become a nun.*

Even though she was an "enrolled nun", Vicka never entered a convent. Twenty years later, she found a young man from the neighbouring parish of Gradina and the two of them were married in Medjugorje. Over two thousand invited and curious guests attended their wedding party. During the wedding festivities, the "seer" went to her new house a few kilometres away from the noise of the wedding party with husband alongside her and had a "vision". Everything according to routine and regular programming. Afterwards they went back to the wedding party.

The "visionary" in the beginning announced Urbi et Orbi–"to Rome and the world"–that she was an "enrolled nun", but twenty years later she travelled to Rome to buy her wedding dress. The "visionary" explained this to a journalist: *The Madonna gave each of us our freedom to choose. Everyone can respond to the vocation they desire. Regardless of the fact that I'm now married, I shall continue to spread the messages of the Madonna, because Christian faith can be witnessed in marriage as well.*

Regarding her religious vocation she is free, yet as regards "spreading the messages of the Madonna" she is obligated!

Marija Pavlović. In response to an Italian journalist's question, "Why haven't any one of you decided to become a priest or nun?" Marija, in 2001, gave the following explanation: *For many years I thought that I would become a nun. I began visiting a convent and my desire to go there was very strong. But the sister superior once told me: "Marija, if you want to enter, you are very welcome; but if the bishop decides that you must not speak about Medjugorje, you will have to obey". At that moment I began thinking that my vocation might possibly be to witness to that which I saw and heard, and that I will be able to find the road to holiness outside the convent* (OP, 28).

Marija therefore came to terms with the demands of religious life in which she couldn't obey the bishop if he were to decide that she shouldn't spread the "apparitions" that the Church even to this day has not declared authentic. And hence she decided to find the road to holiness "outside the convent".

Not God's work. Yet things weren't exactly that way. Marija did eventually attempt entering a mixed spiritual community, where she remained for several months. She then left the community with a written explanation that provoked not a little public astonishment. First of all, it was written that the Madonna, through Marija, had said on 8 March 1987 that that community was *God's plan, God's work*. Later on, when she left the community with her boyfriend, Paolo Lunetti, who helped her leave and write the letter, she denied everything in her own handwriting on 11 July, 1988: before God, the Madonna, and the Church of Jesus Christ, she categorically denied that there were ever any "messages" through her for this community and for this *work of God*, in which she had lived for several months (OP, 30-31).

At that time, in 1983, Father Tomislav Vlašić, OFM, who was the spiritual director of the "seers" of Medjugorje, wrote to the Swiss theologian Hans Urs von Balthasar: *The children have decided to enter the religious life, but they are waiting for the right moment which only they know* (OP, 55). Today the whole world knows that these were only simple stories or children's fairytales. Not all the "privileged" children of Medjugorje entered the religious life, while those who tried quickly left. Only the mature won't allow themselves to be misled by irrational "messages" and children's stories! Is this some kind of "sign", "secret" or "message" of Medjugorje?

Though I believe that it's improper, I will nevertheless compare these "vocations" with the two best-known modern Marian shrines.

At Lourdes the 14-year-old Bernardette once said: *I must become a nun, but I don't know in which Order. The Holy Virgin told me this and I'm waiting.* She received her religious habit in July 1866. Though infirm, she held on until her death on 16 April, 1879. Pope Pius XI canonized her on the Feast of the Immaculate Conception in 1933.

Secondly, at Fatima, the seer Lucia became a nun in 1921 and a discalced Carmelite in 1948. Little Francisco and Jacinta died as children and were both beatified by Pope John Paul II at Fatima in the year 2000.

There's something strange in all of this: three "seers" who tried to "enrol" themselves into religious life, who later on dismissed themselves and were happily married, still have regular daily "apparitions". The other "seers", though, who didn't enter the religious life, receive an "apparition" only once a year. Can this be considered a reward for those who didn't enter the religious life?

A grace of God. Keeping in mind the fact that many young boys from Herzegovina who entered the seminary and who later became priests, and the numerous young girls who became nuns (from the parish of Medjugorje alone there are over thirty living priests and sisters) who from what I know, never had any apparition, message or encounter with any supernatural phenomenon, it is indeed odd that not one of the "seers" in these twenty three years (who have had between 770 and 8,270 "apparitions), realized a religious vocation. And this same phenomenon, in a threatening way, demands that Bishop Žanić recognizes the "messages" of Medjugorje as authentic without questioning them. Every true religious vocation is a grace of God and a serious matter. The manner in which religious vocations were handled by the "visionaries" has been shown to be irresponsible. Is this possibly a question of games without borders, regarding numbers, "visions", "messages", "revelations", "secrets" and "signs"?

V. WHAT DO PRAYERS AND CONFESSIONS PROVE?

1. Prayer as a context. Prayer is an important factor in the "apparitions" of Medjugorje. It is in the context of praying the Our Father that in most cases the "apparitions" begin for the "seers". They even cease praying so that the "apparition" can be followed for a few minutes.

2. A Message not to pray. On 16 September, 1981: "She also told them that they need not pray for themselves, because she has rewarded them in the best fashion. They should pray for others instead" (OP, 111).

The Biblical Madonna will never say that people need not pray for themselves and that the "reward of apparitions" replaces personal prayer. This is false teaching. Even Jesus prayed firstly for himself, then for his apostles and then for the entire world "that all may be one" (Jn 17).

3. A Message to pray for Bishop Žanić. Concerning a prayer group of Medjugorje "the Madonna has asked that they fast on bread and water twice a week. Three months later we are fasting on bread and water three times a week. The group is offering the majority of their prayers for him [Bishop Žanić]. We often offer our adoration, rosaries and visits to the place of the apparitions where we pray long into the night for him. God shall look upon our prayers and fasting" (OP, 126). So wrote Father Tomislav Vlašić, OFM, on 8 January, 1984.

The phenomenon established a prayer group around Father Tomislav Vlašić, OFM, who in a letter in 1984 presented himself to the Pope as the one "who through Divine providence guides the seers of Medjugorje" (OP, 56). This group has been praying and fasting just so that the bishop would give in to their hallucinations. They also built a convent in Medjugorje with close to one hundred beds and didn't even think of asking the bishop for permission to do this. Then the "mystifier" Father Vlašić was recently removed from his guiding role in the prayer-group, after having mixed the spiritual with spiritualism in Medjugorje during a retreat!

4. He could have but didn't want to? In an interview in 1993, during the height of the war, the "seer" Jakov said: "The Madonna has asked me today, as every day during these last twelve years, that I pray for peace in the former Yugoslavia. The Virgin convinced me that I could stop the war with my prayers." (OP, 37).

If this weren't so naive, a normal believer would ask himself: If the "seer" was capable of stopping the war in ex-Yugoslavia, then why didn't he go pray and bring it to an end? Yet during the war over two million people were displaced, over two hundred thousand were killed, thousands of religious sites and tens of thousands of homes were destroyed, and then the unjust Dayton accord was imposed upon us!

5. Can prayer be considered proof? There are people within the Church who say: If the people are praying to God, let them then go to Medjugorje, let them make their pilgrimages and pray. It is better for them to pray than not to pray, better to venerate "the Madonna of Medjugorje" than not to venerate any Madonna at all!

For two thousand years now, the Church has been teaching and suggesting to the faithful that they pray, fast, do penance, go to confession and convert. She doesn't prohibit anyone from praying to God where they please. But she doesn't allow "pilgrimages to the place of the apparitions" to be endorsed in churches from the altar, that have not been accepted as authentic. She does this so that the truth may be separated from falsehood, and true doctrine separated from false doctrine.

As if it were really necessary for someone to travel thousands of kilometres from Korea or Ireland to Medjugorje just to pray a Rosary or to make a confession. Yet Jesus teaches us to go into your room and pray to your Father in heaven! (Mt 6:6).

Do those who say that they have travelled to Medjugorje over thirty times really prove by saying this that they have "converted"? This could be a real sign that they haven't converted (OP, 229-230). A truly converted person would never boast about this but would rather demonstrate it by his life!

If the faithful of the parish of St. James's in Medjugorje sincerely confess their sins and pray, regardless of all the nursery rhyme "apparitions", they thereby certainly receive the same Divine graces that other believers receive who pray and validly receive the sacraments in Catholic churches throughout the world. The local Church has always held this belief (OP, 268-269).

VI. HOW MANY CHURCH COMMISSIONS AND INTERVENTIONS HAVE THERE BEEN?

Towards the end of June, 1981, the sensational news of the "Madonna's apparitions" to children in Medjugorje started to spread in the mass media. In mid-August of the same year, after having spoken with the so-called seers in Medjugorje on 21 July, in his first Statement, the bishop of Mostar-Duvno, Monsignor Pavao Žanić, emphasized that the most difficult question is whether or not this is a "subjective experience of the children or something supernatural?" (OP, 192). Even though he had informed the Pope and the Holy See on many occasions regarding the diverse opinions regarding Medjugorje, the bishop felt it was necessary to establish a diocesan commission in order to study the events.

A. The Chancery of the Diocese of Mostar
The First Church Commission (1982–1984).

Bishop Žanić established the first commission on 11 January, 1982, which worked until 1984 (OP, 43). It was composed of four theologians, two diocesan priests and two religious.

The bishop's new discoveries. The commission hadn't even gathered yet when on 14 January, 1982, something happened that marked the bishop's position once and for all. That day, three of the "seers" came to Mostar with the "Madonna's" message that the bishop, regarding the famous Herzegovinian Affair, acted too hastily, because he sought the removal of two Franciscan associate pastors who were causing problems in Mostar. The bishop, who during his lifetime venerated the Madonna with numerous devotions and pilgrimages, upon hearing that the phenomenon in Medjugorje was accusing him of irreligious disorder in reference to the parishes; that it didn't recognize in him a faithful son of the Church and the Madonna, the Mother of the Church, to whom a year earlier in September, 1980, the cathedral church of Mostar was consecrated; that the phenomenon was defending disobedient religious friars who were obstructing the normal functioning of the cathedral, began to look with suspicion upon the "messages" and the "apparitions" in Medjugorje. Despite this, the commission began its work.

Great sign. The commission held three conversations with the "seers". In 1982, the third meeting brought some results. On the bishop's request, the commission asked the "seers" to write down in double copy what kind of "great sign" shall appear and when it would happen. They were then to put their responses into two envelopes and then seal them. One of the envelopes was to be kept by them while the other at the Chancery office. When the "great sign" occurs, then the envelopes would be opened and the truth verified. However, five of the "seers" refused to answer the questions, because the Madonna did not permit them to. Yet the seminarian Ivan did respond in writing to the questions. He even said that the Madonna did not forbid him from responding to the questions. His response was more than inappropriate. A good number of lies and tricks are tied to this "great sign" which to this day hasn't occurred (OP, 102-108).

The Response to the Holy See. In November, 1983, the Congregation for the Doctrine of the Faith asked the bishop if the commission has come to some conclusions. Bishop Žanić wrote a study on Medjugorje and the Herzegovinian Affair, which he sent to Cardinal Josef Ratzinger. In the conclusion the bishop puts forth the question of the "apparitions":

Are they from God? — The "Madonna" of Medjugorje has brought more disorder and disarray here than there was earlier! Hence, he doesn't see how he can accept this as coming from God.

Is it from the devil? — He has difficulty accepting this hypothesis as well, even though the thought has crossed his mind.

Is it all a hoax? — From the outset one can notice that the children have sometimes lied. At times it's clear that what they say is what they have heard from the Franciscans, especially regarding the "Herzegovinian Affair". The bishop goes on to say that he awaits the judgement of the commission and the cessation of the "apparitions". The bishop waited seventeen years and he saw the Madonna in heaven on 11 January, 2000, (the day of his death) before seeing the "visions" of Medjugorje cease.

The Second extended commission (1984-1986).

In 1984 Bishop Žanić decided to extend the first commission. He wrote to all the theological faculties in Yugoslavia and sought the permission of certain religious superiors to allow their experts to join the commission.

There were fifteen members in the second commission: twelve priests and three medical experts. They held seven meetings in all. The first was in Mostar in March, 1984, and the seventh in the same city in May, 1986, during which the commission completed its work. The members of the commission voted on the following conclusion: *Non constat de supernaturalitate* (eleven voted "for", two "against", one accepted *"in nucleo"*, and one abstained). The commission prepared a draft "declaration" in which were listed the "unacceptable assertions" and "bizarre declarations", attributed to the curious phenomenon. The commission also stated that further investigations were not necessary nor the delaying of the official judgement of the Church. The bishop duly informed the bishops' conference and the Holy See, and he then informed the public during his homily in Medjugorje in 1987 (OP, 47–50).

The well-known negative position of the bishop, which he summarized in twenty-eight points in 1990, is significant since it speaks of the inauthentic nature of these supernatural apparitions (OP, 196).

In August of 1993, Bishop Žanić handed over the administration of the diocese to his successor, who continued his work at a swift pace.

B. The Bishops' Conference of Yugoslavia

The Bishops of Yugoslavia intervened twice, in 1984 and 1985, and asked both priests and faithful to await the judgement of the Church regarding the events of Medjugorje, which shall be given after intense investigations. Hence, no pilgrimages are to be organized as if "the Church has already given a positive judgement" (OP, 193).

The Third Commission (1987–1990).

In January 1987, upon the suggestion of the Congregation for the Doctrine of the Faith, Cardinal Franjo Kuharic, president of the bishops' conference, and Bishop Žanić made a joint communiqué in which they announced the formation of the third commission and in which they asked the faithful not to organize pilgrimages motivated "from above" which would ascribe to the events of Medjugorje (OP, 196). The commission was composed of eleven priests (six religious, five diocesan), four physicians and psychologists and one religious sister as secretary.

The commission held twenty-three meetings in Zagreb at the secretariat of the bishops' conference. The first meeting was in April 1987 and the twenty-third in September 1990.

A characteristic of the third commission was to work on the findings and results of the previous commissions and *ex novo*. Everything was done under oath and no statements for the public were made. The results of their four-year-long efforts were presented to the members of the bishops' conference in Zagreb in 1990. Discussions at the bishops' conference on the "apparitions" were held on four occasions: 25 April, 9 October, and 27 November, 1990, and the declaration on Medjugorje was accepted through a vote held in Zadar on 10 April, 1991: nineteen bishops voted for the declaration while one abstained.

The declaration states: "During the regular session of the bishops' conference of Yugoslavia, held in Zadar from 9–11 April, 1991, the following was accepted:

DECLARATION

From the very beginning, the bishops have been following the events of Medjugorje through the local bishop, the bishops' commission and the commission of the bishops' conference of Yugoslavia for Medjugorje.

On the basis of studies made so far, it cannot be affirmed that these matters concern supernatural apparitions or revelations.

Yet the gathering of the faithful from various parts of the world to Medjugorje, inspired by reasons of faith or other motives, require the pastoral attention and care, first of all, of the local bishop and then of the other bishops with him, so that in Medjugorje and all connected with it, a healthy devotion towards the Blessed Virgin Mary according to the teachings of the Church may be promoted. The bishops will also provide special liturgical and pastoral directives corresponding to this aim. At the same time, they will continue to study all the events of Medjugorje through the commissions.

Zadar, 10 April, 1991,
The Bishops of Yugoslavia

The Aggression. In the years that followed, Croatia and Bosnia-Herzegovina found themselves victims of a terrible aggression. With the formation of new states, new bishops' conferences were established. Despite the declaration of the bishops' conference, *Non constat de supernaturalitate*, that is, that it cannot be affirmed that these matters concern supernatural apparitions or revelations in Medjugorje, the adherents of this phenomenon consistently claim that the "Madonna is appearing".

If our bishops' conference, despite numerous curious visitors to Medjugorje, notwithstanding massive publicity accompanied by charismatic inspirations, had the courage to declare on the basis of serious, solid and expert investigations, that there was no proof in Medjugorje of any supernatural apparitions, this then is a sign that the Church even in the twentieth century is still "the pillar and bulwark of the truth" (1 Tim 3:15)—(OP, 151).

C. The Interventions of the Holy See

The Congregation for the Doctrine of the Faith has intervened four times through two of its secretaries, while the prefect, Cardinal Ratzinger, has also made an important intervention.

In 1985, Monsignor Alberto Bovone notified the secretary of the bishops' conference of Italy not to organize official pilgrimages to Medjugorje.

In 1995, Monsignor Tarcisio Bertone wrote to the bishop of Langres, Monsignor Leon Taverdet, and repeated the same to Monsignor Lucien Daloz of Besançon, France, who were interested in knowing the position of the Holy See on Medjugorje.

Finally, in 1998, the same secretary wrote to Monsignor Gilbert Aubry, bishop of Réunion. All these letters emphasized that pilgrimages, whether private or public, were not allowed if they presupposed the authenticity of the apparitions, since this would be in contradiction to the declaration of the Bishops' Conference of Yugoslavia.

Ratzinger's *Frei erfunden*. In 1998, when a certain German gathered various statements that were supposedly made by the Holy Father and the cardinal prefect, and forwarded them to the Vatican in the form of a memorandum, the cardinal responded in writing on 22 July, 1998: "The only thing I can say regarding statements on Medjugorje ascribed to the Holy Father and myself is that they are complete invention"—*Frei erfunden* (OP, 283).

Conclusion. Not only are these statements ascribed to the Holy Father and Cardinal Ratzinger "complete invention", but the numerous messages of Medjugorje, ascribed to the Madonna are also complete invention. If our faith is considered *obsequium rationabile*—rational service to God, true and healthy spiritual worship, as it rightfully is (Rom 12:1), then it cannot be any person's private fantasy or illusion (OP, 84). The Church is competent to say this. In her name, thirty chosen priests and physicians, working together in three commissions for ten years, in more than thirty meetings, dutifully and expertly investigated the events of Medjugorje and brought forth their results of study. And not one but twenty bishops responsibly declared that there existed no proof that the events in Medjugorje concerned supernatural apparitions or revelations. The believer who respects both principles, *ratio et fides*, adheres to this criterion, convinced that the Church does not deceive.

Regarding Medjugorje, there's a real danger that the Madonna and the Church could be privatized. People could start contriving a Madonna and a Church according to their own taste, perception and deception: by not submitting their reason as believers to the official Magisterium of the Church, but rather forcing the Church to follow and recognize their fantasy.

Naive believers could easily then leave the living fountains of grace in their own parishes to mosey on down to Medjugorje or follow the "seers" around the world, who by the way, thanks to the "apparitions" have good homes and a comfortable existence–at least that's what the mass media say.

There are at least six or seven religious or quasi-religious communities, just initiating or already established, some of diocesan right, some not, which have arbitrarily been installed in Medjugorje without the permission of the local diocesan authorities. These communities are more a sign of disobedience than a real charisma of obedience in this Church!

There exists a problem in this diocese of Mostar-Duvno that in recent years has practically precipitated a schism. At least eight Franciscan priests, who have rebelled against the decision of the Holy See to transfer a certain number of parishes administered by the Franciscans to diocesan priests, have been expelled from the Franciscan Order and suspended *a divinis*. In spite of this, they have occupied at least five parishes through force, and continue to exercise sacred functions. They invalidly assist at marriages, hear confessions without canonical faculties and invalidly confer the sacrament of confirmation. Three years ago, they even invited a deacon of the Old Catholic Church who falsely presented himself as a bishop, to preside at a confirmation and he "confirmed" about eight hundred young people in three parishes.

Two of these expelled priests sought after episcopal consecration from Swiss bishop of the Old Catholic Church, Hans Gerny, yet without any result.

So many invalid sacraments, so much disobedience, violence, sacrilege, disorder, irregularities, and not a single "message" from tens of thousands of "apparitions" has been directed towards eliminating these scandals. A very strange thing indeed!

The Church, from the local to supreme level, from the beginning to this very day, has clearly and constantly repeated: *Non constat de supernaturalitate!* No to pilgrimages that would ascribe a supernatural nature to the apparitions, no shrine of the Madonna, no authentic messages or revelations, no true visions!

This is the state of things today. How will things be tomorrow? We'll leave them in God's hands and under Our Lady's protection!

APPENDIX II
REGARDING THE EVENTS OF MEDJUGORJE: PART 1

Criteria for Discerning Apparitions
Bishop Ratko Perić

MEDJUGORJE, A PARISH IN THE DIOCESE OF Mostar-Duvno in Herzegovina, is known not only to Catholic Croats but to the entire world. For fourteen years now, much has been spoken and written on the "seers", and on the "apparitions" of the Blessed Virgin Mary in this parish. The ecclesiastical ministry of the diocesan bishop Monsignor Pavao Žanić has been marked by commissions, investigations, communiqués, declarations, meetings with the "seers", and persuasions and dissuasions regarding these events. His coadjutor and successor, from the time of his taking over the ministry of bishop in Mostar (1993), has received many letters of varying content, expressing all types of advice and suggestions on the events of Medjugorje. Some have sought to impede these phenomena, while others have endeavoured to have them approved and propagated. He himself *volens-nolens* has been asked in some public appearances and interviews to say something and to explain himself. He never refrained though, from supporting the declaration of the bishops' conference of 1991. He also mentioned the events of Medjugorje at the bishops' synod in Rome, in October of 1994. Therefore, this current and contemporary theme cannot be ignored.

It is impossible to provide a brief summary of the events tied to Medjugorje. There exists an abundant amount of literature from the naive to the fanatic. This article limits itself to bringing out the theological criteria for heavenly "private" apparitions on earth. Many worthwhile articles and books have been written on this topic that systematically and expertly write on "private" apparitions and revelations. For this reason, the aim of this article is to gather criteria that can help those who already know certain facts, to compare them to these rules and evaluate the conclusions. Consequently, to bring forth the official documents and declarations of the Church regarding the events in the parish of Medjugorje in the diocese of Mostar-Duvno and finally, to summarize the position of the diocesan chancery in a few points, keeping in mind the well-known declaration of the bishops' conference of 1991.

1) According to the teachings of the II Vatican Council, the historical person of Jesus, His appearance and revelation, by word and deed, through miraculous signs, passed on to us through his apostles, is the final and complete revelation of God, to which nothing essential can be added or taken away. Therefore, beyond this first revelation, there shall be no other revelation before Jesus' Second Coming. In this sense, the Council is quite unambiguous: "As a result, He Himself—to see Whom is to see the Father (cf. Jn 14:9)—completed and perfected Revelation and confirmed it with divine guarantees. He did this by the total fact of His presence and self-manifestation—by words and works, signs and miracles, but above all by His death and glorious resurrection from the dead, and finally by sending the Spirit of truth. He revealed that God was with us, to deliver us from the darkness of sin and death, and to raise us up to eternal life."

2) **Holy Scripture**. In the Old Testament, the word "listen" is used twice as often as the words "to see" or "to look" (1080: 520). Along with this, the relationship of man to God, including the most humble friend of God, is a relationship of words and not one of seeing or of vision: One cannot see God and remain alive, as was also valid for Moses. God revealed His glory to him but not his face (cf. Ex 33:20-23). On the other hand, "listening" to the word of God is the regular attitude of the believer, the prophet and the king. It is no surprise that the Jewish Credo (I believe), does not begin with the words "I believe in God almighty", but rather with: Shema Israel—Hear, O Israel (Deut 5:1).

In the New Testament, especially in the Letter to the Hebrews (1:1-2), emphasis is placed on the fact that God has spoken many times and in many ways to the fathers and prophets. Yet all revelation—of the Holy Trinity and of our salvation—definitely and completely, is found in the revelation of the only Son of God, who is the reflection of the glory and imprint of God's being. The theology of St. John the apostle and evangelist particularly emphasizes this vision and revelation of the Son: "No one has ever seen God; it is the only Son, who is nearest to the Father's heart, who has made Him known" (Jn 1:18). Jesus is the revelation of the Father, his image and icon. Hence, he who sees the Son sees the Father. Jesus shall praise those who believe and have not seen (Jn 20:29). In John's theology, "seeing" and "believing" are one and the same. The Word of God, the Second Divine Person, did not "appear" in a human body, but became body and lived amongst us, in our human condition, in space and time. This revelation is the substance of our faith and also the highest expression of revelation. For this reason, the religion of Christ is the religion of the Incarnation, which surpasses all types of apparitions. After His death and resurrection, Christ appeared many times in His glorious body, identical to the preceding one He had. These apparitions had a dual purpose: on the one hand, they proved Jesus' resurrection, and on the other, through these apparitions Jesus finished His instructions to His disciples: He gave them the power to forgive sins, He established their general mission to proclaim the Gospel to all creation, He told them to wait for the Holy Spirit, and to give witness to all, so that people could believe, be baptized and saved. After the ascension of Jesus, apparitions are no longer necessary.

3) Theological problems and explanations. Theologians who are professionally involved in studying Revelation are loath to talk about private apparitions and messages. Yet amongst the people, many of the faithful are inclined to believe in such phenomena, because they provide something visible, touchable, something that can be felt or sensed. This is especially true if it is something that becomes visible in their lives in the form

Criteria for Discerning Apparitions

of some kind of emotional aid, a healing or similar experience. Such phenomena and beliefs can easily slide into true superstition and forms of magic, especially if the desired "grace" or "miracle" doesn't occur in the way the person expected and "prayed for". In such situations, it is not uncommon to come across even suicide. Yet it must be objectively recognized that in recent years and decades, tens of millions of people have made pilgrimages to the recognized Marian shrines of the world, such as Lourdes, Fatima, Czestochowa, Loreto, and Marija Bistrica. This is also another reason that so much is written and spoken on the problem of private apparitions. Moreover, he who in his ecclesiastical ministry feels it his responsibility (whether this be in a theological, investigative or episcopal teaching ministry) has the duty to defend the faith of the common folk and not to allow (under the veil of various public religious gestures) the concealing of any superstitions, nor permit the faith of the people to be based upon false apparitions.

Theologically speaking, in order for private apparitions to be accepted as authentic, they must be characterized by some essential traits and be free of dubious elements. R. Silic, a professor of theology in Sarajevo, advised the priests of his time briefly and clearly: "May pastors of souls be careful not to quickly believe in revelations so that they may not be deceived by pious women."

Another Franciscan priest from Herzegovina, K. Vasilj, provides three criteria:

1) The appearing Mary must be in total concordance with Mary of the New Testament;

2) The person who claims that Mary is appearing to him/her must be completely sincere and truthful;

3) That person must also be psychologically healthy, unperturbed by illusions and hallucinations.

A serious theological article on apparitions was written ten years ago by Rev. Jean Galot, a Jesuit professor at the Pontifical Gregorian University in Rome. He presents three problems that should be resolved while questioning the authenticity of apparitions:

1) Did a true apparition occur?

2) Is the person who presented this trustworthy?

3) Can the theology of the apparitions be explained and placed within the life of the Church?

This third problem should be placed first, and the theologian gives it much attention. Describing various apparitions depicted in the Bible, he also brings out his own theological considerations. In the faith, there exists a fundamental light that is shrouded by darkness. Hence, some seek apparitions in order to confirm their faith. They would like to compensate for what they lack in believing by "seeing". "It is exactly this desire which drives a good number of today's Christians towards persons who say that they have apparitions or visions."

The first criterion for discerning authenticity is rarity and exceptionality. Apparitions are essentially very rare occurrences. They cannot replace the Faith. "Hence, apparitions which would continue for a long period of time, becoming a part of daily life of the seers, would tend to transform Christian living into seeing and would then liberate it from the darkness of faith. Such frequency would be a motive to doubt the authenticity of the apparitions."

The second criterion for judging authenticity would be the conformity of the ensuing messages and revelations to the truths of the Faith. If there were to be any doctrinal errors, or affirmations incompatible with the teachings of the Gospel, with Christian love; or if they were to contain slander, to instigate rebellion, to entice "disobedience towards Church authority", in such cases their validity would have to be questioned.

Thirdly, "it would equally be detrimental if the transcendent origin of the apparitions were to indicate a certain human manipulation: when the recipients of apparitions determine the place, date, regularity or programme. They do not then concern a phenomenon from above, but more or less a direct experience of the actors on earth".

Fourthly, one also has to consider the fruits. "It must be observed that the spiritual fruits alone cannot suffice in discerning the authenticity of apparitions. There have been cases

Criteria for Discerning Apparitions

where many conversions were registered, which then only wound up being rejected by Church authorities as unfounded."

Želimir Puljić, once a member of the diocesan commission for the investigation of the events of Medjugorje and who today is bishop of Dubrovnik, emphasizes the necessity of a serious analysis of the following elements for the discernment of the authenticity of apparitions:

- the psychological equilibrium of the person;
- the object or content of private apparitions; and
- the moral implications on the "seer" or on others who accept them.

Other theologians present up to eight criteria for discerning authentic from false private apparitions and revelations. In order to evaluate them, one would have to respond to these questions:

- What is the basic information on the "seers" like, and how are they judged to be?
- Has there been a concrete realization of the seers' announced predictions?
- Is the seer honest and respectful towards his superiors (spiritual director, pastor, bishop)?
- Is an absolutely authentic text of the "messages" obtainable?
- Does there exist any harmony between the so-called messages and revelations to the official teachings of the Church?
- Are the so-called messages useful towards the eternal salvation of people?
- Have the so-called apparitions survived all the difficulties of time and all investigations?
- Have there been significant fruits in every aspect?

R. Fisichella, a respected professor of theology at the Gregorian University in Rome, after making some biblical observations, stresses the following criteria for discerning the authenticity and truthfulness of private apparitions.

- These visions must never overshadow the authentic and radical Revelation described in Holy Scripture;
- They must always respect the mystery and secrecy of genuine revelation; "it is absurd, not to say blasphemous—not only to western mentality—that during a vision one could photograph the face of Jesus or the Virgin!";
- They must respect the mutual completion of charisms, and the greatest of these is love; hence they should not be directed against love, which is the centre of Christian revelation.

Furthermore, for a theological analysis of so-called private apparitions, it is important to keep in mind the social and cultural factors of the place where the apparitions occur, a linguistic verification of the descriptions of the apparitions would be necessary, and finally, a thorough psychological analysis of the seers should be undertaken. One also must recall that apparitions are always something rare and extraordinary; this is an important element for their discernment. "If apparitions were to occur on a daily basis in the life of a believer, or if they were to continue for years, this would obviously create serious problems for the theology of faith". Every apparition must refer to or return to the revelation of Christ, presume it, and lead towards it as well.

Referring to the "scientific research" of Father René Laurentin, a French priest and publicist, on the "apparitions" at Medjugorje, J. Curic, a professor at the Catholic Theological Faculty in Zagreb, provides a few significant critical points that greatly contribute towards clearing up the mentioned difficulties:

- Curic first of all differentiates between the popular term "scientific" as it was comprehended in the nineteenth century and the way it is understood today in the twentieth century. Real scientists today are much more humble and careful, due to the likely rebuttals and replies they can easily receive tomorrow for their conclusions of today.
- While the French scientist lists facts and figures, he remains in line with his historical profession. But when he presents the actual "visions" of the seers, he does not take

into consideration the "experience of the presence" as a significant element of spiritual consciousness. This is one of his greatest drawbacks according to the Croatian Jesuit.

- A three-day stay in Medjugorje during the Christmas rush gave Laurentin the opportunity to establish that the seers were mentally healthy, simple and totally honest. Curic observes, though, that God does not reserve his gifts only to those who are "scientifically" sane. He portrays Laurentin's great leaps to conclusions: "Meanwhile, if he were to come to a perfectly certain conviction that the seers of Medjugorje are totally sincere in their declarations, this would not give him the right to conclude—that the subjective sincerity of their speech proves the objective truthfulness of their visions."
- Following this, Curic poses a general problem of principle: "What if anything can science research and verify regarding extraordinary, miraculous phenomena, whether they be of divine or demonic origin? It appears that *Glas Koncila* did not proceed properly when it reiterated the 'scientific nature' of Laurentin's approach to the Madonna's 'apparitions'; as if the problem of the authenticity of these apparitions (after all our Balkan controversies), could now be resolved in a proper manner—the scientific way." Laurentin recognizes that in the end "the verdict must be left up to the Church".

Curic then responds: "Why would this scientist, having concluded his scientific research, now restrain his scientific conclusions and bow before the unscientific authority of the Church? If science can scientifically establish that a certain virus causes cancer, then no bishop could ever deny this conclusion! Hence, if science scientifically establishes that the Madonna is 'appearing' in Medjugorje, can the bishops along with their commissions deny this?" Here the critic is examining two things:

1) God's grace cannot be an "object" of scientific research;

2) yet, through grace, God can touch a person in such a way that this encounter manifests itself in a miraculous healing, miraculous knowledge, etc.

But science is incapable of establishing the miraculous nature of these happenings!

Curic differentiates between mystical and prophetic types of private revelations. Mystics usually cannot and do not know how to express what they have experienced. Prophetic souls "behave themselves diversely: they are convinced of the truthfulness of their experience and consciously wish to go public, so that people may listen and follow their 'message'". The phenomenon of Medjugorje falls into this prophetic category. Yet the mystical and prophetic types of revelations cannot be verified by science, but only through a spiritual evaluation.

Curic also presents the differences between public Revelation, which is absolutely necessary for salvation and which extends for all eternity to all of mankind, and private revelations, which no one has the right to impose upon or extend towards others. This results from the private nature of private revelations.

- This type of private revelation does not lose its private character even after the so-called "approval" or *nihil obstat* of the Church, which can also revoke this "approval". Curic's conclusion is: "Whoever believes along with Laurentin that the Madonna has truly appeared to the seers of Medjugorje—and not once or twice, but thousands of times—that person would have to keep in mind the historical fact that even very noble divine initiatives have ended in failure, because they were defeated by the disproportionate propaganda of various naive and fanatical persons. On the other hand, one should not forget that according to the Bible, God is not bound by our human legal or scientific methods."

4) The position of the Church. Cardinal Prospero Lambertini, who became Pope Benedict XIV (1740-1758), explained the value and strength of "approval" which is given to apparitions, visions and revelations: "It is important to know that the public approval (of apparitions) after serious examination, is provided for the education and benefit of believers. But even though such approved revelations cannot claim nor be given the consensus of the Catholic faith, they nevertheless require the assent of human faith according to the rules of prudence, in virtue of which these revelations are considered probable or piously credible." This wise rule is also valid today.

In the most recent Catechism of the Catholic Church there exists a clear position regarding "private" apparitions and revelations: "Throughout the ages, there have been so-called 'private' revelations, some of which have been recognized by the authority of the Church. They do not belong, however, to the deposit of faith. It is not their role to improve or complete Christ's definitive Revelation, but to help live more fully by it in a certain period of history. Guided by the Magisterium of the Church, the *sensus fidelium* knows how to discern and welcome in these revelations whatever constitutes an authentic call of Christ or His saints to the Church."

5) The phenomenon of Medjugorje and declarations of the Church. From 1981 onward, three ecclesiastical commissions have worked in succession on studying the phenomenon of Medjugorje. They could not avoid taking into consideration the above-mentioned principles and criteria during their investigations. The commissions, the local bishop and the bishops' conference gave certain communiqués, declarations or explanations that were accepted or rejected by the followers or the opponents of "supernatural apparitions". Here are the most important official declarations, signed and dated by the competent authorities:

- In mid-August 1981, in the declaration of Monsignor Pavao Žanić, bishop of Mostar-Duvno, which was open to honest interpretation, it was said that the "most difficult question remains whether this is the subjective experience of the children or something supernatural?"
- On 14 January, 1984, the archbishop of Zagreb, Cardinal Franjo Kuharic, prohibited the seers of Medjugorje from appearing in all the parishes of the archdiocese of Zagreb until an ecclesiastical judgement was passed on the events.
- On 24 March, 1984, the first communiqué of the expanded commission was made public. The commission asked that the mass media refrain from giving judgments of the events until the competent Church commission provides its judgment. It also asked that organized pilgrimages not be allowed; that

the "seers" and Church personnel in Medjugorje not give any statements regarding the so-called "apparitions": "Since the events in the parish of Medjugorje have had a considerable echo in our local Church and throughout the world, the bishop felt it necessary to expand the present four-member commission in order to choose new members from all the theological faculties from the Church in Croatia and Slovenia, from various theological disciplines as well as experts in medical sciences.... [T]he commission does not approve of priests or Catholic lay people organizing pilgrimages to Medjugorje, or public appearances of the seers before it has made a judgment on the authenticity of the apparitions."

- On 11 October, 1984, in the second communiqué, we read amongst other things: "The commission has decided to further study all the experiences of the children and the interpretations of these experiences by the pastoral workers of Medjugorje, even though it already notices some difficulties of a disciplinary and theological nature in the messages of Medjugorje."

- On 12 October, 1984, the bishops' conference asked that official pilgrimages to Medjugorje not be organized: "The bishops advise that regarding the events of Medjugorje, it is necessary to await the judgment of the competent Church authorities which shall be given after a thorough and expert examination of the events. Hence, official pilgrimages to Medjugorje cannot be organized as if the Church had already given a positive judgment on these events."

- On 30 October, Bishop Žanić presented the (unofficial) position of the diocesan chancery in a fifteen-point statement demonstrating negative factors and facts tied to the phenomenon of Medjugorje.

- On 8 March, 1985, the third communiqué of the mentioned commission on the results of experts and studies was made known. Amongst other things it said: "The commission feels that the most difficult question arising from the events concerns the ecclesiastical disobedience of two former chaplains of Mostar who refused to be transferred, appealing to the messages of Medjugorje."

Criteria for Discerning Apparitions

- On 18 April, 1985, the bishops' conference once again made an appeal to the faithful against making official pilgrimages to Medjugorje: "The bishops are following the events of Medjugorje in Herzegovina with due attention. During this meeting they reconfirmed their previous directives and decisions regarding these events."
- On 23 May, 1985 came the warning of the Congregation for the Doctrine of the Faith—signed by the Secretary of the Congregation, Monsignor Alberto Bovone—addressed to the Italian Bishops' Conference, not to organize pilgrimages to Medjugorje. Here is the entire text of the letter sent by the Holy See to the secretary of the Italian Bishops' Conference, Monsignor Egidio Caporello:

> Your Excellency,
>
> From many parts, especially from the competent ordinary of Mostar (Yugoslavia), one can gather and lament the vast propaganda given to the "events" tied to the so-called apparitions in Medjugorje, for which pilgrimages and other initiatives have been organized that only contribute to the creation of confusion amongst the faithful and interfere with the work of the appointed commission which is delicately examining the "events" under scrutiny.
>
> In order to avoid enhancing this mentioned propaganda and speculation going on in Italy, despite all that has been expressed and recommended by the bishops' conference of Yugoslavia, could this Presidency please suggest to the Italian Episcopate to publicly discourage the organizing of pilgrimages to the so-called centre of apparitions, as well as all other forms of publicity, especially written materials, which could be considered prejudicial to a sober assertion of the facts on the part of the special commission which has been canonically formed for this purpose.
>
> I take this opportunity to express the assurances of my highest regards....

- On 31 May, 1985, came the fourth communiqué of the mentioned commission in which the themes and difficulties worked upon were presented: "A comparison of the concept of conversion as presented in the Gospels to the phenomenon of Medjugorje; problems of discipline regarding two former chaplains of Mostar who appeal to the messages of Medjugorje; theological problems regarding some of the messages of Medjugorje; and insufficient documentation on the supposed miraculous healings."

- On 27 September, 1985, the fifth communiqué of the same commission was published in which they briefly explained what the participants were doing.
- In January, 1987, on the suggestion of the Congregation for the Doctrine of the Faith that a commission of experts be established at the level of the bishops' conference, a communiqué by Cardinal Kuharić and Bishop Žanić was published:
- "While waiting for the results of the commission's investigations and the judgment of the Church, may pastors and the faithful observe prudence in these circumstances. Therefore, organized pilgrimages or other manifestations, motivated by supernatural attributes given to the phenomenon of Medjugorje are not allowed."
- On 25 July, 1987, during a Mass held in the parish of Medjugorje, Bishop Žanić referred to the so-called apparitions. Here is a paragraph which was cited in many newspapers throughout the world: "It is said that Our Lady began appearing at Podbrdo on mount Crnica, but when the police banned going there, she went into homes, on fences, into the fields, into vineyards and tobacco fields, she appeared in the church, on the altar, in the sacristy, in the choir loft, on the roof, on the bell-tower, on roads, on the road to Cerno, in a car, in a 'bus, on a carriage, in a few places in Mostar, in more places in Sarajevo, in the convents of Zagreb, in Varazdin, in Switzerland, in Italy, again on Podbrdo, on Mount Krizevac, in the parish, in the parish rectory, etc. Surely not even half the places of the so-called apparitions have been counted, and a sober person who venerates Our Lady would naturally ask himself: "Dear Mother of God, what are they doing to you?"

- In 1990 the diocesan bishop, Bishop Žanić, published his position on Medjugorje by summarizing in twenty-nine points what decisively dissuaded him from any belief in the truthfulness of the so-called supernatural apparitions.
- On 10 April, 1991, came the declaration of the former bishops' conference on the basis of the results of its commission, which said that there are no valid reasons that could verify the events of Medjugorje as supernatural apparitions or revelations. The declaration in its entirety follows.
- "During the regular session of the Bishops' Conference of Yugoslavia, held in Zadar from 9–11 April, 1991, the following was accepted:

A DECLARATION

From the very beginning, the bishops have been following the events of Medjugorje through the local bishop, the bishops' commission and the commission of the Bishops' Conference of Yugoslavia for Medjugorje.

> On the basis of studies made so far, it cannot be affirmed that these matters concern supernatural apparitions or revelations.
>
> Yet the gathering of faithful from various parts of the world to Medjugorje, inspired by reasons of faith or other motives, require the pastoral attention and care, first of all, of the local bishop and then of the other bishops with him, so that in Medjugorje and all connected with it, a healthy devotion towards the Blessed Virgin Mary according to the teachings of the Church may be promoted. The bishops will also provide special liturgical and pastoral directives corresponding to this aim. At the same time, they will continue to study all the events of Medjugorje through the commissions.
>
> The Bishops of Yugoslavia
> Zadar, 10 April, 1991

The statement was approved by the bishops with nineteen in favour and one abstaining.

Later on, war broke out in the Republic of Croatia and the Republic of Bosnia-Herzegovina. Followers of the phenomenon of Medjugorje still claim that Our Lady is "appearing". The diocesan chancery has warned on many occasions that one cannot claim or preach in churches on supernatural apparitions due to the fact that it is impossible to confirm that Our Lady is appearing. Hence, official pilgrimages to Medjugorje are not allowed.

6) The Church has still not recognized the supernatural nature of the "apparitions" at Medjugorje. Having in mind the previously mentioned rules, which the commission members empowered with the task of investigating the phenomenon have taken into consideration, and on the basis of which they have suggested to the local bishop and the bishops' conference to maintain the conviction that it is impossible to prove the supernatural nature of the "apparitions"; and also keeping in mind what was said and written in the past and especially recently on the events in the parish of Medjugorje, we present a few basic positions that the diocesan chancery has in various ways made public and of which it has duly informed the Holy See, and still maintains today:

a. **The Case of Herzegovina—Medjugorje.** The local bishop of Mostar, Bishop Pavao Žanić, at the beginning of the so-called apparitions in 1981, was open to news that on the territory of the diocese of Mostar-Duvno, in the parish of Medjugorje, there appeared the Blessed Virgin Mary. However, when the so-called seers in their "messages", which were presumed to be those of the Blessed Virgin, began giving anti-Church statements linked to the "case of Herzegovina" regarding parishes, parish jurisdiction and canonical faculties, defending the disobedience of certain Franciscan pastors of souls, prudence demanded taking a more cautious stance. The competent Church authorities, first of all the diocesan bishop on the basis of investigations made by his two commissions from 1982–1986, and then the commission of the bishops' conference on the grounds of its investigations from 1987–1990, both brought forth the following negative judgement regarding the supernatural nature of the apparitions at Medjugorje: "It cannot be affirmed that these matters concern supernatural apparitions or revelations", of the Madonna or any other saints.

Therefore, it is forbidden to claim and profess the contrary, in churches and ecclesiastical communities, that is, as if Our Lady appeared there or is still appearing.

b. **The fruits**. Despite the numerous people who come to Medjugorje "with religious and other motives", and even though there are religious, priests and bishops, the curious and those seeking physical healings and spiritual conversions; despite the dozens of books and brochures written in favour of the so-called apparitions at Medjugorje, all from the pens of famous writers in the world; despite the hundreds of thousands of confessions and holy communions made, which the supporters of Medjugorje consistently stress, the declaration of the bishops' conference clearly states: "It cannot be affirmed that these matters concern supernatural apparitions or revelations" of the Madonna. The fruits that are so often mentioned are not proof of "supernatural apparitions or revelations" of the Madonna, but insomuch as they are authentically Christian, they can be understood as a product of the regular workings of the grace of God, through faith in God and the intercession of Mary the Mother of Christ, and through the holy sacraments present in the Catholic Church. (And this is not to mention anything at all about the negative fruits associated with Medjugorje!)

c. **The "messages"** of Medjugorje on prayer, fasting, faith, conversion and peace, repeated daily as something new but, in reality, always the same, as if the Madonna conveyed them to the "seers", are already present in Holy Scripture and the Magisterium of the Catholic Church. Anyone wishing to obey and live according to God's commandments and the teachings of the Church can pray, fast, believe, convert and work for peace anywhere in the world. This Christian requirement and duty cannot be lessened or enhanced or strengthened by any confirmed apparition, let alone thousands of unsubstantiated "apparitions" at Medjugorje.

d. **Contradictions**. In some of the statements made by the so-called seers of Medjugorje published in the past fourteen years, there are such contradictions, falsehoods and banalities, which cannot be attributed at all to our heavenly Mother *Sedes*

Sapientiae—Seat of Wisdom, since there does not exist even a minimal guarantee of credibility. On the basis of such statements and the events tied to the statements: it cannot be affirmed that these matters concern "supernatural apparitions or revelations" of the Madonna or others. The talk of a "great sign", of "ten secrets", which Our Lady supposedly conveyed to the children, resembles the scare tactics that are typical of non-Catholic communities and not the sound teachings of the Catholic Church.

e. **Normal people**. Of the six former children of Medjugorje who claimed that the Madonna "appeared" to them, one of them entered the seminary, another entered a type of mixed religious community, and with the passing of time both of them left their respective communities. Five of them have married, including the latter two mentioned. These faithful, even after thousands of so-called apparitions, remain so "normal" in their behaviour, that only their words attest to their "encounters" with the Madonna. They remain "normal" as do all other "normal" faithful who have never seen the Madonna, yet as Catholics still firmly believe in her and fervently pray for her intercession. Our holy faith, which is based upon listening to the word of God and not upon seeing heavenly apparitions, is at the same time an *obsequium rationabile* ("reasonable service") Rom 12:1), that contradicts the insistent propaganda on daily or very frequent "apparitions". Some are behaving in direct contradiction to the beatitude that Jesus uttered to the doubting apostle Thomas: "Blessed are those who have not seen and yet believe" (Jn 20:29).

f. **Charitable activities**. Despite all the charitable and humanitarian aid that has been collected and is still being collected throughout the world during this terrible war in this war-stricken area, through the help of the mass media serving the Medjugorje propaganda machinery (in the name of Medjugorje and also passing through Medjugorje channels to the needy), there exists no reason to profess the claim that "these matters concern supernatural apparitions or revelations", neither of the "Queen of Peace" nor of any other type of supernatural apparition.

g. **Destroyed and undestroyed churches**. Neither can it be considered proof of the supernatural nature of the "apparitions" the fact that the church of St. James the Apostle in Medjugorje was not hit by grenades during this war, while for instance, both of the churches of Mostar and many other churches in Herzegovina, Bosnia and Croatia were bombed and destroyed.

h. **The unrelenting process of "apparitions"**. Those who for the past 14 years have claimed that the "Queen of Peace is appearing" in Medjugorje precisely every day (even though on 30 June, 1981, it was said that there would be "apparitions for only three more days"), not knowing how to stop the process of "apparitions" without stopping those who come there called by some so-called apparitions or with other motives, are certainly not doing any favours to the honour and truth of the Madonna, the Mother of the Church. Nor are they doing any favours to the Church itself, the spiritual Mother of all Catholics who base their Catholic faith in God and devotion to Mary not upon some childish stories and hallucinations, but upon the authentic Revelation of God and its authentic interpretation guaranteed by the Holy Spirit received through the living Magisterium of the Church.

i. **Tourism**. By stating the truth that it is impossible to prove and affirm that the Blessed Virgin Mary has ever appeared to anyone in Medjugorje, we do not wish to dissuade the efforts of the republic and the media to attract the greatest possible number of tourists to our country. Yet let these necessary and useful tourist aims be based upon our praiseworthy Christian traditions and the martyrdoms for the Faith undergone in the past and present, along with the well-known values and beauty of our homeland, which the Almighty has given her, and not upon unsubstantiated and groundless supernatural "apparitions", "revelations" and "messages". The Croatian civil authorities and media should clearly differentiate these facts and keep in mind the official position of the Church, if they wish to adhere to the principle of not intervening in the affairs of the Church and want to remain objective.

j. **No shrine and no pilgrimages**. Neither the diocesan bishop as the head of the local diocese of Mostar-Duvno, nor any other competent authority has ever officially declared the parish church of St. James the Apostle in Medjugorje as a "Marian shrine" and no "cult" of the Madonna based upon so-called apparitions has ever been proclaimed. Due to these discrepancies, the local bishop has repeatedly forbidden anyone from preaching or speaking in churches on the supernatural nature of these so-called "apparitions and revelations", and he has asked that no official pilgrimages be organized, be they at the level of parishes, dioceses or generally in the name of the Church. These and similar warnings were made by our former bishops' conference and the Holy See. Whoever acts to the contrary is directly going against the official statements of the Church, which even after fourteen years of so-called apparitions and widespread propaganda, still remain valid.

A healthy devotion to the Mother of God in accord with the teachings of the Church, especially with the Papal Exhortation *Marialis cultus* of 1974, must be nurtured and promoted in every person, family, church, parish and diocese of the Catholic Church.

Mostar, May, 1995
✠ *Monsignor Ratko Perić*
Bishop of Mostar

APPENDIX III

Extracts from the Diary of Vicka Ivanković

These extracts from Vicka's diary, which Father Laurentin claimed did not exist, are from the archives of the chancery in Mostar. It will be noted that they are not in strict chronological sequence, but this is the case in the original. Vicka's educational standard is evidently not of a very high level, and she makes no use of quotation marks. It is not always completely clear whether a remark is to be attributed to her or to the Madonna. Quotation marks have been inserted into this translation at the points where they appear most appropriate.

Saturday, 19 December, 1981: I asked about the Herzegovinian problem, particularly where Father Ivica Vego was concerned. The Madonna answered that Bishop Žanić is the one most to blame for all this disorder. So far as Father Ivica Vego was concerned, the Madonna said that he was not at fault, but nevertheless the bishop has full authority. She told him (Father Vego) to remain in Mostar and not to leave.

Saturday, 3 January, 1982: All we seers together asked the Madonna about Father Ivica Vego. The Madonna replied: "Ivica is not to blame. If he is expelled from the Franciscan Order, let him remain steadfast. Every day I say: 'Peace, peace', but there is ever more strife. Let him remain, Ivica is not at fault." She repeated this three times. We all heard it, and we told him. "The bishop is not maintaining order and that is why he is to blame. He will not be bishop for ever. I will show justice in the (heavenly) kingdom."[1] This lasted for ten minutes, all about Ivica.

---

[1] There is only one possible interpretation of the remark that Bishop Žanić would not be bishop forever, and this is that his successor would adopt a different policy. This has manifestly not been the case, and Bishop Perić opposes the spurious apparitions as adamantly as Bishop Žanić did.

Monday, 11 January, 1982: Twice we asked about the two priests from Mostar, and the Madonna repeated twice what she has said before.[2]

Friday, 20 January, 1982: I asked some questions about Father Ivica Vego and Father Ivan Prusina, and the Madonna replied to me in the same way. Blessed Mother, the newspapers say that Ivica and Ivan have been expelled from the Franciscan Order. She replied: "They have not been expelled." She laughed. "Tell them just to be calm and steadfast. There are many trials. Let them persevere. Let the papers say what they want. They should pay no attention to that. That is not important." O Blessed Mother, put an end to all this so that Ivica and Ivan have no more problems. The Madonna answered: "I shall calm it down." She also mentioned some friars from Mostar, saying to leave it for the time being: "There will be an opportunity for me to tell them. There are three main ones (friars)." Blessed Mother, what about the bishop? Is he going to change his attitude? The Madonna replied: "I am not going to hurry. I am waiting to see whether he will submit to these instructions of mine, which I have conveyed through you." But this is all very hard on me (Vicka). It is too much for me, let alone for Ivica and Ivan. When we were with the Blessed Mother yesterday, we asked her whether she would recite one "Our Father" for those two (Ivica and Ivan). She replied at once: "By all means." And she began to pray. When we finished, she smiled and said to me: "The only thing that is on your mind is those two." I said: "That isn't so."

Thursday, 15 April, 1982: Ivica Vego and Ivan Prusina. I asked the Madonna in this way to tell me everything about the two of you. She first laughed, and then she began to speak. "They are not to blame in the least." She repeated this twice. "Let them not worry about the subject. Many are against the two of them, who can scarcely wait for them to be expelled from the Franciscans, and to leave Mostar. The bishop is at

---

2 Note carefully that this entry was made on 11 January, 1982 and that three days later, at a meeting with the bishop in the chancery office, Vicka denied that she knew Vego. See May 1990, no. 7.

Extracts from the Diary of Vicka Ivanković

fault here, and there are many who support him. Every day they urge him to expel you so that they do not see you around any more. Don't listen to any of them. Do not reproach yourselves in any way. The most important thing is that you should not leave Mostar. They are doing you a great injustice. They do not wish to act in accordance with God's law, but they are all against Him, and they are delivering heavy blows to the faith and to the Church, and sowing ever greater disorder." O Blessed Mother, you told me that you would in some way show the bishop that they should be left in peace. And so now I beg you to do so as soon as possible, for we are in rather a hurry, and I expect that the whole situation will be calmed down and made better. One hundred times a day, Ivica and Ivan pass by many who do not even glance at them as if they do not exist. O Blessed Mother, you know how things are for them, so I beg you to help them as soon as possible, and to free them from their troubles so that they will be in the same position as other priests.

The Madonna laughed and said: "Be patient. I shall calm the whole situation down and there will not be any more problems. They can say Mass from time to time. Let them be discreet about it until the situation has calmed down. They are not to blame for anything. If they were at fault in any way I would have said let them go and not to be in the way."[3] Then I said no one but you can calm the situation. If you choose to do nothing, then so be it. She replied: "All in good time."

16 April, 1982, in the evening: I asked some questions on behalf of the two of you, and once again the Madonna said: "Many Franciscans are troubled in conscience because of what is happening to these two. They will reveal themselves in their true colours little by little." And she emphasized: "Pay no attention to them. Do the task that is allotted to you." That is all that I have written about Ivica and Ivan. The rest I made known to them, by notes that I sent them. I did not have time to write down everything in full detail.

---

3 The alleged promise of Our Lady has certainly not been fulfilled.

Monday, 26 April, 1982: "In his heart the bishop is completely lacking in Christian charity towards those two. Let Ivica and Ivan not be distressed by the bishop, for he is imposing too heavy a burden upon them only in order to be rid of them. He has begun by persecuting the youngest among the Franciscans, and then from them slowly upwards. This is a sign that this is the last great blow. Let them not be troubled about it. Let them freely wipe it from their minds. Let them learn how to suffer for the sake of righteousness. What the bishop is doing is not in accordance with the will of God. They are innocent and without guilt, yet they suffer so much. God would not have allowed this, but the bishop does not act in accordance with God's mercy, because he is able to do as he pleases. But one day all will see justice the like of which you have not seen for a long time. I shall slowly set work to restore peace, and many of the friars will be filled with great joy."[4]

Wednesday, 29 September, 1982: Father Ivica asked, "Shall we leave Mostar or shall we stay?" The Blessed Mother replied: "Stay!" Towards the end of August 1982, Vicka said to him: "The Madonna instructed me that Ivan and Ivica were not to go away from Mostar."

---

[4] Far from peace being restored, the Franciscans of Herzegovina are now in a state of open rebellion against legitimate authority in the Church, and, as has been documented above, are establishing parishes outside the diocesan structures, hearing confessions and solemnizing marriages without faculties (thus rendering these sacraments invalid), and bringing in a bishop from outside the diocese to confer illicit confirmations.

Ingram Content Group UK Ltd.
Milton Keynes UK
UKHW041119230323
419044UK00001B/16